LEADERSHIP
CHALLENGES

IN MANAGING
ORGANISATIONAL CHANGE

LEADERSHIP
CHALLENGES

IN MANAGING
ORGANISATIONAL CHANGE

Dr. E. J. SARMA

White Falcon
Publishing

www.whitefalconpublishing.com

Leadership Challenges in Managing Organisational Change
E. J. Sarma

www.whitefalconpublishing.com

ISBN - 978-1-63640-571-1

ABOUT THE BOOK

There is a powerful story of the Eagle's life. The eagle is very strong and majestic and fearless bird.

An eagle can live for 70 years but at the end of 40 years life, it faces a dilemma. The talons are long, its beak is bent and feathers are old. It cannot catch its prey and fly great heights. The choice before the eagle is to die or reinvent its old charm and agility.

It then goes to the mountaintop and painfully breaks its talon. Plucks its feathers one by one allowing new ones to grow. Soon it is back into action and lives for 30 more years. Change requires paradigm shift; new mental models.

Change is inevitable and the painful choice must be exercised. This book's theme of Leadership challenges in managing organisational Change is very well reflected in The eagle story. The cover design reflects that theme

CONTENTS

PREFACE

Millions of words have been written on fundamentals of leadership and the effectiveness but the challenges before the corporate leadership in initiating and implementing wholistic transformation is not given adequate treatment. Conventional approaches to implement change seem to be abstract and are like the outdated yahoo map and have become too simple or obsolete as they do not keep step with changing time or complexity of doing business. After spending over three decades with people of multiple culture I came across leaders who ranged from autocratic style to pure democratic type.

The traditional leadership styles do not seem to hold good any longer especially after this fast-paced changes in 2022 and beyond, after two years of forced global economic slump.

Where leadership accepted the challenges, there was abundant agility and visionary zeal. The changes were rapid as well as timely. They depended on people to carry out the changes by championing the cause. The book focuses on these aspects.

There were many CEOs who were opposed to the idea of remote working or work from home before the pandemic. What happened in 2020? Not a single company dared to oppose allowing remote work. It would have been foolish not to fall in line with policy changes.

Those leaders who espoused a no-remote-working policy had to swallow the bitter pill to keep the business going. Personal whims were thrown to the winds. Everyone had to push the company to the untested styles and culture at any cost. Flexibility of adaptation are the new normal for leadership.

Business leaders in the past had a single objective: maintaining the enterprise's profitability and growth. Bankers and investors were pleased if the return on investment was safe with predictable growth. Successful businesses could afford to continue moving in that direction with their current management style. Only near-fatal financial crisis conditions, caused by a few greedy insiders or external influences, prompted the leaders to consider a change.

Changes in consumer tastes, market shift, national economic conditions, and technology shifts are the main drivers of organisational change. They force the leadership to take a more proactive role in dealing with emergencies and changing things in a planned manner. The change starts with initial step of the crisis and emergency management.

The pandemic became the biggest disruptor in 2020 and 2021 and beyond, which ruined many businesses worldwide without exception.

A recent PWC survey indicated about eighty-six per cent of the CEOs in the USA expressing lack of business growth as their chief concern during the pandemic. Therefore, what would they do other than accepting the change in the business climate?

Bringing changes in the business systems is mainly a mighty people management endeavour as it involves leadership perspectives and admirable leader behaviour. The techniques and styles in managing change become secondary. It is an ongoing process to change attitudes to correct the existing state, A strong-willed and courageous leadership alone can handle such culture turn around. One has to begin somewhere to change something and that beginning can be made by the leadership alone.

I recollect my own experience. I was heading HR in a Bay Area California USA, IT services company. I was also the part of executive management committee as member and the committee was the elite decision-making body in the company. The IT start-up had reached a revenue size of nearly USD 100 million in twenty-plus years and had sustained a productive track record.

The system in the company was that the executive committee would meet every week from six am at their Bay Area office, where executives from three time zones would take part. The meeting was inevitable, but it would last four hours or more, even when people showed signs of fatigue.

The CEO had the final say on every matter. Although everyone expressed their views, they would keep quiet and be speechless as the leader would always say "it is my way or no way."

One issue which was brought up week after week by the CEO was falling revenue, profits, the lack of growth and new client development. They were almost reaching the tipping point. The CEO would burst out, "Guys, if you can't deliver, think again about whether this is the place you wish to be in."

The sales managers and other senior people were almost like lifetime employees. Therefore, one was embarrassed to hear such an outburst.

The stunted growth leading to falling profits were real, and the CEO was whipping the lame horse. Their issues were not about the poor performance but a faulty, non-functional business model. The CEO would not agree with that theory.

The CEO's status quo mindset would not let him think of alternatives other than raising the target every year.

He had a strong belief that unless pushed to stretch-point, employees do not deliver their best. His tactics were not showing any result, and this was an indigestible truth for the leader.

There was a complete failure on his part to understand the extensive rebuilding of the business model and reformulating the offerings according to market demands was inevitable.

I had to assert myself against the idea of raising the target alone was counterproductive. I suggested the idea of moving up the value chain by transforming the offerings and strategy. It took courage to challenge the high-level authority on the outdated business model. My genuine concerns might have struck the right chord with a few members of the senior team. They tasked me with challenging the status quo mentality of the founder and his peers who had spent long years in the same business without changing their ways of thinking. Clearly, the change initiation needed someone other than the founder to be the initiator. The CEO wanted to test a hypothesis and the seeds of change were planted.

This book is not a traditional textbook. Instead, it has been created out of an experiment with moments of truth and best practices for successfully implementing change initiatives in organisations that are staring at death. It is a combination of practice with theory and concepts.

We don't find scarcity of publications or literature on change management, but this book will approach the subject from a different angle and provide a new methodology for successful implementation.

Organisational changes need the deployment of tried-and-tested, state-of-the-art tools and methods to meet the challenges of large-scale transition.

The book integrates the people management facets of change management with creative robust processes and systems for success. It is proven transformation efforts succeed only by changing people's attitudes, their mindset, and not with the best technology or tool alone.

The stated goal of any socially responsible business organisation in the 21st century is merely to delight the customers, create wealth for investors and employees. Of course, every organisation espouses these ideals, but few live up to the claim as an organisation cannot truly walk the talk unless it is headed and supported by value-driven, solid leadership.

One can find many ways to manage complex projects, programmes and risks with the best practices, tools and methods in any technology-driven changes. However, managers rarely discuss change management related to *people* and how the people are fundamental to achieving success during transformation.

Whatever is the scale of change, it always becomes a test of leadership ability. It expands this expertise to the limit whenever leaders take decisions on high-impact enterprise-wide modifications. Transformation decisions are always at the crossroads between logic and sentiment, and they all know that.

The risk of leading change is like sitting in the driver's seat of a Ferrari Formula One race car. The expert race driver deploys technique and logic to handle every challenge and crisis while racing through the most challenging route.A reason for the race driver to respond to sudden unplanned emergencies is extensive training. The race car represents the complex data. The race driver directs the car on the specially prepared race track, and his chances of winning the race are high. Otherwise, the vehicle and the driver end up in a big mess.

They may even meet with a fatal outcome, not to point out the unexpected impact of others' mistakes.

Change initiatives create disorder, and in most situations, people do not have any coping techniques with chaos or ambiguity. The fluid conditions that develop during change are incredibly traumatic for many.

A massive overhaul for a better future is feasible through the contribution of a decisive leadership during the challenging transformation phase. Any exemplary leader will take up the change challenge. The idea of writing about organisational change management (OCM) was born out of my experience in high-risk transformation project initiatives.

This experiment made me conclude that experiential learning is the best way to understand the pains of transformation and change.

The urge came from my motivation, compelled by the principles of the 4Ls (Living, Loving, Learning, and Leaving a legacy) which Steven Covey espoused in *7 Habits of Highly Effective People*. Businesses face turbulent developments in the external environment, and the global pandemic is one great force that changed business ways.

Few insulations exist for business organisations to function trouble-free. Those volatile changes affect every business. Right from the beginning, in the early fifties, Britain suspected France when their prime minister engineered joining the European Union. No one expected Britain to exit in 2020.

The impact of change varies from obliteration to need-based changes. Instead of quick hits or small incremental process changes, Re-engineering requires massive overhaul and aims at a massive leap in results. The top leadership is to be responsible for designing escape routes before events can drive an organisation into any crisis. Business processes, marketing and delivery, product portfolio mix, communication, internal and external messages and people's tastes need to change for a successful escape to a better future.

One can harness tools and technology to establish process changes, but they cannot be used to convert the behaviour of people. However, one can feasibly expect changes in people's mindsets and attitudes when both the leadership and the people fathom the essential steps and principles behind managing changes.

Three robust and key attributes can steer the escape to the future state from the past and present:

1. Courage and conviction of the leadership to initiate change and the leaders' personal characteristics that will drive changes until the end.

2. The determination to separate away from the status quo and comfort zone.
3. The ability to drive and motivate people and create the required climate and urgency for change.

Leadership needs to make sure that the change initiatives gain momentum to propel the organisation to next level.

Constancy and consistency to keep the momentum alive are essential for success in any change initiative. Every change project needs to operate, at least, with a minimum speed. The change actions have to move at incredible speed to propel the entire organisation from the current state to a better one.

Like the satellite leaving the orbit of gravitational pull needs a threshold level speed, change needs to have a base speed of acceleration.

An organisation may have the best leaders in command who start the changes, but these leaders can fail if the creative tension is missing. Unfortunately, enough evidence exists to show us that leaders who relied on technology and tools had ignored people's facets when they initiated changes.

This book reflects the mainstay issues on how to architect the change while touching upon other significant problems to successfully implement change programmes of any size.

This book is a blend of powerful concepts from diverse disciplines, psychology, human behaviour, creative thinking, co-creation, shared responsibility, social networking and practical examples of tested methods in shaping the change programme.

It covers important suggestions that are crucial to leadership. The challenge for any leader is not staying on course but making the hard decision. The decision has to be made by choice. Most leaders find it challenging to make such a decision for various reasons, viz., tenure of appointment, risk-taking ability and fear of lack of support from peers.

A recent survey covered over 40,000 CEOs in America, found that 25 per cent had PhDs, another 25 per cent had MBAs, and 16 per cent had no advanced degree. The oldest CEO was 92, and the average age of a CEO was 56-plus. Fewer are indeed the risks taken at later life stages. So, what is the reason behind the cautious approach in their advanced years? It has been one of the many mysteries of human behaviour.

Researchers have found the answer in brain scans have revealed that changes in the grey matter might predict risk-taking behaviour more than a person's age itself. Age and grey matter together can affect risk-taking ability in advanced ages.

People at 90 are not less competent, but their ability to cope with dramatic changes is questionable.

Warren Buffett is over 90 and is the oldest CEO in America. 10 others over 80 are working as CEOs or chairpersons.

Sheldon Adelson, the CEO, chairperson and treasurer of Las Vegas Sands, was 82 years old. Roger Penske, head of Penske Automotive Group, is 79. Leslie Wexner heads L Brands as CEO and chairperson, at 78; the year 2016 marked his 53rd year as CEO of L Brands, and he is the longest-serving CEO on the Fortune 500 list. Finally, Alan Miller is the CEO and chairperson of Universal Health Services at 77.

They are all the super seniors. Older people are risk averse, yet they do not vacate the chair.

The belief system is, "Longer is the track record of successful existence, greater is the comfort level and the hidden forces inside the organisation that work to pull back and resist moving through changes."

An escape to the expected future is the answer if the leadership does not ignore business purposes. Whenever leaders placed organisations before themselves and attempted to change in tune with changing business climate, they face with a dilemma: should they think of large-scale change initiatives only while facing a crisis?

Should one start a change process proactively? What is the best time? Unfortunately, we do not have Nostradamus in businesses to predict the future.

"Hundreds of closed hedge funds will go bankrupt, and the international exchange market will need to close in a short time; maybe even for a week, to stop the panic of selling shares, that will slowly envelop the stock markets," said Nostradamus; also predicted the crisis of 2008 and 2021.

The exchanges markets registered slump and created panic levels. The end of the crisis is still out of sight. The world's leading economies have been facing economic stagnation for several years and the economic fundamentals are no longer applicable today. How many businesses have a contingency plan for change, even if the downward spiral come true?

The *right time* for initiating changes does not exist because the business environment constantly changes, faster than organisations can keep up. Rapid technological and economic advancements make time very crucial. Developments in the external environment engulf and make the business environment volatile.

The force is like tsunami waves striking with a deadly force.

Few experts would have predicted about China or India to become economic superpowers. Instead, both countries turned the excessive population around and converted the disadvantage into an advantage.

They changed their ailing economy and became the fastest-growing one.

Not a single product or merchandise sold by the American superstores and corporations across the world is supporting "Made in China" label. Communist China has gotten more and more support from capitalistic American enterprises, with Chinese leaders finding it easy to bury the ideological differences and change for their economic gains.

This ideological shift from communism is the outcome of managing change.

The Information Technology explosion has caused every unresponsive organisation to degenerate because of the inability to take correct and timely decisions. The core of architecting any business strategy is the sensitive understanding of the environment by the leadership and making the internal changes proactively.

Changes initiated to accommodate external changes are reactive, and any leadership with vision will not adopt a reactive style.

A leader who can take well-articulated action and inspire their employees will make changes easy to execute.

However, enormous stress happens while attempting changes, even if the change impact is positive.

Minor cosmetic changes of reorganisation and restructuring do not bring windfall results because sporadic small doses of change are inadequate to keep pace with the rapid external changes.

What only the mainframe computers were doing is now possible for mobile phones to execute. Standard cell phones can boast 6 to 8 GB, but 256 GB memory phones are now available.

Bihar and Uttar Pradesh have many illiterate women in India, but they handle dual cell phones through two different carriers. The mobile phone is used not merely for calling but for its photographic power, social networking, photo sharing, money transfer, cab hiring and shopping, food ordering, table reservations in restaurants, etc.

More speed is built into every communication as technology adds versatility, variety and speed. As a result, frequent interactions happen among people worldwide, and nothing remains as an isolated incident.

Substantial volumes of data and instant analysis contribute to robust corporate decision-making and help create change initiatives more than ever in the past.

This book provides insight into the human psychology of greed, leadership effectiveness, behaviour modification, and the influence on communication decisions. One needs a proper approach to succeed in any change effort. Therefore, a new simple ten-step model for implementing change is presented to contribute to the body of OCM knowledge.

The alternative model lays the foundation for leaders and organisations to initiate change. The model outlines the process steps for everyone to go through to reach the objectives for change.

This book provides extensive practical tips for leaders and managers responsible for making change initiatives. This book might be most beneficial to management students and end up empowering them to gain insight into the subject as they think deeply about augmenting their knowledge through further research.

The dilemma before corporate leadership is to decide on the scale of change initiatives. The power to change things lies with founders and leadership, but they are emotionally attached to their creation and are reluctant to abandon what they created.

The two case studies presented here prove the point.

The management myopia or status quo comfort eventually kills change initiatives.

Change management is fascinating because it deals with rewriting and reconfiguring, reshaping organisations and people's destiny and emotions. Executives responsible for managing people and using their creative mind to intervene, should delve into this subject and learn to make work-life meaningful. People come to the organisation with dreams and do not expect a steadfast leadership or organisation; instead, they align with adaptive ones. The book addresses the leadership challenges for managing changes because the impact of success or failure falls on the administration, and room for failure exists.

CHAPTER 1

WHY INITIATE ANY CHANGE?

"Whatever got you here may well prevent you from getting there."

Marshall Goldsmith

"When the going is good, why rock the boat?" is another objection we hear often whenever any change is proposed. If you were part of the senior management team or decision-making body, invariably, you have heard this response whenever anyone proposed organisational level changes. If any change initiative comes up, the immediate reaction is one of defence among senior managers.

A frog enjoys the warmth and feels comfortable if we put it in a beaker filled with water and heat it slowly to a boiling point. It will continue to stay there, enjoying the warmth till cooked and dies. Instead, if we heat the beaker quickly, the same frog would jump out. The question is, should one wait till it reaches the boiling point to change?

Most managers and leaders develop the "frog in the beaker" mentality if they spent many years in the same culture. Crisis management is the only weapon most of them know, and is the only one they use to react and manage.

The management's reactive behaviour is similar to the frog in a beaker of steaming water; they brush aside any external pressure prompting change. The death of giant organisations viz., Steuben and Kodak and their insensitive leadership are examples.

Business organisations with uninterrupted success for a long time behave like the frog in the beaker. But, unfortunately, only a few takes proactive steps to stay relevant to the volatile market needs.

Banks lend vast sums even today, ignoring basic rules, leading to collapse and loss of faith in the entire system., CEOs and chairpersons in authority bestow undue favours, risking the bank and investors in trouble because of selfishness and greed. Recent examples in India are Yes Bank, ICICI Bank, and Punjab Maharashtra Bank.

The most recent case is of Punjab and Maharashtra Cooperative (PMC Bank) in India, which shocked millions of small depositors, and many investors lost their life savings — dying of heartbreak.

The corruption by the chairman and other senior executives of the bank was a significant cause, as it always happens with Indian bank frauds. The PMC's top management had conspired to grant massive loans to companies doing housing development.

The bank had loaned over 70 per cent of its lending (over Rs 90 billion) to the bankrupt HDIL. The bank officials defrauded further by hiding 44 loan accounts of HDIL. All these happened even as surveillance by the Reserve Bank of India was started.

RBI placed restrictions on Ahmedabad-based Madhavpura Mercantile Cooperative Bank, as there was a colossal fraud.

The two local banks viz., the Indian Mercantile Co-operative Bank Limited, with a base in Lucknow, came under the cloud of suspicion in June 2014 and Kapol Cooperative Bank Limited in Mumbai went under the scanner in March 2017.

The scamsters spread all these frauds over two decades, while RBI's guidelines and directives remained static, and the apex bank did not achieve any different results in its regulatory measures. Did anything change in the banking supervision?

In India, politicians manipulate the cooperative sector banks and small rural banks, and the central bank is always reactive, resulting in a considerable loss for the investing public all the time. The banks lend huge sums with no securities, hide bad debts, and do not classify as non-performing assets. Despite knowing this, the apex bank has never attempted to change its method of oversight.

VG Siddhartha was a highly influential and wealthy Indian business owner. He owned the Café Coffee Day, booming chain coffee shop and also owned large coffee plantations.

The news broke that he had jumped out into a flooded river, abandoning his car and driver early one morning.

Yes Bank started in 2004, had Rs 15 billion of exposure to VG's business through a maze of small plantations, and the bank landed in big trouble. The Reserve Bank of India contained and prevented the collapse and fired the founders. However, the bank had abused the priority sector-lending rules of the RBI.

A consortium of banks loaned huge sums to Vijay Mallya, Nirav Modi and Mehul Chokshi, ignoring all basic lending principles.

ICICI Bank is another curious case of illegitimate lending by the CEO, the wife of a key official in beneficiary companies.

The bank had earned a name for itself and yet, lost its reputation because of the greed of one senior executive who acted with no conscience and killed the golden goose.

All these are examples of failure to learn from the past blunders.

The entire banking system in India behaves like a frog in the beaker, evidencing insensitive and ineffective leadership. The lack of agility to be adaptive and change has killed many businesses. The banks' resistance to learn from numerous past mistakes contribute to the reluctance to transform. As a result, multiple crises keep happening and changes are few in the system.

Shifting consumer tastes and preferences is another big reason, forcing organisations to adapt to market needs and change.

McDonald's and Coke found their sales dropping year after year and found out about consumer preferences shifting. It forced Coke to change and diversify into bottled water and other drinks.

The second powerful cause is the massive advancement in information and communication. It forces organisations to fall in line to be efficient in manufacturing and delivering to every global customer. Amazon focuses on speedy delivery while providing service and keeping fulfilment costs very low.

The third is the fact that static organisations cannot sustain themselves forever. They will experience the pressure to speed up progress and enable speedy progress.

Therefore, one has to find newer avenues for expanding and changing, which means a departure from the current.

Steuben died because they were not sensitive to changing consumer needs. Digital technology replaced traditional photography, and the refusal to adapt to change killed Kodak.

The technology driven high speed internet has revolutionised has shaped the way people buy goods and services. Mobile technology further adds acceleration to doing business globally, and exploit reporting methods will give value.

Techniques and methodologies like scorecards, dashboards, KPI, metrics, OLAP, ad hoc queries, etc., deliver a retrospective analysis for fine-tuning the strategies.

Technology companies focus on data analytics in the new era, and businesses use data to predict the future, though it sounds mystical. People are increasingly accessing the internet for day-to-day existence, and they are being tracked, monitored, and exploited. The data generated by surfer's social media is used heavily by marketing research agencies.

The Eastman Kodak Story

Steuben dug its own grave despite catering to the niche market of the super-rich and famous. Eastman Kodak was a mass market consumer product company, unlike Steuben. It created a colossal market for photography and defied the need to change someday. Kodak remained blind and refused to adapt and change to fight the emerging threat from technological changes and got killed by disruptive technology innovations.

Innovator and philanthropist George Eastman founded Kodak in 1892, and the Eastman Kodak brand became the undisputed king in America and the world. Kodak became an American icon-along with Bausch and Lomb, Xerox, and Gannett. Anyone who was born affluent lived till their death in the American city of Rochester, because of Kodak.

Their market share was as undisputed as 80 per cent in film sales and 85 per cent in camera sales. They employed 1,45,000 people in 1988, but downsized to 20,000 in 2009 and 6,500 in 2015.

That is how dramatic the decline was. Kodak's competitor, Fuji, was making moves to pose the biggest threat.

In 1990, the company launched the Photo CD as a digital image medium and it was an investment gamble. Despite this threat, Kodak got stuck in its status quo mindset that film would never die. This attitude was identical to Steuben's attitude in refusing to change.

The status quo mindset showed at peak performance level, and the CEO emphatically stated that there was no need for change.

Kodak was obsessed with the timing in the picture business.

Kodak performed well for over a hundred years and gained a market leadership position, but that success did not guarantee continued survival. By the mid-1980s, 100 years after George Eastman invented paper-based film, the digital revolution had ushered in a sweeping change.

Kodak did not see the enormity of disruptive threats and thought of how to change, instead of focusing its strategic moves on the emerging digital technologies, they continued to stick to the old.

Kodak made a few diversifications to acquire pharmaceutical giant Sterling Drug for USD 5.1 billion and set up a brand in the battery business.

These moves only added to Kodak's financial woes and losses. The decline started in 1990, and by 2012, Kodak filed a bankruptcy petition under chapter 11. This Bankruptcy Code of USA provides for reorganisation, of a corporation or partnership firm (*A chapter 11 debtor usually proposes a plan of reorganisation to keep its business alive and pay creditors.) (Individual's setup can also seek relief in chapter 11)*. After a series of moves of patent sell-outs and downsizing, Kodak began to restructure, and it emerged out of bankruptcy in 2014. But unfortunately, it shut its most extensive research and production unit in Rochester, known as Kodak Park. As a result, Kodak's brand was wiped out from the market.

These two examples prove the point that change is not a choice. 100 years of existence is no guarantee for survival for the next 100 years. The answer lies in change and transformation.

CHAPTER 2

GIANT EVENTS THAT SHOOK GLOBAL BUSINESSES AND ENFORCED CHANGES

External Triggers and Management Inertia

External triggers, specifically artificial crises, drive changes for many organisations. For example, a natural disaster forced changes earlier, but now, changes result from human actions more often.

Jack Welch said, "When the rate of change outside exceeds the rate of change inside, the end is in sight". 21st-century organisations face a higher probability of disasters triggered by external events of economic, political and religious fundamentalism than ever before, which forces changes in the way corporations do business. Every industry, be it financial services, insurance, airlines, travel, and tourism, healthcare and security, face compulsions to initiate massive changes in dealing with investors, markets, governments, and customers.

We cite a few examples of reactive actions in airlines, travel and tourism. The most significant contributor to organisational changes is always human greed for money and power. For instance, large-scale financial frauds are motivated by an individual's desire to amass wealth and lead lavish lives. Not only were the organisations they managed destroyed, but the entire industry they operated got traumatised.

It is not that people from one geography, culture or country are fraud-prone, but one can find a common denominator in the combination of greed with power. Whether we speak of scams in Wall Street, USA or Dalal Street, India, the people responsible for organisations' positions of power have always been behind any massive frauds.

Greedy and corrupt politicians, public servants, and even statutory auditors who were supposed to function as watchdogs have backed such fraud.

People who were intelligent and studied the system's weak points committed fraud by exploiting the weakness, the legal system's inefficiency, and the slow administration of legal procedures. Another common trend is the non-existence of any limit to the greedy person's action until it reached massive unmanageable proportions and found its dead end. These engineered crises trigger reforms and changes, which bring in more restrictions, besides erosion of trust in the entire system. As a result, the perpetrators of fraud end up drowning themselves and destroying profitable businesses along with them.

Steven Hawking focused on the threat posed by human greed. He considered the capitalist greed to be "more dangerous to the future of human civilization than robots, aliens, or quantum particles".

The Steuben Story

Steuben Glass Works, founded in 1903, specialised in handmade art glass and crystal ware, featuring blown, cut and etched designs and animal sculptures. Corning had 108 years of glorious existence with exclusive and super-rich customers. Unfortunately, the business had to fade away by closing down a prestigious factory in Corning, NY, and its flagship store on Madison Avenue, which became a prestigious landmark in 2011.

Steuben was as famous as Hollywood heroes and heroines and remained the most preferred choice of the super-rich and elite when it came to gifts and collections. Wealthy and privileged customers spent enormously on a wedding gift. Prince Charles gifted the Steuben to his lady love Diana in 1981. Steuben had such a high brand reputation and image, that it became the prestige symbol for elite consumers and all of America. The glass was clear; one could walk through a sheet of Steuben and not even notice it; the clarity and quality of Steuben is still unparalleled.

The Hollywood blockbuster film of 1983 was *Risky Business*. It was an offbeat comedy and an action movie. A rebellious teenager turns his parent's home into a brothel while his parents are away to repay his accumulated debt.

Tom Cruise acted as the rebellious young lad, while Rebecca De Mornay co-starred as the liberated call-girl Lana. *Risky Business* was the most influential film of the generation. The film propelled Tom Cruise to stardom besides launching another superstar, Steuben, as the most sought-after gift. So naturally, the capitalist American elite and super-rich strata of the entire world wanted to have Steuben.

The movie also featured the famous Phil Collins song "I can feel it coming in the air tonight", and it played over a steamy, hot scene depicting Tom Cruise and Rebecca on a subway train. In addition, the super-rich family of the teen was shown to exhibit Steuben collections. Because of this publicity, Steuben got positioned in the best premium segment. Hollywood rarely launched a film unless it had huge money-spinning potential, and Steuben was a money-spinner product.

Risky Business projected typical American cultural values of capitalism, materialism, losing childish innocence and the child's coming of age, besides the super-rich American's characteristic obsession with a status symbol — Steuben.

In a scene in the film, Joel, a prime character, is having a nightmare, where he sees the police circling his house and arresting him for rape while his friends and family watch in horror.

Joel makes a phone call to a gorgeous call girl, and they end up having a steamy romantic outing.

The call girl Lana demands USD 300 for her services, and Joel goes to the bank to get cash. But unfortunately, Lana disappears with the expensive Steuben crystal egg, a gem in his mother's proud collection. Joel traces Lana to a restaurant and demands the Steuben egg back, but Lana's pimp, Guido, confronts him and draws a gun to shoot him; Joel escapes.

The rare Steuben egg actually reappears later in the film.

The movie revolves around Steuben gets a prime place in the film and after the release of the film, among the top stars.

"America just became less beautiful. On every Valentine's Day, for 20 years, my wife received a Steuben heart.

Now my heartbreak" Loyal wealthy customer. It was the tearful emotional outburst of a loyal customer reflecting the emotional attachment". The exclusive Steuben customers had an emotional attachment to this exquisite product range. For many families of the generation, Steuben became an indispensable symbol.

Corning Glass Works, New York, acquired Steuben, and converted it as Steuben Division.

For decades, Steuben had been the only product which had easily resolved the million-dollar question for the wealthy and famous when it came to gifting. Steuben proved to be the obvious and only choice for kings, queens, presidents, celebrity brides, wealthy government officials and heads of state.

Past American presidents were the biggest fans and gave Steuben glassware as gifts to visiting heads of state. Steuben, thus, was a national symbol for America.

None of the top leaders in Steuben expected a fatal end to a glorious brand. It would have been simple to foresee the fall, but the emotional attachment of the founders to their brand overshadowed the vision.

Steuben's founder and designer Frederick Carder either ignored or failed to sense the decline in demand for the premium expensive crystal ware. The tides were turning, but it did not affect the company which was credited with creating the most exquisite things for the likes of Louis Comfort Tiffany or Rene Lalique. Instead, the world identified it for its art nouveau and aesthetic.

Rene Lalique was a famous French expert in glass designing and artful creations. They were exceptional and involved those creative brains with Steuben's product. They are priced at a premium sum and are positioned to cater to the super-affluent and famous. They created exclusive crystal ware, partnering with designer Ted Muehling.

All the success, name and fame, earned over the years could not save them from collapse. The Steuben owners turned blind to issues like revenue generation or finding new customers as they were obsessed with their past glory and status quo mindset, and were in the ultimate comfort zone. Steuben's management did not think of changing to cope with consumer tastes and market conditions.

The new generation shifted to mobile phones, video game consoles and iPads, and away from expensive crystal glass as gifts.

The primary dealer of Steuben in New York disclosed the reasons, and Steuben's demise was inevitable. "They lost their way. "You are doomed, whether you're making Steuben glass or Twinkies if the design department is pathetic, the costs are prohibitive, and the marketing vision for the future is unsuccessful" - said another dealer.

The economic condition in the country couldn't breathe life into Steuben's recovery, either. Steuben stands as one of the classic cases, of attempting to survive on a glorified image and not willing to stick to the business purpose of commercial success.

The Steuben story established the need for transformational change leadership — *the sine qua non* for everlasting and meaningful organisational existence.

WorldCom Information Technology

WorldCom was set up as a long-distance discount services company in 1983 and did a series of aggressive acquisitions and mergers to speed up its growth. As a result, it became the second-largest long-distance phone call service company in the US in 15 years.

No one, including the management, would have expected to face a downward slide 20 years later in 2002 and resort to a job cut to its global workforce and face investigations from government and regulatory authorities. WorldCom announced the merger with MCI. It was the biggest merger in the United States of America.

When fortunes turned, Moody's and S&P lowered the credit rating to junk. The company loaned excessive sums to CEO Bernard Ebbers, which were questionable and faced scrutiny.

"Life in an internal audit department could be very boring," a WorldCom employee had stated. When one stumbles upon an accounting entry for USD 500 million for computer expenses, the boring life becomes a nightmare. Any auditor would be shocked beyond belief to find there are no supporting documents.

What was needed was accounting common sense. For Worldcom, a few forces in the internal audit department with questionable integrity and plenty of common sense hid the frauds.

An auditor who smelt mischief and suspected about some mischief with the entries reported his findings to his boss. He suspected the company's transactions, based on grapevine information he had received of the misdeeds and the accounting irregularities. The team soon figured out the gigantic fraud.

Frauds to the tune of USD 3.8 billion in misallocated expenses and phoney accounting entries were detected. It marked the biggest accounting fraud in US corporate history. The actions sent WorldCom into delisting, and the bankruptcy left thousands of their employees jobless and truncated the stock market.

The corporate custodians had clearly been dishonest.

There was one group of middle managers who did not fit into cowboy culture. They took their professional ethics as principles, and commitment drove them to extraordinary heights.

These honest employees stood firm amidst dishonest executives. Rapid erosion of profits and an accounting scandal which created billions in non-existing profit haunted WorldCom. That was an enormous price paid for a greedy strategy for the exponential rise and aggressive acquisition of new companies.

The company had accumulated over 40 billion in debt.

They called off a crucial merger with Sprint in the year 2000.

To hide the financial condition of the company, Scott Sullivan (CFO), David Myers (Controller), and Buford Yates (Director of Accounting) resorted to supporting falsified numbers and inflated the revenue with fictitious entries; they misrepresented operational expenses as capital expenditure. Probably these acts, later on, inspired the Enrons of the world to follow a similar route.

This fraud got Bernard Ebbers 25 years in jail. The company now operates as MCI Inc. and is a part of Verizon. This is an example of collective leadership failure and fraud driven by greed.

Most often incidence of fraud is created by people in power. They started with personal greed and ended with the system's failure to learn from past events. These crises affected many unrelated organisations fatally and shook the trust of people who invested in them.

The organisation's leadership is solely responsible for any unpreparedness for a situation that accompanies change.

The Lehman Story, America

The financial world saw Lehman Brothers' unmatched strength and recovery from the destruction. Lehman created a conservative management culture but when the crisis struck, they quickly adjusted and changed. But, when faced with another challenge, the same agile culture and leadership failed to guarantee revival.

Internal forces concealed the greed of leadership. The organisation, which was moving extraordinarily to adapt, revealed its dark side. This leadership style not only killed them but also killed many allies who trusted them. The organisation and its system were not ready suddenly to take part in a challenge to change.

Lehman Brothers possessed three floors of the World Commerce Centre in Manhattan, New York. They never expected their prestigious assets to crumble in a day and become dust. It is an unplanned and undesired change.

When the terrorists crashed huge jet planes into the twin World Trade towers, among the many who lost their lives were Lehman employees. The attack ruined the most important financial centre of the world and disabled Lehman.

The office of Lehman was in shambles. Lehman's management faced the challenge of thinking deeply and act to put the business back on the rails. The task included relocating over 6000 employees. The crisis turned everything topsy-turvy for the employees who were accustomed to plush air-conditioned offices and high-power technology-driven, real-time trading floors.

They had to move the operations to makeshift offices in the rented Sheraton Hotel. Employees had to work from home, something they had never done before. Business recovery actions had to be rapid; they moved the trading operations to makeshift offices in Jersey City, New Jersey. Less than 48 hours after the collapse, stock markets reopened on 17 September 2001, and Lehman was back in action in full swing.

It was a demonstration of adaptive ability to dramatic changes even when said change was forced on them suddenly.

"Many finance professionals who had the least technical experience were fixing computer issues for months. Many were working 24/7 for seven months" an employee; fine example of collective responsibility in dealing with a crisis.

This is the definition of engaged employees who are loyal and committed to the employer.

Unfortunately, on 15 September 2008, the same agile company took the most painful and tragic bankruptcy step. Internal forces of misdeeds drove it to collapse.

The epicentre of the leading financial earthquake was in New York City, and the shock waves spread. It caused a financial tsunami, and the impact was global. The Lehman collapse triggered a wave of change in the American financial services sector, particularly in the world markets, compelling government and regulatory authorities to bring sweeping changes to protect investors' interests.

They caused the most significant loss to investors and loss of trust in markets around the world.

Lehman never recovered when the collapse was imminent; Lehman had accumulated a debt of USD 619 billion, rendering the bankruptcy the largest of its kind in the history of Wall Street. Size did not guarantee permanency in existence for this company which was the fourth-largest US investment bank.

It also gained the bad name of being the most conspicuous victim of the US subprime mortgage crisis.

The world trade disaster contributed to USD 10 trillion wipe-outs in market capitalisation from global equity markets, and it was the worst and the biggest-ever fall.

The organisation came out of one disaster and became the centre of another global crisis. While sensible management coped with one external turmoil, they did not come out of another internally manufactured crisis.

The engaged and loyal employees of Lehman did not consider it necessary to stand with the leader who engineered the fall this time.

The evil actions of this financial giant taught many lessons, but the complex instruments in the mortgage and home finance market continue to break the innovative minds to create more significant frauds.

The outcome was to merely make a few cosmetic changes in regulatory and compliance standards.

Fannie Mae and Freddie Mac: Mortgage and Finance Industry, USA

Another example of an artificial crisis is of Fannie Mae, Freddie Mac companies in America. America had created these financial market Goliaths, which held an unchallenged and dominant position in the mortgage market.

Over 50 per cent of all outstanding mortgages in the United States, including a massive share of subprime mortgages, were controlled by these two organisations.

The subprime crisis was artificial chaos, which snowballed to affect the entire mortgage industry in America. Greedy financial company executives approved the home mortgage loans without observing the basic norms of verifying borrower's repaying capacity. Instead, they teach every banker the basics of three Cs: The Character, Capacity and Capital, and the compulsory verification of borrowers on these parameters, and it did not occur to any of the intelligent bankers.

The greedy actions by these financial institutions triggered foreclosures, and led to the downfall of many lending institutions and hedge funds.

The financial disaster in the mortgage industry affected the global credit market, pushing up the interest rates and reducing credit availability.

Of course, we can attribute the reason to the selfishness and greed of people in power. But unfortunately, neither the law enforcers nor the investigators bothered to control it.

The **power elite theory** postulates, "the life and death issues for a nation are decided by the single elite group and not by a multiplicity of competing groups; leaving trivial matters for the middle level and nothing for the unsuspecting common poor people".

"Therefore, the power elite always disrupts and detests the unequal and unjust distribution of power wherever it finds."

India prides itself being the world's largest democracy. It has a free government but witnesses' politicians and a few power elites always driving everything. The world's 1 percent rich people have more than twice as much wealth as 6.9 billion people. The power elite spent massive money on elections, and the elected candidates quickly recovered the money many times over through corrupt means. The elite power influences each decision of the government in power.

The common citizens of the modern democratic society are powerless elements as the leaders of armed forces, corporate leaders, and politicians manipulate them. Social conflict theorist Wright Mills highlighted the interwoven interests of these power centres in controlling American lives. The crisis created in the mortgage industry demonstrates the hold of the power elite of every modern society.

The situation caused more damage to all the vital segments of the economy viz., banking, insurance and automobile. Future generations should learn the values, morals, ethics and principles alone can save nations' economies in the long run.

Wall Street experts saw the brewing subprime crisis, which would seal the fate of many banks in America.

The event happened when 22 banks had shut down because they could not bear the adverse impact. Lehman Brothers had a 138-year history and had to file for bankruptcy, followed by the biggest Washington Mutual Funds. Many small and medium-sized banks went bankrupt. The shock waves hit the financial markets not only in America but also the world economies.

The subprime mortgage crisis affected the banking sector far beyond Wall Street, as stock markets tumbled in every nook and corner of the world. The stocks nosedived in every significant exchange viz., Frankfurt, Tokyo and New York.

The European Central Bank rescued many banks in Europe by injecting €95 billion cash assistance.

The Central Bank of Japan injected 600 billion yen or 3.6 billion euros. The funds given out for this purpose were many times more than the money given out after the terrorist attack on the World Trade Centre. The shock waves hit the IKB Deutsche Industriebank in Germany (Europe).

French bank BNP Paribas created an unprecedented step of halting withdrawals, as the bank had no clue of the extensiveness of impact on its assets. The bank came out of trouble with the infusion of USD 11.1 billion. The bank had an enormous exposure in the mortgage segment.

Deutsche Bank attempted to fight the impact by redirecting or re-routing euros worth 100 million of the bank's funds. German federal agency BaFin, the German regulatory authority which supervises over 4,000 financial institutions, resorted to hiked rates of interest which brought lending to businesses and choked liquidity in the money markets. The entire system of interbank borrowing and lending got upset.

The world changed after the dropping of atom bomb- and now years later the global economy faced the crisis. Yet, American International Group (AIG), a global insurance company, survived because of the US government's USD 80 billion bailout money. Likewise, Citibank wrote off USD 60 billion as bad debts but got rescued by the US government's bailout plan. These are events and changes of high impact and magnitude, triggered by external events.

AIG story, USA.

American International Group (AIG) is not an amateur player in the insurance market and has always been a different global insurance giant.

They do not follow the beaten track as they are a unique in insurance business. They provide insurance cover to even the weirdest items, e.g., shrunken skulls collection, a 15th-century witchcraft book printed on human skin, trophies of stuffed animals, a model of Marc Quinn's self-sculpture made of his blood, et al. They go to extreme lengths to settle or even deny claims.

A customer had damaged his Ferrari Enzo that was insured and wanted the same car back. To satisfy the customer, they remade it in Italy.

AIG was always a high-risk buyer, and its financial products division was a synthetic buyer of varieties of asset-backed securities.

Profit declined, and AIG started denying more claims.

Even their client Metro-Goldwyn-Mayer Studios

Inc. had once accused the AIG unit of failing to support, despite a statement which said that it would defend the studio against lawsuits at a crucial trial over ownership of the James Bond movie franchise.

AIG settled after a California state court judge found the AIG unit had dropped the coverage. Many consumer lawyers had opined that the company's business strategy was to refuse the claims.

AIG's debacle was because of the outcome of an aggressive culture, which was reflected in their investment strategy. They bet on the housing market and other asset classes without buying the bonds backed by mortgages or other assets. AIG's investment strategy has been incomprehensible one to ordinary people. To the average observer, AIG appeared to be insuring mortgage bonds backed by banks, while AIG's misplaced belief was there wouldn't be even a remote chance of making a pay-out. Goldman Sachs and Merrill Lynch, too, contributed to the messy business.

AIG reported results and said the swaps had declined in value by USD 352 million. The condition deteriorated, and AIG's image changed to one of a demon. AIG built their big businesses with questionable methods by their senior sales executives by creating relationships with influential business and government leaders, who obliged for personal gains.

They found new markets, invested in developing economies, and recruited the best, most talented and dedicated workforce. They had 1,00,000 employees.

Seizing opportunities at high risk is normal and acceptable in AIG's culture. For example, AIGFP- a division of AIG in London- saw potential new business opportunities and made windfall profits by insuring CDOs against default. It came through a financial product, named a credit default swap. However, it was doubtful if AIG was concerned about the high risks of covering a volatile market.

This new risk insurance product became a money-spinner as the revenue jumped to over USD three billion, contributing 17-18%.

It meant heavy incentive to those who architected this new money-spinning product. They did not worry or even bother as personal greed won even as company interest was buried.

The economy behaved adversely, and foreclosures rose to high levels. As a result, AIG's calculation of no pay-out went non-functional and it had to end up paying a vast amount on what their insurance covers. Analysts ascribe the problems to AIG Financial Products. There is always an allegedly unregulated, irresponsible derivatives dealer hiding within an otherwise solid insurance company. In contrast, the company got into a tough spot by lending securities from its life insurance companies' portfolios.

Short-term cash from collateral was diverted to long-term investments with the hope of no decline in values even as it hoped to rake in huge profits; obviously, this went utterly wrong.

In six years, the securities lending programme shot up from USD 10 billion at the end of 2001 to an excess of USD 80 billion.

AIG could not pay the demands due to a lack of liquidity. As a result, the borrowers ceased renewing their loans, returned their securities, and requested payback; revenue and profit were severely harmed. As a result, the division's loss was USD 25 billion, which impacted the parent company's stock price. In addition, accounting issues and irregularities aggravated the situation, increasing the extent of the losses.

As AIG's credit rating declined, it was required to provide additional securities for its bondholders, affecting the already stressed finances and equities that the New York Stock Exchange was caught up in.

AIG remains the world's biggest insurance company, which covers anything and everything for individuals and companies. AIG's culture is of high-flying life that suited AIG's top executives. Management encouraged risk-taking and seizing every chance for a business that brought huge cash returns to the "band of brothers". As a result, the team revolutionised the insurance business by building a multibillion-dollar industry.

AIG symbolised the capitalistic American dream, and the work culture had been demanding. Therefore, it was unsuitable for the weak-hearted and suited those eager to bet every cent to make huge money, fame, and a fast-paced lifestyle.

AIG had created a profit addiction approach among top executives, which drove them to make another team of aggressive managers with deep knowledge and an enormous desire for money, driving arrogant behaviour propelled by success.

The top executives bragged about shaking hands with a slew of American presidents, from Nixon to Clinton, to demonstrate their capitalistic lust.

Greed breeds greed, and when greedy people rub shoulders with power centres, a scam culture is always lurking behind the masks. Falsetto, a former vice president of human resources at AIG's life insurance branch in Manhattan, was one such veiled visage mentioned in every newspaper article. In exchange for payments, he siphoned off business funds to numerous fictitious firms.

Thus, the jet-set mentality of senior executives who went after everything money could buy was fuelled by aggressive incentive plans.

AIG truly reflected the capitalistic culture where money is everything. According to *Time* magazine, Mr Joe Cassano, a founding member of the product division, earned USD 280 million over eight years at AIG at the time of his exit; he got USD 1million a month through the end of 2008.

They credit AIG with the repayment of every penny of their dues by 2013, even though they received immense help. Robert H Benmosche, AIG president and the chief executive officer, did not mix any words when he expressed his appreciation and pride for the support from the government for returning every cent. So, what began as the bailout in 2008 ended in 2012 when AIG claimed full repayment. However, it has raised doubts and questions about how the federal authorities accounted for profit post-bailout by 2014.

AIG posted a double-digit jump in second-quarter profit, announced solid results in its core operations, and made significant gains after the worst crisis. By the year 2007, the net income was substantially higher. After five years of restructuring and repayment of the rescue package, Peter Hancock was at the helm, driving changes in the company's worldwide operations. Even today, capitalistic America's new super-rich are corporate chieftains of Wall Street financial insurance service companies and banks. The destructive potential of the nuclear bomb was known to America. Similarly, AIG was aware of the destructive potential in the complex world of strange financial instruments such as credit default swaps.

But unfortunately, the financial service and insurance companies are again active with an added craving for creative destruction, and they are loaded with new tools.

Reforms and Compliance Measures

The subprime crisis in the USA brought along significant changes in the way business is conducted and reported to stakeholders. Control measures increased in the mortgage industry across America, and stringent regulatory standards were introduced from every government agency. The change impact was enormous in the internal operations and operating procedures of insurance and financial companies.

A completely new and retooled job descriptions, regulators and legislators-imposed actions regarding lending methods, bankruptcy protection, tax policies, affordable housing, credit counselling, education, and licensing etc emerged.

While the operational risk was the prime focus area for larger lenders, credit and interest rates were important factors for small lenders. This perception difference caused varying degrees of change in initiatives in the internal operation, control and management, employee training and reskilling in those organisations.

The most significant change induced in America after the Enron exposure was the Sarbanes Oxley Act of 2002. The Securities and Exchange Commission of the US tightened its grip on how the companies had to report financial figures. The Sarbanes Oxley Act comprises 11 different parts and six significant sections.

First, the CEO and CFO of the company have to certify in writing that they write the financial statements accurately and truthfully to the best of their knowledge.

Secondly, the Public Company Accounting Oversight Board would investigate and punish auditing firms that do not adhere to the Generally Accepted Accounting Principles.

The third gives the power to hire, fire, and compensate accounting firms that audit the company's financial statements.

The fourth step was more regulations on audit firms staying away from businesses with a conflict of interest.

Fifth is providing internal checks to ensure that the shareholders and future investors have transparency and adequate disclosure.

Last, penalties in the form of up to 20 years' imprisonment for anyone involved in altering or destroying any documents.

The Sarbanes Oxley Act, known as SOX, brought changes to the corporate governance methods of public companies and fixed the responsibility of external auditors.

The Act established the Public Company Accounting Oversight Board, which set forth the standards for public accountants and limited the conflicts of interest. In addition, it prescribed the lead audit partner's rotation every five years for the same public company.

Similar legislative regulations are equivalent to SOX in different countries:

Japan — J Sox-April-2008.
Australia-CLERP 9 (Corporate Law Economic Reform Programme) (Audit Reform and Corporate Disclosure) Act 2004.
Canada — Canadian Sarbanes Oxley Act or C-SOX-Ontario, Canada-Bill 198-October 2003.
India — Clause 49-December 2005.
European Union — Euro-SOX- (The 8th EU Directive or the audit directive)
England — Combined Code of Corporate Governance-1998.
Italy — Law 262/2005 - (The protection of savings and regulation of financial markets)-2005.
France — Financial Security Law of France, July 2013.

Enron-India

The Enron story is an archetype of the big, wealthy and powerful capitalists exploiting the weak and powerless third world governments and businesses. It is a typical example of arrogance and greed.

Kenneth Lay and Jeffrey Skilling were in command in Enron during the peak of their criminal intentions when Enron collapsed. They caused the job loss of over 20,000 people and ruined the life savings of thousands of investors. Enron and its leaders were timeless examples of human greed, hubris and self-deception.

They were open to experimenting in deregulated markets and never admitted that it would expose them.

Enron was another typical American capitalist business owner, Kenneth Lay's creation.

The duo and their team were aware of each manipulation by Kenneth Lay, as he presided over the company for many years.

He watched it grow into an energy-trading global monster.

Enron merged two gas companies, i.e., Inter-North & Houston Natural Gas, and created one significant entity. Enron's principal business was in natural gas, electricity, commodities and services. Because of its tremendous demand, the company became the world's primary energy company and earned an honour by *Fortune* magazine as "America's Most Innovative Company" for six consecutive years. In addition, they were once admired as the most innovative company.

However, it filed the biggest bankruptcy case in American history. Initially, profits soared, and shares were surging, and after the exposure of the fraud, shares that were quoting at USD 90 suddenly plunged to USD 1. The scandal surfaced in October 2001, and it led to the demise of one of the top five audit and accounting firms, Arthur Andersen.

The fraud involved concealing financial information through fraudulent accounting strategies and ambiguous financial reporting with the connivance of the auditors. Even the examiner appointed by the bankruptcy court found out larger-scale violations of GAAP (Generally Accepted Accounting Principles) and SEC regulations. Yet, it took the federal government over three years to unearth the dubious accounting methods and irregularities.

The significant reasons for Enron's fall are:

(i) Non-existing board oversight; the board itself comprised dishonest people.
(ii) Disproportionate financial incentives for executives.
(iii) Lack of ethics, principle and culture; reflecting in the discipline throughout business organisations.
(iv) Opportunistic leadership with selfish motives. The company could hide huge debts through the creation of dubious accounting entries. As a result, they managed the lies, inflated profits but concealed billions of worth of debts.

The resulting bankruptcy amounted to USD 63 billion. Auditors at Arthur Andersen paid the price because they also turned blind to the unethical business behaviour of the leaders.

The deception resulted in a loss of jobs for 85,000 people at Anderson. The world-renowned audit firm was sentenced and fined a substantial sum.

This was an example of a crisis hitting unprepared management. Instead, they preached corporate governance and best practices. In 1992, Enron entered India's energy sector with the help of the IMF, which exerted pressure on the Indian government to start deregulation and privatisation in the country's power industry.

The power generation and supply were with the government, and Enron chose the target through the IMF.

At least, one honest and strong-willed leadership driven by principle could have averted Enron's collapse.

Instead, Enron's shareholders lost billions, and employees lost a vast wealth of their benefits. A leader with moral principles would never have let that happen.

British Banking

Greed is a universal phenomenon irrespective of practice. Greed intoxicates all those who are in positions of power and incites them to abuse power and manipulate all others in their favour. However, there exist gaps in the system which greedy individuals are able to navigate with their cleverness and capability.

One person's greed combined with power and the skill to manipulate brought Barings Bank of UK to ruin. The CEO Ramalinga Raju could distort facts with unbridled power. Kenneth ruined Enron.

Managing crises goes along with robust risk management system. Everyone in the financial segment understands the need.

Barings Bank's fraud is an unforgettable example of management arrogance leading to unpreparedness in handling any crisis, and showed the complete lack of leadership. In February 1995, one man single-handedly demolished a large bank, even though the bank had a long and respectful history for over two centuries.

The bank's history prompted them to boast about the funding of the Napoleonic Wars, the Louisiana Purchase, and the Erie Canal with British pride. Founded in 1762, no other British bank had the privilege of being Queen Elizabeth's bank.

The fraud was committed, although the bank's management was conservative and known to have well-established practices. Nick Leeson got the nickname "Rogue Trader" after destroying Barings Bank.

He was the derivatives broker who had been given the authority to handle low-risk arbitrage opportunities between Singapore and Japanese exchanges. But, as if a wild elephant had been let loose, once Nick Leeson was given the position of general manager in faraway Singapore, he had complete authority over both the trading and back office, and threw away all established checks and balances. All the senior managers had merchant banking backgrounds, and risks involved in speculative trading were not their domain.

Nick Leeson unleashed the freedom available to indulge in rampant speculation in stock-index futures and government bonds.

These speculations were like high-risk poker bets, and the outcome of highly leveraged trade would lead to huge gains or huge losses.

Barings Bank's culture and style of management would not have tolerated the size of speculation. Yet, in one month alone, he opened up positions worth USD 29 billion through reckless speculative trading. Leeson was aware of the risk, and he committed to playing the high-risk game. The market did not move as expected. Instead, the slump was like a tidal wave that caused the bank's liabilities to go out of reach.

IT Sector, India

Frauds by greedy individuals in power are not confined to the financial business of the rich and larger economies. They appear wherever the scope for making colossal money exists. One greedy person who founded the company and had usurped the powers orchestrated Satyam's fraud. The CEO acted in collusion with the CFO. Even the external auditors, collaborated in certifying falsified accounts.

He took the investors and the legal machinery for a ride. Employees and the investors and bankers were fooled, as there were no extraordinary revenue or profits and the stock prices kept going up. If one man in power has evil intentions and access to a volume of cash, the bureaucracy is willing to cooperate and abet the misdeed. If one is in power with no fear of fraud, the system and the bureaucracy help in illegal ways.

Exposure in real estate gave the company the grit and motivation to undertake more extensive fraud by buying land cheaply from unsuspecting villagers. It established Satyam Computer Services in 1987 as a private company. It floated public equity issues five years into incorporation, timing it utterly with the IT boom and the craze for IT shares by investors.

The enterprise expanded globally, built a customer base of 44 Fortune 500 companies and over 400 multinational corporations.

Every expert overlooked the obvious steps which the fraudster took. But Indian TV channels, newspapers, and other media were too eager to shower praise on Satyam and rushed to run reports on the CEO.

Investment in real estate and land allowed substantial capital gains and accumulated unaccounted cash. By adding another family-owned company, the intent was to build a conduit for draining off the money generated in Satyam.

Through these means, they grabbed 9,000 acres of land across major cities in India.

The company got listed on NASDAQ, and immediately, the shares started trading at double the face value on the first day itself. Sensing that there was an opportunity for big bucks, Satyam floated an ADR. A leading share broker of the Bombay stock market helped in manipulating the share price.

What began as a falsification of revenue and cover-up of performances in one quarter later swelled to a fraud of Rs 7.8 billion. This fraud triggered many changes in the whole IT industry.

They cleverly networked with all the supply chains, including private institutions that would generate bogus training certificates to buy H1B visas.

The Information Technology industry in India had shown a massive surge during the late nineties, and Satyam benefited the most from that opportunity. They grew from a few employees to 53,000 who were employed in back-office work for clients in 66 countries.

This exponential growth was engineered in a few years, leading to even the New York Stock Exchange listing in 2001 and the listing on Euronext in 2008, which were instrumental in creating a big image.

Frauds by greedy leadership are not confined to the banking or the commercial industry but can happen wherever there are opportunities for making huge money quickly exists. Satyam took the investors for a ride every year; they took the legal machinery and the government for a ride. They recreated another Enron fraud.

The corrupt government officials were eager to incite the company's progress with large value government contracts in return for personal favours.

Neither the employees nor the investors had any clue of the reason behind astronomical stock prices.

Ironically, Satyam was the recipient of the coveted Golden Peacock Award for Excellence in Corporate Governance. India's common practice for award committees is to run after corporate CEOs to confer titles and awards for reciprocal business favours. Raju was conferred The Ernst & Young Entrepreneur of the Year. *Dataquest*, which was a leading IT magazine of that time, gave him the IT Man of the Year award in 2000. CNBC gave him the Asian Business Leader - Corporate Citizen of the Year award in 2002.

Such organisations have rules but have no ethics or values, or moral standards for guiding their actions. Even the central nodal agency for IT organisations in India — NASSCOM (National Association of Software Services Companies) may be guilty of a dishonest act. The industry and media helped create a monster after projecting the CEO as the pioneer of the Information Technology business in Indian organisations.

The CEO's biodata included an MBA from Ohio State University, USA, and a stint at Harvard Business School. The fact that he had dealt in real estate before gave the employees of the organisation courage and motivated them. Employees did not sense the fraud. The enormous fraud was using illegal methods to buy land at throwaway prices from poor villagers.

The launch of the IT company projected Satyam as the most promising global IT company to start in the Indian IT service sector. The company expanded globally and soon built a vast empire.

Unfortunately, every expert outside the organisation who analysed the reason for frauds overlooked the apparent steps that had been taken by this fraud initiator. The lure was the greed for power and effortless accumulation of wealth.

So, they bid for the Hyderabad Metro Rail project by creating many subsidiaries. As a result, Hyderabad in India developed into a significant IT centre, and Satyam played a crucial role in the transformation. These events materialised in a matter of a few months since its incorporation.

The NY exchange listing in 2001 and the securing of a place on Euronext in 2008 were significant events that enabled the creation of the global brand image for Satyam.

Like any other company on the NY stock exchange, Satyam had to conform to corporate governance works, and the company appeared to be compliant on its records.

If greed drove the fraud, guilt drove admission to declare that he had engineered systematic falsification of financial accounts.

The firm's balance sheet had presented an existing non-asset as cash and loans from the bank amounting to Rs 53 billion.

The Sanskrit word 'Satyam' means 'absolute truth' and ultimately truth triumphed, though the company officials fed lies to everyone around. Enron did much the same fraud of providing misinformation to its investors.

Stock Market Crisis, India

A crisis can force order and bring about changes in the system and process of the organisations. Yet, failure to learn from artificial problems is rampant despite massive negative experiences. One such case is that of the Indian Stock Market Regulatory System. From fake banker's receipts and warehouse receipts to bull and bear manipulation of Bombay Stock Exchange or National Stock Exchange, several misdeeds continued with little learning even after repeated scams.

Nothing much has changed with the financial management systems, except for a few cosmetic changes.

People in power commit big-time frauds all the time. Bollywood made a superhit movie on Harshad Shantilal Mehta's life and made more money.

Mehta was a high-profile stockbroker and hit the headlines for the notorious Bombay Stock Exchange security scam of 1992. Popularly known as the Big Bull, he was born in a Gujarati Jain family.

Paradoxically, the Jains preach a simple, pious life and advocate about not amassing wealth beyond one's needs. They consider it as is theft. Harshad Mehta and many other wealthy Jains continue to amass wealth beyond a level. While his guests would drink, he was always a non-drinker, and said he got a kick out of being a bull operator. The Jain monks walk barefoot and even sweep the road before walking, so they do not unknowingly hurt an insect.

The Jains are fanatical about karma, resolution, and a disciplined and simple lifestyle. The reason Jains are wealthy is that their religion teaches self-help as the best form of life.

Jainism, which was born in India around 500 BC, is an active religion.

The word is derived from 'Jina', which means 'Conqueror'.

These are the foundation tenets of Jainism:

(i)   All animals, plants, and humans are living souls and be treated with equal respect and love. Therefore, Jains do not consume meat and are strict vegetarians. However, the new generation eats eggs.
(ii) One need to trust in self-help and not any divine power.
(iii) One need to have faith in reincarnation (rebirth).
(iv) Believe in the five great vows that lead to liberation:
      (a) Ahimsa: Non-violence, aka, not even mental torture.
      (b) Asteya: Steal nothing.
      (c) Brahmacharya: Sexual restraint.
      (d) Satya: Speak the truth or be silent.
      (e) Aparigraha: Do not have attachment to any possession; an extension may cause greed, jealousy, selfishness and other negative emotions.

(v) Jainism has no priests. Instead, the monks and nuns lead strict and ascetic lives.

(vi) Everyone should respect all living beings and prevent hurting any.

(vii) Jains are divided into two sects, Shvetember and Digambar. Monks belonging to Digambar sect don't wear any clothes, excepting when walking outside their temples. Only men may be monks in their society. The Shwetambar monks always wear white clothes, and women can become monks.

(viii) Jainism is an ecologically responsible religion.

(ix) Believe that the life's aim should be to perfect the soul.

(x) Avoid delusions and distractions.

(xi) Believe in the concept of three jewels:

 (a) Right faith - right perception: Never believe what you hear or were told and jump to opinions.

 (b) Right conduct (samyak charitra): Do not harm other living beings and be free from attachment and different impure attitudes and thoughts.

 (c) Right knowledge (samyak jnana): Have the right, proper mental attitude.

In India and Antwerp, many of the super-rich people are Jains. Palanpur in the state of Gujarat in India has the history of being the first place where the diamond business began in 1909. The Mehtas and Shahs from India control three-quarters of the diamond business of Antwerp.

Antwerp has a few thousand people in diamond cutting and polishing work, while Surat in India has over 5,00,000. Nirav Modi of the recent diamond scam has been overseeing three generations of the diamond trade in Belgium and had lived the most luxurious life, contrary to the Jain belief system. Jains support each other intensively.

As far as diet is concerned, Jains follow a strict code of conduct; they eat nothing taken from the ground like potatoes, onion or garlic. There are extreme cases of followers excluding green vegetables.

Fanatic Jains take the vow, called anastasia, aka, not eating after sunset. They vow not to consume food which has been stored overnight.

The Jains have taken over Antwerp in the world's diamond trade from the Jews. The Mehtas and the Shahs and not the Epsteins and Finkelszteins of Israel rule Hoveniersstraat which is the hub. The Jains from India control seventy five percent of the Antwerp's diamond industry.

Jains believe in an extreme form of self-sacrifice and charity with no expectation.

Mehta was not like many of his community members. He grew up in Mumbai, the metro city where his father was a short-time business owner. But, with media backing and prodding, he managed the transformation from a modest broker to a big-time player and was nicknamed "Big Bull".

First, Mehta had a brief stint on job with a general insurance company. He changed his affiliation to a BSE affiliated stockbroker, became a jobber on the BSE, and soon became a sub-broker for leading stock brokers. (The Bombay Stock Exchange traditionally has been the stronghold of the Gujarati community.)

A company established by him called Growmore Research and Asset Management Company Limited began trading. By 1990, traders associated Mehta's name with bull runs.

He used to buy the shares of the blue-chip cement company (ACC-Associated Cement company)) heavily to exploit the investor confidence in that script.

He would inflate the price of a cement company, creating a 4400% jump in its price.

By 1991, Mehta had elevated himself as the most prominent player, and the media propelled him to get into that orbit.

But the power elite was also in full force. Mehta's close-knit associates, community members, and bank chiefs blindly supported and helped by empowering extensive manipulation of the share market in the BSE and exploiting the gaps in the Indian banking system to syphon off funds.

After locking in cash through dubious means to borrow, they bought stocks at a high premium across many industry verticals. The sensex rose dramatically due to artificially inflated price push. A few banks who lent money noticed Mehta's intentions, and they demanded the money back amounting to billions of rupees; once this news leaked to the press, the sensex collapsed dramatically. This crisis affected many financial companies, and investors lost money for no fault of theirs. The government slapped over 70 criminal cases and over 600 civil cases on him.

Mehta's illegal methods of manipulating the stock market were exposed in April 1992, not by any government or regulatory agencies but by a financial columnist of *The Times of India*, the leading daily newspaper.

Finally, Mehta and his brothers were in jail, tried and convicted.

Mehta died while serving a sentence, though many cases are still pending against him in courts. Growmore died on its own.

If Mehta changed the BSE brokers' trading style, the scam changed the BSE's trading controls. The Securities Laws (Amendments) Act was passed in 1995, had widened the scope of the Securities and Exchange Board of India (SEBI), to strictly monitor and control depositories, FIIs, venture capital funds, and credit rating agencies.

Stock Market Scam 2: Bombay Stock Exchange, India

The Bombay Stock Exchange can boast of many scandals and frauds. Ketan Parekh was a chartered accountant the Indian equivalent of an American CFA and he was a stockbroker based in Mumbai, India. He destroyed that life when he became a much-publicised convict in 2008. He architected the largest scam of technology stocks in India's stock market during1999-2001.

Parekh belonged to a family of stockbrokers, and the community he belonged to was famous for its participation in the stockbroking professions. This was an advantage as blind community faith usually adds to one's strength.

Parekh was a shy person, and the hype elevated him as the sharpest share market predictor.

Two people with similar intentions and from the same community, created two big scams.

Mehta belonged to the lower-middle class, while Parekh's background was that he came from a family of stockbrokers. Moreover, many famous stockbrokers were his relatives, which made collaboration easy.

The Indian economy was a protected one, and the stock market was getting modernised. This situation helped Mehta operate undetected, as he used other people's money and the community support to exploit the weaknesses in the system.

Market people understood Mehta as one with flashy lifestyle with a super luxury Lexus car and many other cars, as well expensive sea view apartment in Mumbai. The tactics adopted by Parekh included planting stories on the shares and selling the inflated claims to institutional investors.

Parekh attracted the attention of brokers and investors of all capacities. Everyone watched his moves, believing that everything he bought would turn into big-time profits.

Nicknamed "Pentafour Bull", he kept a low profile for a while deliberately.

By 1999-2000, Indian IT companies started growing and were going public. These stocks became the golden goose and displayed signs of hyperactivity as well. His strategy was to target a few IT companies to inflate the prices. Many investment firms which were under the thumb of promoters of public companies were helping Parekh in price manipulation.

The local cooperative banks and even the private banks from other countries fell head over heels to lend to Parekh.

He deployed the capital that had never belonged to him to inflate stock prices.

Once the investors got the news, the stock prices he was targeting saw an upward spiral. Another IT company, VisualSoft's stock, was quoting at Rs 625 and that price shot up dramatically to Rs 8,448 per share.

Sonata Software, another small computer software company's stock was artificially inflated from Rs 90 to Rs 2,150. Mere price rigging was not fraud. Parekh found a safe place to dump increased stocks in big financial companies through the connivance of their corrupt officials, such as the Unit Trust of India. The usual industry practice in India for companies issuing an IPO is to take the help of unknown stockbrokers to back the issues and help in hiking the post issue prices.

Ketan Parekh had tactfully created a network of brokers in smaller and lesser-known towns. The advantage of hiring known people or blood relatives is obedience, and they merely do what they are told.

However, the companies commit unaccounted financial transactions to evade tax in what Indian's call 'benami', aka, 'nameless or without a name' transactions.

The deal consideration for immovable property transfers title to a virtual person or a stranger who cannot be traced to the family. Even the cab drivers, personal servants and housemaids are made such benami owners by paying cash as rewards.

The person who pays for the property is the ultimate beneficiary of the property in the future.

Such a property is named benami. Industrialists and politicians who amass wealth illegally used this method to launder unaccounted cash.

To prevent money laundering fraud, the government made these types of transactions illegal under the Benami Transaction (Prohibition) Amendment Bill, 2015.

Parekh widely used benami means, to purchase stocks in the names of unknown poor people living even in Mumbai's slums. KP had borrowed vast sums from a private bank, Global Trust Bank, and profited much through price manipulation.

The Global Trust Bank kept on understating the loan amount of Rs 2.5 billion. Another small community bank, the Madhavpura Mercantile Cooperative Bank, loaned again a huge sum. The bank violated Reserve Bank of India's regulations on the maximum amount it could lend a broker (Rs 150 million).

A bear cartel finally collapsed and crushed the flaring prices in February 2000. Despite attempts by Ketan Parikh and his allies to prop up the prices, they could not rescue falling prices.

The banks loaned with no discretion, and two of them, viz., the Global Trust Bank and the Madhavpura Cooperative bank, faced the heat to go under.

The Bank of India, another government-owned bank, had loaned the vast sum. They filed a criminal complaint, and the Central Bureau of Investigation (CBI) stepped in to stop Ketan Parekh's two-year dominance of the share market by arresting him.

As with dishonest dealings by Nick Leeson of Barings Bank, Parekh had to meet his failure because of greed. This crisis did tremendous damage to the Bombay Stock Exchange and destroyed the trust and confidence of millions of investors, especially the amateur investors who had blindly followed Ketan Parekh. The scam also impacted many shares, which lost their value heavily, and people who had blindly followed Parekh's moves lost their entire life savings. In addition, many banks, including government-owned banks, lost significant amounts of money.

Parekh's intention was not understandable to any clumsy and casual investor. Media was the culprit as they fuelled a celebrity image of a Bollywood movie hero. A few national dailies had even interviewed and quoted him as an economic expert on India's Union Budget.

The white-collar criminals are always a step ahead of the systems that try to prevent the crime. Harshad Mehta's scam of 1992 exposed the miserable inadequacy of the regulatory system, and later, Ketan Parekh's fraud reinforced the inadequacy. The Securities Exchange Board of India (SEBI) and the Reserve Bank of India (RBI) are unable to prevent frauds and remove the inadequacy of the systems,

Reducing the trading cycle from a week to a day and banning the carry-forward system in stock trading called BADLA were all examples of such steps, which were merely an eye wash. SEBI approved forward trading as exchange-traded derivatives to protect the futures market and eliminate stockbroker hold over stock exchanges.

SEBI officials had the misdirected perception of their role as watchdogs to check stock prices rather than be responsible for fraud prevention. However, SEBI made few extreme changes.

They banned the short sales and increased the margins. These measures troubled a frustrated system and the investors, leading to cash shortage. The volume of trade shrunk to one-sixth of the average level.

The action included dismissal of all the broker directors from the Bombay Stock Exchange and Calcutta Stock Exchanges and blacklisting of bear operators while launching a detailed inquiry into their alleged short sales.

The fraud changed the way business was done. India's stock markets became cautious and safer. The crisis was a factor in forcing inefficient financial policy-makers to bring reforms into the system.

The ban of individuals and entities from trading in the stock markets as a penalty for manipulative practices are never effective. Bans are of no use, as the participants in the system know how to beat the system and work around technicalities. Enforcing the ban is extremely complex compared to the punishment. One can start a private limited company, appoint a few relatives or a close acquaintance as a director, and invest through that firm, drawing no one's attention.

These massive frauds brought sweeping changes to the management systems. However, few organisations took proactive steps to install checks and balances, while others pretended to be insulated.

Human ingenuity always moves ahead, and few greedy leaders always bring crises.

The moral of the story is obvious: one has to learn from others' mistakes and change.

CHAPTER 3

CONVENTIONAL APPROACHES TO CHANGE MANAGEMENT

Any change is a drastic departure and a planned action to meet the market forces and challenges in business. It is not merely about designing and installing a new process. To be effective, the changes have to positively impact the company, increase revenue or profit, improve the work climate and last long-term.

Process change, or structural change is necessary, but resurrecting any failing organisation requires a creative strategy and action plan. The impact of well-orchestrated change is on all those affected by the change and the entire organisation benefits.

A famous statement is "yesterday's methods cannot win tomorrow's battle". So, every process gathers momentum with discontent, growing among the majority with what is being done.

Change is perceived as unnecessary waste by those who don't learn from past actions' ineffectiveness; decisions and inertia may lead to the organisation drawing its last breath (e.g., Kodak, Steuben). Even if the idea to change incubates in leaders' minds, much damage is done before disclosing it to the surrounding people. The idea of accepting change needs enough time, which varies from one organisation and individual to another.

Change is a reformation to the existing state or condition that defies the present belief systems of people and their behaviour. Change is a deliberate action to modify a current set of rules or processes or even the offerings for survival to enable sustained and better performance.

It is human to define how the world should work for us. Therefore, another way of interpreting change is to define change as an action inconsistent with the self-created definition of the world around.

Change is starts as vague however well planned, and reactions to change initiatives unfold subtly during the progress of change process.

Organisational change and people management is a structured process for empowering, conscripting, encouraging people to accept, adapt, and align with planned changes.

Crucial Steps

Any planned change at the bare minimum, have actions to include:

(i) Need analysis.

(ii) Organisational SWOT analysis.

(iii) Shared vision and proliferation of the shared vision.

(iv) Readiness assessment, aka, finding out how soon the change process can be initiated in the organisation.

(v) Strategy for implementation and communication

(vi) Identification of change champions and agents to drive the change and gain momentum.

(vii) Milestones and interim measurement plans, goals, results combined with review process.

(viii) Impact measurement for the success of the plan.

Change materialises by deploying basic management principles such as planning, organising, coordination, control, evaluation and feedback. Change helps organisations carry individuals and teams from an existing state of as-is to a better future to a to-be state of rejuvenated performance.

Planned changes impact people and are always a sensitive issue. Therefore, the need is evident for anyone involved in leading change to master the subject.

21st century organisations face increasingly pressure from external forces and they compel changes. But transformations have to be a thoughtful act carefully articulated, well-structured and planned.

Prompted by a desire to be opportunistic and grab the advantages of escaping to a future or even taking reactive action to face a threat is change. Moving an organisation from the 'as is' to a 'to be' state involves tremendous efforts.

The leadership actions to change always have to "come out with the end in mind"- Steven Covey- and be influenced by reasons for assessing the current readiness along with capabilities.

Change in an organisation becomes expedient to stay profitable in the long run and grow by adapting to changing customer needs.

Established Approaches

Action Research

Business Action Research is a variation of participatory research. It is done to discuss and solve an immediate problem. It is a reflective process of problem-solving, led by team members working with others. The principal reason for undertaking Action Research is help in improving or refining the action steps.

Unlike controlled laboratory experiments and assessments, Action Research indulges in action and evaluating while implementing change.

This technique can help one to experiment with different approaches with discrete groups, especially when groups exhibit resistance for various reasons.

One uses this problem-solving approach from a general idea, followed by fact-finding, planning, auctioning, evaluating, and planning a second action.

It is leans towards practice. Action Research is "self-reflexive inquiry," carried out to "improve rationality and justice".

Action Research is more popular in educational research and is used to improve educational outcome using change interventions. However, its critics would claim that the drawback lies in objectively selecting subjects and participants.

Just as the criticism posited about any other research methodology, here too, questions are raised about the integrity of choice of subjects and respondents' honesty.

Therefore, those who use this method analyse, evaluate their current state and make changes to improve.

Lewin's Three-step Model

Kurt Lewin's introduced in 1947, a model and it is relevant even today, despite being criticised of being over-simplistic. Subsequently, newer methodologies have been developed around this approach. The method supports the three stages viz., unfreezing, change and refreezing. He hypothesised, that change is not an isolated event but a process.

Lewin's model stated about motivation to change, communications and empowering people to embrace novel ways of working (change) the process. They all end when the organisation reaches stability. Stability through new, changed ways is necessary for establishing the confidence to embark on the next wave of change.

This second stage occurs as everyone makes the adjustments to change as needed. Refreezing a stage of stability is reached once the changes have been imbibed, accepted and they've become the new normal. People form new connections and experience the routine in their unique ways.

This over simplistic approach seems to be inappropriate in modern times.

Lippitt, Watson and Westley Extended Model

A seven-step model was created in 1958 which emphasised the role and responsibility of the transformation agent.

The seven phases of change are elaborated under Lewin's three-step model. These steps shift the change process and include the role of a change agent through the progress of the change.

Phase 1: Detect and establish the problem.

Phase 2: Measure the motivation and dimension for change.

Phase 3: Evaluate the resources, inspiration and commitment of the change agent, their power and stamina.

Phase 4: Establish stages and milestones of change.

Phase 5: fortify the role and responsibility of the change agent to ensure they are understood by communicators, facilitators, and subject experts.

Phase 6: Keep the tempo of communication, feedback, and group coordination alive.

Phase 7: Decide the exit point for change agent as the changed process is embedded and becomes the new organisational culture

John Kotter's Eight-8 step Model

John Kotter said, "Leaders who transform businesses do eight steps, and they do them in the right order." His change management model was developed on these lines. Kotter's work on *Leading Change* remains authentic and relevant to many corporations who undertake change as an appropriate intervention to keep going profitably. In the modern complex scenario, it is not sure the over simplistic model will any more deliver results. Kotter, in his work, *Leading Change*, introduced the eight-step model:

Step 1: Create urgency. Changing it helps if the entire company accelerates the intensity to change.
What is needed is the intense urge for change, which will act like a spark; it is similar to the role of ignition in the car.

Step 2: Form a powerful alliance. Develop the conviction of people about why change is important by giving them hard facts.

Step 3: Create a vision for change. Link the thoughts to an overall vision which people can accept, whereby it becomes a shared vision.

Step 4: Communicate the vision frequently, powerfully, and embed it within everything. Talk as often as possible about change vision.

Step 5: Remove obstacles. Create the structure for progress monitoring. Resistors of change progress must be dealt with.

Step 6: Plan quick but short wins. Nothing equals winning — it is the most inspiring thing. The success during early life of the change process always acts as catalyst in accelerating further efforts.

Step 7: How to enhance progress by building on success? Small wins lead to a long-term change.

Step 8: Implant the changes into corporate culture. Finally, it should become a part of its core values to make any change stick. A corporate culture where everyone is aligned with the vision of the top person often determines what and how soon many new initiatives are to be done.

The values behind the vision are reflected in the attitude and behaviour exhibited in the day-to-day work.

A variety of models have contributed to the evolution of OCM.

McKinsey's 7-S Model

In Search of Excellence, published in 1982, remains the best-selling and most widely read management book in time. Tom Peters and Waterman, the authors, found eight common themes leading to companies' success. These have become pointers for corporate leaders and managers ever since.

The McKinsey 7-S model formed the base for the famous work of Tom Peters' *in Search of Excellence*, focusing on the customer, people and action. However, Tom Peters would go on to claim to add **speed** as the demanding element besides the eight factors discussed in his book, even by his admission.

The model elements are:

Strategy, Structure, Systems, Shared Values, Style, Skills, Staff.

Everything contributes to shared values.

Organisations can deploy this "never say die" approach at even project level. The model is constituted by three intricate and four soft elements; they display the interdependency of various forces driving every organisation.

MRP Systems

Japanese manufacturing techniques brought a fresh wave of creative approaches to enhance efficiency. The just-in-time technique is "to produce what was needed and eliminate waste"; this was the crux of the Toyota production system. Another Japanese technique Kanban and Kaizen brought holistic changes in many of the manufacturing practices in Western and Asian organisations.

Quality Focused Management Systems

Starting with the earliest work of Edward Deming to the modern avatar of Lean Sigma, the ideas attempt to focus on isolating the root causes of performance problems and changing the existing methods. A significant push to the transformation movement came with Michael Hammer's Re-engineering ideas in 1990, as it created a tsunami of change.

Many experts, including Michael Hammer, argued that the minor tiny improvements might not significantly affect the strategic actions. Instead, it asks "what an ant can do to the elephant" - forgetting that an ant could even kill an elephant.

A few visionary leaders took advantage of these novel approaches to change their organisations, while many struggled to unlearn and relearn new ideas.

Most change management activities concentrate on retraining one or other skills to implement change successfully. Awareness of the interplay between the organisation's environment and the individual is crucial for change in organisations.

One has to first seek to change the system to understand. Lewin called this "Action Research". The core philosophy of Lewin's approach to change addressed changing groups rather than changing individuals.

Models rely more on the systems. They do not rely on the psychology of people to get convinced and change their behaviour.

People don't buy the CEO's vision and swear by the loyalty when change happens in a big way, and uncertainty creeps in hard; it takes more than plain sermons. Change requires mental preparation before motivation can be created. All three stages need to be executed with force before the ultimate step can be made easy.

The three stages are:

 (i) Mental preparation.
(ii) Motivation.
(iii) Being propelled to action.

Initiation of change involves mental preparation; hence, the first three steps address the preparation stage.

The steps that follow create the motivation to act before the passion triggers the next four steps. The final three steps discuss the nudge needed to reach the finish line. The goal is vision realisation.

We cover the new model details elsewhere.

CHAPTER 4

DOES ANYONE LEARN FROM PAST CRISIS?

Business means risk. Risk mitigation involves dealing with a crisis, both expected and unexpected. Yet, although many crises have destroyed businesses in the past due to their huge negative impact, few organisations in the world can boast of equipping themselves with a robust defiance strategy to face all sorts of crisis. Yet, every one of these affected organisations would boast of brilliant talents carefully selected and nurtured over the years.

Fraudsters are like hawks in behaviour and are always creative in inventing new methods to cheat. Everyone in corporate leadership knows that every tiny crisis, however small, if ignored, has the potential to snowball into monstrous proportions and spin out of control. Any unresolved problem can cost an organisation and destroy everything it has built for years.

Jerry Sandusky's child sex abuse episode at Penn State in the USA illustrates this point. The scandal exploded out of the blue, years after it was committed.

There was no strategy to manage the crises, and the entire leadership of those bodies involved was caught unaware.

Blind faith leads to the crime being buried and leads to disastrous consequences if left unchecked for a long time.

It affected the university at many levels, including the demolition of its fair name and reputation. What followed was sanctions placed on it by the NCAA, and the job loss of many executives, including the president and vice president and athletic director.

In October 2013, Penn State ended up paying nearly USD 60 million to 26 victims. Thus, capitalism was the unfortunate tool used to squash the issue; aka, money was thrown around to hide the crime. It should be remembered that while insurance companies may pay the damages, losing reputation is massive and can never be compensated.

While emergencies come in many forms, it invariably places the onus on the current leadership to face the challenge. If the leaders don't answer the challenge, someone else will. When others narrate a twisted story, it won't be to the liking of most of the affected parties. Without the leadership's response, the people will draw their own conclusions based on what is circulated by the media.

The way of conveying is as serious step as the message itself. When one takes a defensive stance of "no comment", things might only worsen.

Organisations need to have an articulated, strategic action plan as few crises catch any leadership off-guard. An example is the recent Covid pandemic when millions of businesses, big or small, were caught unprepared.

Large companies often have to handle social media crises and few manage the media-created problem effectively. Many have no clue about handling social media even now. Television channels are often eager to sensationalise - and the public, whether or not affected, get restless and active.

In this digital world, news breaks thick and fast with comprehensive coverage at the click of a button.

Twitter, Facebook and other social network platforms make it easy for any news to go viral. Any organisation facing a crisis is left with little time to react. Arguing with the public in the media, especially when one knows there are innumerable social media users watching, is not always a good idea.

Nowadays, even employees have many avenues through social media to speak about their employers and bosses.

Be it Glassdoor, LinkedIn, Twitter, the world can hear what they say, and ignoring the message or being defensive is never a good strategy.

One example is that of Applebee, when it tried an offensive public posture. It took on social media when the latter erupted in protests about the wrongful termination of an employee.

An Applebee employee was once serving a customer who was a pastor. The latter, when presented with the bill, had written that he would not pay the suggested 18 percent tip as he planned to give 10 per cent to God. The employee posted a picture of the bill on Reddit. Applebee fired the employee for "violating consumer privacy".

Two weeks before the incident, the company had posted a receipt, complimenting the servers. However, the espoused standards were not the same which attracted angrier reactions and public comments made by agitated people. It did not take much time for the news to spread to other social media platforms.

Applebee escalated this to Facebook, and there too, met over 10,000 negative comments. Undeterred, it reposted the same message, trying to make its point, but only drew angrier remarks by social media users who scathingly criticised Applebee.

Two days after the original post, there were over 19,000 comments. Applebee hid the comment, which further incited rage. Applebee's strategy at the time had been to take an offensive approach, but it only added fuel to the fire.

The moral is, "With public and mass communication; one needs to be thoughtful". This holds good when people ask uncomfortable questions when change issues are being communicated. Some say, "settling scores or being right is far less important than being united". This rule needs to be followed in change communication.

Apologies are effective only when the apologiser takes full responsibility for the action or impact. For example, DKNY -a famous clothing brand did respond with apologies when faced with compensation claims from another person for using the photos in a window display.

The person who had taken those photos posted his claim on social media and mobilised community support for his demand that DKNY donate USD 100,000 to a local YMCA. DKNY apologised immediately. Unlike Applebee, they admitted the genuineness of their mistake and ascertained that they had no intention to violate copyright. They donated USD 25,000.

They realised their mistake and accepted the claim. DKNY was quick and balanced in its approach, which defused the crisis which otherwise could have snowballed into a PR crisis.

These examples of communication strategies to handle the crisis created by social media prove the need to define communication strategies and plans to face the situation.

In April-May 2015, a massive earthquake in Nepal claimed 5,000 lives and nearly destroyed the economy of the Himalayan nation.

The 2011 Tahoka earthquake caused tsunami which devastated Japan and caused damages worth USD 300 billion (25 trillion yen).

The Japanese government's estimate showed the earthquake had struck a crippling blow to the economy. These disruptive forces remind governments as well as corporate management that crisis management plans are critical to any operation, and that survival will be at stake without that.

Even a minor crisis can spiral to global proportions, severely disrupting operations and damaging the good name among customers.

Most crises at the beginning appear to be random and unexpected events.

The failure to recognise the potential problem and foresee the probability of them becoming fatal puts companies of all sizes in jeopardy.

The majority of crises are the kinds that smoulder. They begin very tiny and should one be perceptive, they could probably be fixed before assuming significant proportions to run out of control.

Satyam, Enron, Lehman are examples of this disruption which indicates a dire need for systems and methods to resolve them.

Every crisis takes a toll on the bottom line, leaving the recovery task to the leadership and management.

Industrial accidents, devastating oil rig fires, financial fraud, management scandal, government intervention, labour strife, white-collar crime, physical accidents of Chernobyl explosions, chemical, oil spills, and workplace violence can have a crippling impact on business.

A business leader can expose the organisation to risks if they believe that the company is immune to any crisis.

CM's 2010 Annual Crisis Management Survey said, "Crisis because of external forces, account for twenty per cent of the crisis potential, while ineffective leadership, bad management account for over fifty per cent of crisis and employees contribute to the remaining thirty per cent."

This is demonstrated in the Satyam, Enron and RCom examples cited elsewhere.

The leadership in managements with forward-thinking capabilities, use crisis management planning as a tool to effectively manage their business and lessen the impact of external events.

Business is not insulated from any form of crisis. Public anger leading to consumer litigations, product failures leading to recalls, non-compliance leading to government actions are some of the external actions that usher in trouble for a business. Therefore, one requires a solid, fast-paced implementation plan of action when an adverse event happens that negatively affects business.

Crisis in business is well defined by The Institute for Crisis Management "a problem that disrupts how an organisation conducts its business".

Many crises lead to negative financial consequences for the company (an estimated penalty of USD 18 billion for Volkswagen), unless tackled with prompt and effective corrective actions.

Recent crises, which are intentional, have generated severe adverse reactions to Volkswagen. The company has been accused of whole probability throttling defeat software on cars that manipulated emission data. Nestle India was embroiled in a crisis over Maggi noodles in the country (although they eventually disproved it); Nestle went on to face a government ban for non-compliance with food and drug control standards.

These are crisis examples that derailed regular business through substantial financial repercussions.

Threats exist for every organisation and can hit in any form, including natural disasters such as fires, floods, and earthquakes. In this technological era, data security breach is a dangerous threat. Other human-made crises include workplace violence, embezzlement, fraud, industrial accidents, and sabotage. Therefore, one needs a robust communication strategy and action directed to all stakeholders to tackle the crisis.

Managers need three crisis management plans: operational, communication; recovery to return to normalcy and set up continuity. The risk estimation, the probability of occurrence through review and analysis of current operations is the starting point for setting up any crisis management. In addition, the risks associated with location, type of operation, supplier, governmental and political risks are triggers for depth analysis.

Reflect on this story. A fast-growing marketing company in India marketed itself successfully at a national level. They became the sole selling and servicing business for Cannon photocopiers in all the states.

Photocopier shops with the long-distance calling (subscriber trunk dialling facility) services provided a unique employment opportunity for many in rural India.

This innovative retailing services business boomed with the help of bank finance and government subsidy. It became a unique model for employment generation, with a low capital of USD 500, to millions of unemployed school dropouts.

This break allowed this company to capture most of rural India's business by selling and servicing photocopying machines. Consequently, a colossal revenue amounting to Rs 100 million was generated in a few years.

Most of it came through the sale of consumables and maintenance service contracts.

The business was running smoothly for over three years until one fine day, the CEO hurriedly convened an executive committee meeting and told the stunned group that she had decided closing down the business.

The CEO did not assign any reason for the unexpected decision, though it was viewed as breach of trust later on. They came to know from field sales; they had opened a retail outlet in prime locations, which was blatantly violated the exclusive sole selling agreements. The snap decision led to the layoff of 300 full-time employees. The company had to pay retrenchment compensation. It terminated all legal agreements that involved spending a heavy amount as penalties. The company had accumulated an enormous cash reserve, and the business that had been nurtured for three years got wiped off overnight. This crisis was a creation by one person's whim. Was it avoidable?

Yes, if only there were a plan for crisis management in place.

Corporate governance raises its head everywhere purely due to many large-scale frauds that cause massive corporate collapses.

Corporate scandals of various forms and sizes have caused public and political uproar, demanding regulation through proper controls. For example, Enron, Worldcom and other frauds caused the American federal government to pass the Sarbanes Oxley Act in 2002 to protect and restore public confidence in corporate accounting. By the same token, scandals and failures in Australia (HIH, OneTel) triggered eventual passage of the CLERP-9 reforms. (Corporate **Law Economic Reform Program Act 2004.**)

Another business set up as a family-run unit in 1961 grew its dairy business by leaps and bounds and became a global giant. They had over 200 subsidiary companies spread over 48 countries.

But unfortunately, the people running the show created the biggest frauds in Italy. The scam's modus operandi was similar to Enron or Satyam, aka, it covered up losses through manipulation, forgery with deliberate intentions to defraud.

They made dishonest claims and reported massive cash in the books when nothing was available; they resorted to inflating revenue by double billing to fool investors customers and financial institutions. The fraud got multiplied when statutory bodies, instead of being watchdogs, connived.

Few smart analysts can always smell the foul deeds. Few analysts from Meryl Lynch had forewarned the company's borrowing through bond despite having colossal cash, but no one listened.

The company even resorted to financial re-engineering to hide borrowing and show it as equity.

The fraud attempts began with the steady financial performance decline and steeper falls until 2003. The management intentions to defraud by disguising facts were identical to the other colossal frauds. Therefore, Italy had to enhance its regulatory measures with the Parmalat Episode.

These large-scale frauds have set the tone for much robust oversight in many nations. Corporate governance refers to the mechanisms, processes, rules by which organisations with public accountability control and direct their activities while behaving responsibly.

Governance requires conformance to the rules with the identified distribution of rights and responsibilities among various groups or individuals who take decisions.

In any corporate entity, big or small, the board of directors is entrusted with good governance. They run the day-to-day affairs, utilising the money of investors.

One would expect the auditors to deploy fair accounting and standards. The governance procedures affect uniformly all the stakeholders. Corporate governance requires a disciplined approach to be pursued in the regulatory and market environment. Steps include reporting, monitoring actions, policies and decisions of corporations and their executives. In addition, corporate governance practices are aimed at protecting the interests of stakeholders and investing public.

In India, the Ministry of Corporate Affairs and Securities Exchange Board of India are mainly responsible for protecting shareholder wealth and regulating compliance. They took few steps to safeguard the public investment and their interest.

It took over 15 years for various committees to decide on the improved norms. There have been reforms in the corporate governance framework during the last 5 years, starting with Kumar Mangalam Committee in 2004. SEBI issued the revised guidelines on Corporate Governance. The aim was to change the definition of independent directors and strengthen the audit committee's actions, and improve the quality of financial reporting.

The next move was by the Narayana Murthy Committee in 2006 which voluntary guidelines which was followed by a series of guidelines on corporate governance based on the recommendation of the Adi Godrej committee. The revision of the Companies Act 2013 facilitated corporate governance norms by SEBI (2014). It amended the Companies Act 2013 to give the basic level of corporate governance relevant to all companies.

It took the big scams to force changes in the Companies Act and elevate the bar on governance standards for companies.

There has been a constant demand for transparency on conducting board matters, the roles and responsibilities of the board, various mandatory board committees, and independent directors' duties. Meeting the global standards on corporate governance of the mature markets and economies was the main goal.

The UK Companies Act, US MBCA, US-DGCL, UK FRC Code, Stewardship Code and SOX are a few such examples. However, the responsibilities of a board of directors are vital to the overall governance.

The Securities Exchange Board of India reconfirmed this condition after a series of financial scams and frauds. However, the responsibilities of the board and various board committees were either ignored or not defined.

CHAPTER 5

REGULATIONS, DISCIPLINE AND GOVERNANCE: RESHAPING THE CONDUCT OF BUSINESS

Corporate frauds and scandals of immense magnitude have impacted corporate governance worldwide; reforms have continued to emerge since 2018. The latest in the fraud list is the Petrobras (semi-public corporation in Brazil in the oil and gas sector) scandal in Brazil. In addition, recent stock market incidents in India exposed the way regulations were bypassed.

The Toshiba accounting scandal in Japan and Volkswagen's emission fraud had a substantial impact on corporate governance measures in those countries across the globe.

There exists a constant demand for stricter measures to promote management accountability and transparency from companies, especially of their boards of directors.

As institutional investors are getting global, they demand more transparency and stricter controls as their holdings and cost of governance and staff cost have increased manifold.

Global investors demand governments to enhance compliance measures to protect shareholder rights and responsibilities whenever a scandal erupts

Reforms in the USA

The milestone legal measures were Dodd-Frank Wall Street Reform and Consumer Protection Act in July 2010. They hoped to control Wall Street's misdeeds. In addition, the law was aimed at preventing more financial meltdowns by regulating the financial industry and protecting customers.

Millions of dollars and voluminous reports of the 2,300-page document provided severe actions against all possible financial frauds, and everyone expected it to prevent the frauds equal to AIG, Lehman.

The law was expected to address reforms to stop the large-scale financial corruption which caused the global economic crash in 2008.

The president stated, "the reforms represented the most robust consumer financial protections in America". Laudable goals, but no political unanimity.

The act merely created several new federal agencies hoping to achieve consumer protection and financial regulation. The Financial Stability Oversight Council (FSOC) and the Consumer Financial Protection Bureau (CFPB) were new. The FSOC monitors the risk that significant banks play in the US financial system. The CFPB concentrated on the consumer protection side of Dodd-Frank. Whistle-blowers were created with expectation to blow the lid off the illegal ways of their employers.

This Act is yet to be translated into action, and the country is yet to realise what was intended. The expert reactions are split even now on the outcome between too many restrictions tied to too good results.

Two years later, the law has been nearly scrapped. It has been a non-starter, proving the point that anyone trying to control and rewrite Wall Street rules is bound to fail.

With new political team at White House and the new administration in control from 2017, several changes were made to Dodd-Frank to undo many industry regulations. But, with these changes, the regulators had something to say about their honest intentions to be fair and truthful to the investing public.

Reforms in Brazil

The South American nation of Brazil is part of the six-nation group constituted by the emerging economic power. That group is called the BRICS; Brazil hosted the sixth BRICS summit. The tides turned, and

Brazil's economy in 2016 faced its worst recession in three decades following the price drop of oil, iron ore and soya. In 2015, their economy shrank by 3.8 per cent to hit its worst decline since 1981, and inflation reached 10.7 per cent. Unemployment increased to 9 per cent in 2015 and is predicted to go into double figures. Brazil's currency declined in value substantially against the dollar in 2015.

Ms Rousseff's recent ouster and impeachment moves have added fuel to the fire. But unfortunately, the Trump administration's approach does not help them.

World economists aptly describe Brazil as an example of modern-day tragedy with its slow decline from its high point.

However, the rise and fall of this country's economy is similar to its once-famous football along with the glory of Brazil's world-class football heroes.

Pelé, born on 23 October 1940, was named after the famous Edison. He became a superstar with Brazil's winning performance in the 1958 World Cup. When Brazil lost the 1950 World Cup, Pele's father had cried uncontrollably. The young Pelé had promised to win the cup for his country one day.

Pelé played for Brazil for two decades, winning three world cups for his country. FIFA named him Co-Player of the Century in 1999.

Garrincha, another younger player, rose from the depths of extreme poverty to become the most outstanding Brazilian football player in the country's history. Garrincha began playing football professionally at 19, despite his low socio-economic background. He lived in the worst conditions.

Brazil, as a nation is famous for coffee and football. The economic history is one of rise and fall. Twenty first century marked heavy unemployment and inflation.

Lava Jatz is a Portuguese phrase that can be translated to 'car wash', that is what Brazil's biggest corruption was nicknamed with.

Investigations revealed the large-scale corruption in Brazil's Petrobras with a host of financial and political problems. Exposure in 2014 was estimated to have been creeping in over the past 10 years.

The scandal came to light with an inquiry that traced the movement of billions of Brazilian Real abroad. The corporate sector paid considerable sums to senior officials and government officials to approve inflated contracts with the state oil company. The bottom-line hit was to the tune of USD 34.8 billion in 2015.

Crude oil price collapse was indicated as the reason for the depreciation of the Brazilian Real.

The Petrobras scandal went on to trigger the changes in corporate governance rules, which changed the ways business is managed.

For the conduct of state-owned enterprises (SOEs), they mandated more independent directors. Ministers were banned from directorship and appointment to audit committees.

The Brazilian Institute of Corporate Governance (IBGC) instituted a comply-or-explain approach for corporates, which changed the system.

Reforms in European Union

Europe is emerging out of the most significant recession in 80 years. The EU is taking measures for financial restructuring to introducing new initiatives of the banking union, capital markets union, and deepening economic collaboration that should change the micro and macroeconomic and business environment.

Each of these measures is expected to make Europe's financial and business dealings robust, efficient and competitive.

Volkswagen is not only a famous German car supplier but is also a global brand. It has production facilities in 11 countries outside and sells cars in 153 countries. In the global market Volkswagen is the most successful brand. Established and true to its name, it has been accepted as the people's car. The VW Beetle is so famous that the movie *Herbie Go Wild* featured it; the movie was a runaway hit.

The city of Bern in Germany, in 1933 witnessed a historical event. The three bigwigs who met were the German chancellor Adolf Hitler and Daimler-Benz's Jakob Verlin, and the inventor and developer Ferdinand Porsche. The plan was to create the future for the German automobile industry.

Hitler wished to have a German car which was an inexpensive and reliable.

Ferdinand Porsche took 10 months to develop a prototype that met all of Hitler's requirements. The Volkswagen Beetle hit the market and it soon was the best-selling car in history. The Hollywood comedy movies had Herbie as the principal character; it starred the Volkswagen Beetle.

Volkswagen sold over 6,00,000 vehicles in the United States, which amounted to 6 percent of its global sales.

The hard-earned fair name and brand reputation, however, got ruined after the scandal. The company was facing USD 18 billion in penalties from the US Environmental Protection Agency and had to pay the price for the scandal over rigged emissions tests. Even the solid German economy got shaken up by the scam.

What could have been the driving force for this company and its leadership to breach integrity and ethical business practices and commit this fraud against governments and its customers?

Volkswagen remained the ranking brand globally but had tarnished its fair name by forcing itself into admitting that 11 million of its vehicles had been equipped with software used to rig emissions tests. This was not similar to other scandals where one person's greed destroyed many interests of stakeholders. Instead, the scandal's outcome was that it again brought ethical and governance questions to the surface.

It proves the hypothesis that dishonesty and greed are not confined to one culture or a few nations. A more realistic system of pollution control was revealed in February 2016, the European Commission,

The carmakers negotiated the deals, but the contract contained major flaws which angered environmentalists. So, one would expect them to react considerably to block the new limits at the European Parliament.

Stock Market Reforms in India

Bombay Stock Exchange is located in a narrow single lane street called Dalal Street in India; it is unlike the spacious wide road at Eleven Wall Street, where NYSC is located. Established in 1875, Bombay Stock Exchange is as much a power centre as Wall Street. It is the first and fastest exchange in Asia, with a median trade speed of 6 microseconds. It is the world's eleventh largest stock exchange which boasts of a listing of over 5,500 companies. Unfortunately, it has also been the hunting ground for greedy stockbrokers, year after year who try to take undue advantage of the loopholes in the rules and the system.

Nearly 24 years ago, one rogue trader took the BSE investment community for a ride. Named as the Big Bull, Harshad Mehta wreaked havoc on Bombay Stock Exchange, and subsequently, in 2001, another trader defrauded a vast scam. These frauds dealt a body blow and drowned the nation's investors and the stock market. Since then, the legal market monitors and lawmakers have been trying to discipline truant companies and bring in reforms.

The lack of political will has disappointed the innocent ordinary citizens by denying the strong governance and well-defined transparent reporting arrangements. A strong need to continually set up, drive and check stock exchange operations without chaos exists throughout the world

India's significant reforms are in liberalising Foreign Direct Investment (FDI), and the economic growth of 7 per cent is being fuelled by reforms in company law, employment laws.

Reforms in Japan

Despite a strong value-driven culture, Japan is not insulated from corporate scandals, and even the 140-year-old Toshiba was tempted to inflate profits to the tune of billions. Olympus Corporation, the biggest camera maker, had hired a British CEO, and he was soon fired for questioning suspicious accounting. In Japanese culture, one never challenges seniors.

Along with inadequate governance standards, the corporate crisis spread during low economic growth. The new corporate governance and stewardship codes and an amended Company Law took effect in June 2015.

The impact of the reforms in governance was expected to be seen starting in 2016. The focus was on gender diversity with more independent women directors. Women's boardroom representation was targeted at 30 per cent, but it was never achieved, and the goalpost was shifted to 2030.

Japan is strong in adhering to the status quo, and change comes slowly. Therefore, every attempt to change well-set processes will face resistance.

US initiatives drove the 2015 corporate governance norms and reforms in Japan. In recent years, international asset managers have demanded higher levels of transparency and director independence.

In addition, investors scrutinise boards and independent directors much more closely now because of increasing malpractices.

Essentials of Implementing Change Programmes

In any change management programme, it is fundamental to set up and define the roles and or lines of responsibility of everyone leading the change for driving it and communicate to avoid chaos and project delays. Changes will always need disruption of the standard pre-defined familiar hierarchy, which will be the case if the change programme stretches across the global boundaries of the organisation.

Managers are compelled to take on the additional role of driving change. Therefore, they should decide on related issues quickly. Everyone has to understand these temporary arrangements.

Effective change management governance means strict adherence to roles, responsibilities, and operating within the organisation to successfully progress the change project.

It outlines a fundamental change governance framework that could be a model for establishing governance. To succeed in the change initiative, every responsible organisation must create at least a norm most appropriate for governance.

Programme Leadership Committee

This committee provides the leadership and adequate oversight for the change initiative programme. Their task is to set the direction and provide stewardship to manage the change progress. Key people need to be supporters of the shared vision. Change sponsors must be designated to be a member of this leadership committee.

The change sponsors are responsible for project kick-off and accelerating the change's commitment, particularly from people to the lowest level across the organisation. The CEO and all the direct reports will have to be change sponsors to be authentic.

Influencers

The next level is the influencers who will manage the overall day-to-day change management process and progress of implementation, mind change, removing mental blocks, and devising communication strategies. It makes them the Work Output Owners. Based on the programme complexity, the change initiative be broken into bite-size projects that small work groups can handle.

This group prescribes the steps and activities that lead to an outcome and identifiable gains, bit by bit. Thus, this body can secure the achievement of change outcomes/benefits.

Its responsibilities should include:

(i) Budget approval, setting goals and establishing programme milestones with outcomes ensuring that appropriate risk management processes are implemented.
(ii) Decision on timelines.
(iii) Policy and resourcing decisions.
(iv) Approval of changes,

The leadership committee consists of senior managers from all the business units that are affected by the change. It would also be prudent to have a committee member from outside the organisation, or from the part of the organisation that is likely the change, to give a 'reality check' — similar to the role of the third umpire in a cricket match.

The committee meetings have to be regular and frequent, discussing issues affecting the programme, and deciding how the change project is to progress. The success factor of change is how the leader with direct responsibility can lead from the front. The leaders are to be empowered to control resources and spend in the change process. Global change initiatives with complexities require senior executive level representation to lead. For minor projects, a department supervisor may fill this role.

This role is of a sponsor, and change sponsors is to champion and be a coach, and be accessible for individual coaching. They have the primary responsibility to enable stable progress of change programme from the start to completion.

The sponsor's support includes championships for the change, mitigating any resistance to the change, and close monitoring of the progress of programme management issues that arise. Change requires managing internal politics, and it tests the sponsors' skill in handling the politics.

All stakeholders are expected to engage actively throughout the project and build collaboration with others across the organisation. Any leader without adequate authority, power, energy and time to resolve any conflicts that impede the change projects do not accelerate.

Usually, the change sponsor should chair the steering committee meetings.

The strength of the steering committee comes from the sponsor to gain commitment from the organisation for any additional resources (outside the project budget) to achieve the required level of speed in the change.

Change Agents.

To succeed, change programmes always need dedicated change agents to give day-to-day project management and support. The change agents are responsible for planning and organising the daily activities of the project execution. The change management process has to focus on business process, workforce and infrastructure changes. Another critical responsibility of the change agent and the team is the daily coordination of communications relating to the change progress and information sharing with relevant stakeholders.

The capacity for creative problem solving is vast with people. If agents create conditions that are supportive than dictatorial, employees will be change agents. The change agents finally report to the steering committee, and they escalate issues for discussion and decision. The team's number will largely depend on the change's size, scope, and complexity. For example, a change team comprising representatives from each work unit across the organisation may manage a substantial organisational change.

The team's composition be kept flexible depending on the progress, as unique skills are required for different phases of the change. The team's design and overall project management responsibilities are determined based on the skills necessary to complete the tasks that secure the change programme's success. Therefore, adequate preparation of teams is required. No heroic leadership can ever deliver results on change programmes; however, the leadership may try to achieve the result.

Team Effort

Well-prepared teams and strong teamwork can alone deliver the result. The 2015 IPL T20 is an example of exceptional team preparation. Mumbai Indians won the cup, though no one ever expected them to reach the qualifying rounds in the immensely popular championship. This sports event is more popular than the New York Yankees, and Boston Red Sox meets for America's super league.

Mumbai Indians had the best advisers and the best international level players, yet they started with four losses in the preliminary rounds and ended up at the bottom. They later demonstrated what teamwork can do by winning their next nine matches out of 10 and reaching the qualifying rounds, where they beat the top-ranked team Chennai Super Kings by a vast margin of 41 runs. What made them tick and brought such a dramatic turnaround? The answer is simply, team preparedness. Their coaches worked on the following measures:

(i)   The team was made to commit every day that they had one core issue: to win the cup.
(ii) The team set a target for each match every day, raising the mark on the bowling, wicket-taking, and runs to score being scored, fielding and catching. The coaches ensured every member realised the team first policy and the individual, next. They were focused on complete alignment with the core idea of winning the cup and the team collectively believing in victory.

(iii) They emphasised individuals need to sacrifice their gains for the team's good in each match, and everyone to realise there was a price to pay for being part of the winning team and be prepared to continue paying the price till the end. The team effort and contribution cannot be one match affair, and every member to accept they are representing the team 24/7 on and off the field.

(iv) Commitment for success had to be 100 percent and 24/7 till the end. The prescribed rule was the captain and the coach would serve as master strategists, and they would have to know the laws of the game and interpret them in case of unforeseen happenings such as rain interruptions.

(v) The captain, coach and physio et al. in the team had to know all members' strengths and weaknesses and exploit them to the team's best advantage while picking the team for the day.

(vi) The team has to aim at peak performance, and this would need reflection, enquiry and continuous learning from losses and failures. Constant attempt to re-energise be everyone's role and responsibility. Team communication would be the responsibility of the captain and coach; briefing has to happen both vertically and across every day. The communication rule was, there should be no room for ambiguity and doubt once the briefing is over.

(vii) Each member to dream of holding the cup after every match.

(viii) There has to be synergy until the end as the team's individuals were highly competent and skilled in their way, whether batting, bowling, or fielding.

(ix) Every team member to know the rules and procedures for handling exceptions during every match.

(x) Emotions would have to be kept under control all the time. Response to each occurrence to be as per team values and principles of honest play.

(xi) Everyone has to play with a "Just Do It" attitude in their heads, aiming to reach the final, even if a few matches were` lost.

(xii) Each member was to be self-driven to strive for the best endeavour.

(xiii) Instructions were given to treat a match loss day as one bad day, and it was typical to fail once or twice, but not many times over. Performance enhancement was based on trust in each other, and collective belief was mandatory. If any member felt otherwise, they have to say so and opt out. The team needed to agree extraordinary results would come from exceptional battles alone.

So, the existence of immense power to create high-performing teams during change is cited here.

Ownership for Profit

The unit level and work output owners are to be designated to implement specific tasks depending on the project module's size. Comprising specialists are responsible for implementing, delivering the results within timelines and milestones. They have to report to the change agent on the periodic progress of the project against the plan.

CHAPTER 6

CHANGE MANAGEMENT IDEAS, TOOLS AND TECHNIQUES

Often, management takes shelter under the "no precedence" logic to suppress any new change initiative. The mindset of most of the leadership and employees is "such a thing has never been attempted before. Therefore, any attempt will fail

In 1995, Robert Metcalfe, founder of 3Com, and the inventor of Ethernet, had promised to "eat his words" if his prediction on internet collapse went wrong. At a conference in 1997, standing by his word, using a food processor liquefied a copy of the article containing the mistake and drank it.

Decision Inertia, in the event of a crisis, is another sure reason for the failure of change initiatives.

Management and leadership are expected to handle crisis issues before letting social media and news channels sensationalise and convert a minor crisis into a major problem.

Even established big brands have experienced how well-conceived promotional communication moves can go completely wrong and have had to resort to significant damage control. For example, McDonald's set up a Twitter hashtag: #McDStories with all good intentions of promoting customers to share fun stories based on their visit experience. However, instead of generating fun, McDonald's faced flak when customers started using the hashtag to post their worst experiences at the outlets.

McDonald's could put the backlash behind them, and it learnt to encourage customers to question than writing stories on their website.

Preparation

Failure to prepare for an issue may hit the organisation can turn into a crisis and generate terrible publicity. Unfortunately, management has inadequate preparation to handle events like random boardroom battles, workplace violence, sexual violation and harassment, theft of corporate documents, and a host of other problems.

There have been countless incidents where a person in position has said something and words have been taken out of context or a "source" and accused of disclosing a piece of company information. These need a sound strategy. The best thing is to communicate their side of the story, and at times the problem can get resolved, as with JC Penny's experience. Rumours started about JC Penney reverting their decision to use celebrity talk show host Ellen DeGeneres as their new spokesperson. The company's CEO made a simple statement clearing up all rumours and firmly not dropping Ellen.

Business Performance: Erosions and Slippages

Business Performance Management (BPM) uses technology to harness analytic processes and deploy measure display techniques. BPM enables businesses to define strategic and operational goals and measures to manage corrective actions effectively.

The continuous assessment and monitoring of business processes related to operations, its effectiveness, and examining short- and long-range plans, data consolidation and reporting methods, and the analysis are absolute necessities.

Every business is monitoring the key performance indicators as per linkages to strategy. The Business Performance Management (BPM) methodologies commonly deployed are the Balanced Scorecard and the Key Performance Indicators (KPIs); though many BPM ideas and tools have evolved, businesses continue to harness these methods.

The Key Performance Indicators are necessary to track whether the progress is on course as per the goals set. This performance measurement method is to evaluate the success of an organisation.

Often, success is measured in terms of repeatability of achievement levels, e.g., manufacturing defect rates, employee satisfaction levels, etc.

The choice of appropriate KPIs depends upon the importance of the indicator to the organisation's continued success.

It is indispensable to capture what is critical and relevant in business monitoring. Present-day managements have various options of tools and techniques to assess the state of the business accurately. These assessments end up in potential improvement opportunities. A commonly used method is KPI and tools like the balanced scorecard.

Most of the time, failure to confront a crisis effectively occurs, with no pre-defined process for highlighting and identifying performance abnormalities. In the absence of significant and qualitative measurement parameters of the results and early warning signals, trouble creeps in much faster.

To stay continually profitable, the organisations have to scientifically measure performance against the financial targets at the organisation level and individual levels. One would use budgets and budgeting for allocation of the money for specific reasons, and budgeting is a crucial part of the operational management activities of any organisation, regardless of size.

Modern formal budgets are estimates of expenditures, but they forecast income, profits, and expected returns on investment a year ahead.

They have evolved these means of control and change. They utilise the process for determining rewards of profit-sharing and bonuses. Budget processes to ensure success has to be a collaborative process in which every operating unit develops the plans aligned with corporate goals. A story involving the chief justice of America's Supreme Court judge, Justice Oliver Wendell Holmes, goes like this. Confronted by the ticket examiner of the train, the passenger was struggling to find his ticket. Despite the ticket examiner saying he could travel without the ticket; he was adamant about showing his ticket and began to empty his suitcase to find it. Finally, the examiner told him he recognised the Supreme Court's chief justice and said he couldn't imagine the chief justice travelling without the ticket. He could go home and mail back, as and when he found it.

Justice Holmes, however, told him he had to find the ticket.

The examiner was confused about why the passenger was so adamant and wondered why the older man was restless. He looked at the ticket examiner and finally said he had to find the ticket because he had to find out where to get down. He had forgotten his destination.

Knowing the goal is important. As the saying goes, "If you do not know where to go, it does not matter which road to take". The budget is, thus, the visible end, as it contains the projection of what is being added for the following year.

As a collaborative process, the exercise involves each unit presenting its plans and budget for review by top management and incorporating changes resulting from negotiations. Once approved, the budget is the road to travel for the operational journey for the year. The budget review process tracks performance variations.

The review process includes modifying the budget numbers and approving the revisions based on external data sources on market and economic conditions. The performance is evaluated against the budget for rewards such as incentives and bonuses at year-end.

This collaborative process impacts lifestyle and culture changes through people-oriented change management. In addition, the regular quarterly budget review enables early catching of any potential pitfalls or other problems to initiate changes and corrective actions.

An operating budget reflects expenses, expected future costs, and variations from forecasted income. Operational budgets are prepared in advance, detailing projected income and expenses.

This budget is updated with actual numbers on pre-defined intervals, and projections are adjusted for the year. This helps make tactical changes.

There are two kinds of budgets. A cash flow budget details the cash inflow and outflow by month to month and supports correct variations.

A capital budget estimates new investments for acquisition, market expansion, and R&D investments for product enhancement in the new product offering or the growth of the production capacity. It is helpful as a tool for long-term strategic change initiatives.

Breathe Life into Mission and Vision

The vision and mission set the organisation's tone "for being and doing" business. They serve as guiding principles for changes whenever a deviation occurs.

Vision statement (desired end state) is an explicit statement describing the purpose is soul stimulating and enables long-term change.

The vision to change includes refocusing continually on future state and articulating to spell out for the understanding of everyone by the leadership. A well-articulated vision statement is inspiring, vibrant, unforgettable and succinct. A well-articulated vision statement makes it easy for leaders to communicate to all employees to remember the one common purpose, provides clarity on the mission, and enables focus on the future.

One example of a powerful vision is one of the Make-A-Wish foundation, which is: "Together, we create life-changing wishes for children with illnesses."

Vision always starts as a mental creation of one person's dream but gets shared and supported.

What are the shared vision advantages? The most powerful contribution is changing employee attitudes from one of "my company" to "our company".

It creates a unified sense of commonality to achieve and is meaningful and fulfilling for those who get aligned and associated. A logical reason for diverse activities becomes the cause by generating the stimulation to transform an ordinary company into the most preferred employer. Collaboration in work despite individual aims was the message.

It created an exclusive identity and a sense of commitment from employees. It encourages newer ways of acting and behaving. It gives courage, fosters risk-taking and experimentation.

Without the sharing, the vision of the leader that has been painfully architected becomes a pointless exercise.

The learning culture in an organisation cannot be created without a shared vision. When a robust common weaving thread as a shared vision exists, everyone has a unified picture of the future state to strive for. People are motivated to collaborate and work together with a common goal, supporting and enabling each other. The requirement for collaborative change in the environment is: a principle-centric leader.

Such a leader encourages open communication, discourages office politics and work as a facilitator to help learn an alternative way of acting.

One or two attempts will not be enough to elicit the planned change in behaviour. It takes time for many fence-sitters to embrace change ideas and practices. Creative ideas are not readily accepted by people and create a willingness to change. Time and facilitation are needed to help people examine what works and doesn't work and accept the new paradigm.

The best outcome of the change happens through the vision mapping process. It is a technique for all stakeholders to explore and articulate an attainable future state. The vision mapping process is about the processes, people and technology elements.

Vision mapping uses the change drivers to communicate the fundamental principles, and mapping identifies high priority actions and initiatives emerging because of change.

The map can become the base or foundation for detailed project planning and programme management activities required for implementation. It is a valuable communication tool for the change programme to help stakeholders visualise work that needs to be carried out to achieve the change vision. In addition, the participatory nature of the vision building session can give participants a sense of ownership for the change process steps and enable them to share and communicate the experience.

Management Dashboards

Technology-driven management decision tools rely heavily on dashboards, which give a real-time interactive graphical representation of data. The tools display patterns of all the key performance variables. They are robust multi-layered reporting systems which present micro-to-macro level insights to multiple decision-makers of all different levels. BY being automated systems, they are free of manual dependencies.

Dashboards enable management to make better decisions by providing real-time monitoring systems. They utilise a large volume of data. Dashboards are now replacing manual systems using a spreadsheet called MIS. They are simpler to read with the one-page display. The graphical presentation of the current level and historical trends of an organisation's key performance indicators make the interface user friendly.

Informed decisions enhance the management efficiency in decision-making. In simple terms, the dashboard is another form of an instant progress report or scorecard.

A dashboard application is tailor-made for levels of management.

Staying competitive depends on timely decisions, and the Management Information System (MIS) helps leaders' control and avoid delayed decisions. The extensive use of business intelligence (BI) makes conclusions robust. It links to any enterprise system and enables intuitive interaction. It integrates a reporting solution for top management for information on all the processes. In addition, the system provides historical data, and current state and future projection about events inside and outside the organisation.

BI applications use emerging technologies, XML, AJAX, Lotus Domino, Flash and Web services capabilities. The dashboard often displays on a web page, charts and graphs that link the database and allow updates of the report.

It used to take two to three weeks for human resources to collate and present data related to the performance of HR. With HR dashboards, all types of data on recruitment, retention and cost per hire, average days per hire and much more are available instantly. This information display can be effective in tactical decision changes.

Six Sigma / Lean Sigma

Six Sigma methodologies rely on a quantitative approach and collaborative team effort to improve yield quality by systematically eliminating defects that lead to waste.

In addition, Six Sigma is data-driven and well-rooted in mathematics and statistics.

The Six Sigma standard is 3.4 defects per million of the output measures. This technique focuses on eliminating eight kinds of wastes. They are defects, overproduction, waiting, non-utilised talent, transportation, inventory, motion, extra-processing or downtime.

Any continuous improvement initiative always brings change to the organisation. Six Sigma and Lean Sigma systems deployment are for eliminating waste and creating the most efficient system. These quality systems follow different routes for achieving this goal. They differ in identifying the root cause of wastage.

Lean Sigma prescribes locating waste wherever there are non-value-adding unnecessary process steps in the production process. Six Sigma insists on the identification of wasteful deviations within the process. Both quality systems have been impactful in exponentially improving overall business performance. The qualification criteria are green belt level for the person executing six sigma. The oversight is by black belt masters. This type of involvement and participation brings in emotional connection without bonding, either physically or intellectually.

Those company managements who want to pay attention to competitive advantage through quality, deploy these tools and bring the planned changes.

Benchmarking

In olden times, the land surveyors chiselled some marks in stone to show levels and heights as reference points from which they could calculate the elevation. A bench was formed by placing angle iron within the cuts on which they set the levelling rod, which allowed repositioning of the levelling rod.

Global Positioning Systems or GPS is replacing the old-style maps. Later, the term took a broader meaning and became pet management jargon, especially with IT designers and architects. In an organisational context, benchmarking is a process deployed to decide the best in class in similar activity and set up goals to equal or surpass them to improve.

A formal definition would be the systematic process of identifying best practices.

The competition which is doing better, for comparison and improvement, and identifies innovative ways and highly effective operating procedures leading to superior performance.

Benchmarking is used to compare how good performance is about the market segment leader regarding important attributes, functions, or values associated with the products or services. Every day measured items are quality, time, and cost which directly have the bottom-line impact.

Organisations have been developing strategies on continuous improvements or changeover to adopt specific best practices, ISO and Six Sigma, to enhance operational effectiveness.

Benchmark is a standard operating procedure, and it was put into use by many of the robust businesses.

It has been a widely used process since the mid to late eighties by many Fortune 500 companies. In addition, it has been in use as a continuous improvement tool to bring in changes.

The rapid changes in the business environment can leave a company far behind the competition unless they measure, benchmark and improve. Xerox reworked business processes using the benchmarking system and developed a five-phase benchmarking process containing 12 significant steps to enhance product quality and delivery.

Xerox became a world-class organisation and won the top American and European Quality Award in 1992.

Six Sigma initiatives were born after a benchmark study in Motorola during 1986. They identified gaps in quality, when compared to the Japanese products and substantially improved productivity

They had nicknamed as, 'Bandit Project', and stole every best practice from the competition to benchmark against the best and transform its pocket pager business.

The investment in Six Sigma paid off and in 1988, Motorola won the Malcolm Baldrige National Quality Award and established worldwide excellence as the brand. Both organisations benefited from these change initiatives of quality excellence. Even today, they continue to be world-class organisations.

Many product designers use technical benchmarking to ascertain the capabilities of products or services compared to the competition or the best-in-class products or services.

Balanced Scorecard

Traditionally, finance provided the figures for financial performance. This tool measures non-financial performance measures. This tool became a recent addition and displaced conventional performance measures. Aligning strategy is much more robust with this tool for business organisations. The decision-making became broad-based, with a balanced approach towards all performance areas — including financial indicators. The balanced scorecard concept came into use in the early 1990.

The roots run profoundly, and General Electric contributed to the performance measurement and reporting in the 1950s. The French analyst created the Tableau board, which formed the basis for the dashboard. A traditional approach to using financial numbers from accounts became ineffective, as one can only analyse financial figures after the event.

A scorecard uses the selection of a few data items to monitor financial and non-financial parameters.

The approach is a typical example of a, capitalist mindset where anything drives profits is embraced.

Management Cockpit

In the 18th century, American cockfighting, which always led to a bloody and fatal end for the birds, was as popular as any national sport. Betting was a significant driver and a large part of the bloody sport. The birds chosen for fights were massive and solid, and had been reared to last long bouts. They were made strong and ferocious, and stood out from other fowls in those historical eras; even now, the same practice continues where the sport is held.

The birds were armed and the terminology used was "dubbed", which refers to a practice in which a bird's wattle and comb were removed so that the opponent could not latch onto them in a fight. The battle conditioned cocks were fitted with deadly knives in their legs and were bred and trained for combat readiness. The roosters slashed at one another ferociously while the crowds screamed and enjoyed the spectacle with bets.

The term cockpit originated from the sport of cockfight, aka, the pit in which people make the cocks fight till death. Even today, cockfighting is a popular sport in the rural areas of the southern Indian states of Andhra Pradesh and Tamil Nadu, where people spend Rs 2 billion every year on betting.

The cockfight is an industry in the south Indian states where over 2,000-3,000 cockfight organisers engage in these sports during the harvest festival.

There are trainers for these hybrid birds, and they hire specialists to tie two-inch knives on the bird's legs to inflict bloody wounds on the rival bird during the fight. The breeding includes special nutritious diet of consisting of pulses, nuts, minced meat (kheema) and eggs. In addition, the birds are given hormone injections which makes them ferocious for the fights.

They categorise birds as dega (eagle), kaaki (crow), pearl and nemali (peacock) and rate them, based on their training —similar to seeding in the grand slam tennis matches.

The word cockpit was used to refer to the scene of combat, such as the World War battlefields. The term was liberally used for any cramped spaces in later years and was also used to describe the pit space around the theatre stage that had seats on the lower level. The location of the war ship's rudder controls was named coxswain's station, meaning the 'boat servant'. It originated from the cock, or a cockboat, which meant, a small vessel kept aboard a ship. Swain, an Old English term, came from the Old Norse 'sveinn' meaning boy or servant and refers to the small, cramped room below decks; later, it was transferred to refer to aeroplanes and cars. Finally, cockpit refers to the driver's seat of a vehicle, especially a race car, and this is official terminology in Formula racing cars. This modified term, management cockpit, represents the fourth generation of reports, financial reports, scorecards, and prospective dashboards; it is a control room for management in the modern era.

Imagine the setting for a large corporate organisation where each manager can access every information. In managing change, these control points can be highly effective in providing corrective action needed without delays. The tool is helpful despite a few drawbacks. Data overload is one such disadvantage.

Behaviour Modification and Employee Reward and Recognition Schemes

The HR community flags the employee reward and recognition programmes. Instead, HR uses the management of people to manipulate the performance or specific behaviour of the target group.

They found the rewards on the hypotheses that positive reinforcement can lead to repetition of existing behaviour and repetition. Incentives are applied to change behaviour in education, and by making contributions to the public good. However, incentives give rise to a conflict that arises between the direct extrinsic effect and intrinsic motivations.

Does rewarding people to deliver results make them work harder? The answer depends on what kind of results are aimed to be reached. The evidence suggests that rewards succeed at bringing only a temporary change.

But for a lasting difference in attitudes and behaviour, neither reward or punishments work effectively.

Once the reward is withdrawn or loses shine, people revert to their status quo behaviour. Therefore, most bonus plans are extrinsic motivators and cannot change the behaviour permanently.

Research based evidence indicates that the effectiveness of rewards depend on the design and the form and the way they affect the intrinsic motivations and social motivations.

Change and Enterprise Risk Management (ERM)

A risk management system in the enterprise is necessary to look at the highly unpredictable risks of external triggers.

Risk management is the process of establishing sound methods and processes, and managing events triggered by unforeseen events, and minimising or eliminating adverse impacts.

Assessment is based on the probability of occurrence, estimating the magnitude of impact, deciding a response strategy, and monitoring progress. By identifying and proactively discussing risks and opportunities, business enterprises can protect and insulate from catastrophic consequences. Unpreparedness is evident when one looks at Lehman's risk exposure.

Lehman Brothers had invested over 35 per cent of its net tangible equity in three commercial real estate investments. A few people at the top saw the concentration in few investments and the scope of high-risk and reckless endeavours with investors' finance with no ERM in place.

It is surprising how the most brilliant financial brains failed to take risks, making it appear as a deliberate oversight. Change management becomes more manageable with ERM in place.

How does one measure and control intangible assets?

The strategy map is the tool. It summarises the organisation's strategic story that explains what the organisation is seeking to achieve.

Use Big Data Analytics

The explosive growth of data volume can be gauged when we see that 2.5 quintillion bytes of data are being generated per day, and that explosion is not over the years but in the last two years. Data is generated through various sources like satellites, social media sites, YouTube, Instagram, Amazon, online shopping, and mobile phones and GPS signals, to name a few.

Big data is far more than the data size of MB or GB. Big data analytics examines data sets containing various data types in petabytes of structured and unstructured data. The objective is to uncover hidden patterns, unknown correlations, market trends and customer preferences to gain valuable business insights.

Traditional performance measurement approaches give way to innovative analytics approaches as the focus is on gaining competitive advantages. Therefore, the focus was on collecting and reporting a few KPIs to monitor the strategy execution.

Managements can access financial management data with future scenarios by using predictive analytics. One can get interactive performance reports in cell phone devices with up-to-date data visualisations.

Organisations with the goal of top performance have robust strategic and operational performance metrics. The insights gained are generated from traditional KPIs and analysis of social media data. It uses past knowledge to predict future performance and estimate new opportunities and risks. Business performance management today involves data consolidation from various sources, querying, and analysis combined with forecasting. Big data analytics is the tool for competitive advantages and agile and relevant decision- making.

With the help of evolving data science, data extraction and analysis are creating overall demand for data and analytics.

BI platforms give a range of capabilities for building analytical applications. Oracle OBIEE, SAP Business Objects are the most popular ones.

Many choices and combinations of BI platforms, capabilities and use cases are available, including many emerging BI technologies such as memory analytics, interactive visualisation, and BI integrated search.

Advanced analytics can manage large volumes of data and deal with highly complex settings beyond any human ability. Digital businesses are adopting data science methods in reducing storage costs. Advanced analytics isn't another elaborate form of analytics.

Descriptive analytics is used in reporting what has happened. Another way to describe descriptive data is as "content without context", i.e., facts representing a particular phenomenon without meaning or relevance; advanced analytics uses predictive and prescriptive techniques to solve problems.

Can anyone tell the future outcomes of customer behaviour? Prescriptive analytics techniques precisely forecast the future.

For example, preventive maintenance has been revolutionised with the use of predictive analytics, preventing unscheduled and costly disruptions.

Data aggregation and data mining techniques were used to give clarity about the past. Statistical analysis and forecast techniques are used by predictive analytics to state about future status; the skills typically include statistics, machine learning, and operations research.

Sentiment Analytic is a Change Driver

Sponsored surveys no longer generate data on public opinions and sentiments, but they are out on social media for anyone to harness. They considerably influence change management strategies as they can trigger changes in product design or marketing. The sentiment analysis involves data mining and retrieval. Other terms for sentiment analysis are opinion mining or emotion AI.

"Natural language processing, text analysis, computational linguistics, and biometrics are used to systematically identify, extract, quantify, and study affective states (affective states are longer lasting mood states (such as anxiety or depression) which are not caused by a single stimulus but results from accumulation of experiences.) and subjective information." In this age of internet explosion and mobile technologies, consumers express their opinions on various blog topics through product/service reviews. For example, Twitter generates 8 terabytes of data daily.

Sentiment analysis is determining what emotions lie behind the words, which a writer uses. The consumer attitudes, opinions, and emotions are uninhibitedly expressed in online messages, forming such an analysis.

The way is established for social media monitors to gain an insight into public opinion behind the subject. Modern tools such as Brand watch analytics make the process quicker and easier than ever before through real-time data monitoring capabilities.

The application of sentiment analysis is done across many areas. The capability to extract insights from social media data is a practice that business organisations use. Analysts watch for the shift in the public sentiment expressed on social media. They have established that the changes in the stock market sentiments correlate with social media sentiments.

In the 2012 American elections, the Democratic Party extensively used the opinion mining technique to measure public opinion and campaign messages ahead of the presidential election. One can read the sentiment behind the words used in forum posts, Twitter, WhatsApp or even articles; one can strategies actions for the future.

Customers associate Kia brand cars with fuel efficiency and the value for money, but the makers want Kia cars for "grand design and cool technology".

The changing consumer perception and ensuring an emotional connection are the brand challenges.

Kia deploys a tool that can regularly analyse huge volume of data extracted from the web, blogs, etc. Including the Twitter and Facebook.

Mass Opinion Business Intelligence can deliver continuous, real-time feed of relevant consumer sentiment gathered from millions of sites. The emerging technologies can now indicate to the decision-makers the people's sentiment on a particular product or service, current and ex-employees' perception about the company and its executive leadership, stock behaviour, advertising campaign, et al. If a company can measure and monitor customer sentiment faster, changing for success becomes easy.

The computerised processing of text to decide the sentiments, attitudes, thoughts, and judgments of the people expressing those sentiments is automated.

Unfortunately, several pitfalls confound the detailed analysis of the sentiments expressed in online statements. Design of systems enabling a computer to identify sentiment within content through NLP is automated sentiment analysis. Sentiment measurement platforms deploy multiple techniques and varieties of statistical methodologies to evaluate opinion. A few rely 100 per cent on automated sentiment, or employ humans to analyse sentiment, and use a hybrid system.

Automated sentiment is meaningful when dealing with huge volume of data to give directional insight and set the tone for depth analysis.

Managements use sentiment data, that is a handy metric when combined with other data, because context is crucial to form conclusions in devising a change strategy.

For example, when people use the terms "bad culture, low pay, and won't recommend anyone" on Glassdoor, a company needs to take time to contemplate of change in policies.

Every company's annual planning meeting sets aggressive revenue and profit margin goals, only to see it slipping most of the time, quarter by quarter. When the goals are not met, change is initiated as a desperate measure. Technological advancements have taken BPM ten notches higher. The focus is on storage, retrieval and reporting performance using large databases and dashboard solutions.

Companies can now integrate strategic and operational data with the flexibility of approaches using analytics. Analysis of all data and performance reporting on financial management, risk management or project management is now possible and can be done in far less time.

Predictive and big data analytics and root cause analysis on past and future data combine and integrate BPM platforms with the analytic capability and root cause analysis. The decision-makers can now visualise data in graphs and reports on mobile devices.

Globalisation

Globalisation involves broadening, deepening, and speeding up worldwide reach and access in all facets of life, from the cultural to the financial to the political environment. The Internet, computing power and mobile communication technology have changed the ways of doing business. It has come to a stage where no global company can exist without adapting these technologies to drive business methods.

Everything must be available on the web and mobile, without which business can lose the race. As business becomes global, opportunities emerge in the different geographic marketplace which the organisation needs to pursue to stay competitive.

Power of Trade Unions: Changes Through Internal Pressure

Employees, particularly those with an organised labour union's support, often pressure management for wage hikes, triggering other change initiatives by management to cope with increased cost. The trades unions always react in a hostile manner to any changes in the working conditions as they perceive it to be violation of their rights. Worldwide, there has been a trend towards resistance by unions when automation through computerisation happens.

Trade unions indulge in restricting the supply of workers in a company or industry to push up wages. Unions secure the wage gains for workers that have to come out of business earnings.

Thus, wage demands lead to higher costs, compelling prices to go up to cover these costs, which leads to loss of market share in the entire process. Does it work better with no union? Studies have shown that unionised companies earn lower profits than non-unionised businesses. Unions stay everywhere. Every time a contract negotiation comes up, the company managements try to initiate organisational changes to cope with the wage rise.

Trade unionism is a global phenomenon. The union evolution and growth has been the inevitable by-product of industrialisation. The union movement in India started in 1854 within one primary textile mill called The Bombay Spinning Mills, and the number grew to nearly 75 mills. The growth of textile mills in Mumbai, jute mills of Bengal and the laying of the railways in 1850 triggered the union movement in India in 1875. The British appointed the first Factory Commission in Bombay in 1875, and India passed the first Factories Act in 1881, with the view to protect women and children from being exploited. The managements' exploitation influenced the proliferation of unions in India; it was the wretched working conditions for workers and exploitation by the owners that made a union turn militant in its approach. There were prolonged strikes and violent clashes, even as multiple unions tried to gain control.

The two legislations viz., the Indian Trade Unions Act in 1926 and the Trade Disputes Act, 1929 by the British, and the Industrial Disputes Act of 1947 gave enough recognition to unionism in India.

The proliferation of trade unions in the post-independence era has been in tune with the rise of political parties. From the beginning, the Congress Party controlled INTUC, (Indian National Trade Union Congress) and the Communists controlled the AITUC. (All India Trade Union Congress)

A popular trade union was the Hind Mazdoor Sabha (HMS), which aligned with the political party Praja Socialist Party. However, they split up to form Bhartiya Mazdoor Sabha (BMS), and they are part of the major national political party Bharatiya Janata Party (BJP) which runs the government.

The Communist Party has always been at the forefront of the labour movement, but they are divided into various factions and the unions are controlled by them; the United Trade Union Congress (UTUC) and the Centre of Indian Trade Unions (CITU) were, reborn. Later, a group went their own way to form another UTUC.

The Indian local parties have become powerful, and many have entered trade union activities because of power-mongering. This regionalism has resulted in the widespread proliferation of trade unions in the country. Thus, the progress of the trade union movement in India has reflected fragmented politicisation.

As of 2021, there are eight major trade union organisations. In addition, four significant federations have a national network to control the union activities. They are the All-India Trade Union Congress (AITUC), Indian National Trade Union Congress (INTUC), Bhartiya Mazdoor Sangh (BMS), and Centre of Indian Trade Unions (CITU).

In a show of strength on 28 February 2012, 100 million workers belonging to various trade unions demonstrated their power by going on strike for 24 Hours; it was termed the biggest strike in world history. However, they failed to achieve much despite this show of force.

Mergers and Acquisitions

Mergers and acquisitions create vast changes in several areas, often negatively impacting everyone to face cultural challenges, besides operating ways.

In 2004, GlaxoSmithKline merged with Burroughs Welcome India Ltd (BWIL). In India, it made a significant impact and involved massive changes and adjustments for the merged entity.

Change for the Sake of Change

Often, to prove a point that one is doing something, a new CEO will make changes for the sake of it.

Another reason organisations may institute changes is that other organisations in the same category are doing so. For example, the drive for ISO certification was motivated by companies wanting to stay competitive.

Selective Abandonment

When decisions are made about dropping a line altogether based on the profitability of the line, its contribution to overall strategy and brand management, it can trigger organisational changes.

For example, an IT data and analytic services provider faced stagnant five-year growth because of a poor overall business strategy. As a result, it repositioned itself to be a BI consulting organisation and enabled massive retooling, rebranding, remarketing efforts and colossal investment to unlearn and relearn new skills.

Changes in product pruning, abandonment of markets, or shutting subsidiaries can lead to a simple reallocation of resources to massive R&D and innovation and investment to capitalise on new opportunities.

As the customer needs keep changing, new demand for entirely new products and services can expose new change opportunities to meet those needs. Changing rules is the priority to stay in business, as no business can remain competitive without change, though change ideas are more challenging to sell than to manage. GlaxoSmithKline, commonly known as GSK, has been well known for its respiratory drugs for many years. However, shrinkage of opportunities in the respiratory drugs business because of generic competition and pricing pressure had forced GSK to abandon respiratory R&D and divert the funds to growth areas, viz cancer research and immunology.

The decline in sales of Advair prompted GSK America to do away with jobs at its largest organisation in North Carolina and Philadelphia. The company concentrated drug research work in Philadelphia in the US and Stevenage in the UK, which affected their R&D. The company filed a report eliminating 900 jobs. Exit from the respiratory segment was a massive change for GSK, as they had been involved in that segment for more than four decades. They provided one-third of the world's asthma and chronic obstructive pulmonary disease (COPD) medicines.

Macro-Economic Changes

The government's move to change budgetary policy impacts the economy involving interest rates, consumer confidence, stock market activity and employment. Regulatory measures affect the cost of compliance. Changes in tax laws, supply shortages or natural disasters substantially sway finance and profits as they directly impact business activities. The government's economic policies positively or negatively affect business organisations, and they are challenging to handle.

A robust economy spurs demand for products and services and propels companies to consider expansion.

They expect to generate more revenue, market coverage, and profits. These organisational changes impact individuals positively through new opportunities.

A weak economy creates problems at the corporate level, forcing complex changes that can impact individuals by layoffs, downsizing, pay cuts and shrinking benefits. These steps adversely affect the overall quality of life. Therefore, balancing and managing the entire spectrum is needed for organisations to retain growth and strong relationships.

Non-Technological Drivers

Technological changes create pressure to retain a focus on their long-term vision. While employees prefer the present, the leadership has the responsibility to shape the future. Despite material inflow and outflow, the living organisms have self-protective mechanisms that sustain their particular form through self-regulation and self-reference (autopoiesis). Organisations are not like them. Organisations need leaders to consciously attempt to perceive change.

There comes a time of crisis in the life of most organisations; at such a time, it is the need of the hour to harness strategy and tools for change in transitioning individuals, teams, and organisations from a current state to a desired future.

The organisation often reaches a fork in the road, and a question that arises is "what do we do now and which road should we choose?" Organisational crisis happens because of management inertia and inability to adapt.

Nature of Organisation and Change Initiatives (Continuous and Multidimensional)

Expansions, Mergers and Acquisitions

The creation of mammoth global corporations through joint ventures (TATA Motors's acquisition of Jaguar in the UK), mergers Burroughs with Glaxo, alliances; (Starbuck - Barnes and Nobles; HP and Disney) other kinds of inter-organisational linkages have become increasingly widespread and created massive change impact.

These expansions surely bring in organisational restructuring and change that adversely affect individual and job performance and organisational commitment. Job insecurity becomes high among the employees. Restructuring creates downsizing, which leads to the loss of skills and knowledge that built the image.

Among organisations of all sizes, ideas such as agile manufacturing, just-in-time inventory management, and unconventional organisation structures impact management's ways on their organisational reporting pattern. However, few leaders would dare to carry out the demolition of the traditional hierarchy.

The traditional one-size-fits-all arrangement was the way in the early stage of reorganisation. The current level of belief is that changing organisational hierarchies, decentralisation, and localisation are necessary for competitive success. India's corporates do not espouse the policy of getting it made; making has become the first choice for management to focus on their core competencies.

Outsourcing and offshoring can always bring enormous changes to the company's management style and operations. There has been no better example than Apple's move to cease manufacturing its phones in America and preferring to make them in China. Over 50 percent of Apple's suppliers are in China.

Flexibility, speed, and the capability to scale up or down have been the Chinese's significant advantage. Apple supports 5 million jobs in China.

Apple felt that make in America is an impossible dream when America does not have the skills it needed with a proper work mindset. Make in the USA did not make a financially workable choice for many capitalist corporations, including Apple. It is not the cost of labour but the flexibility, diligence and industrial skills of Chinese workers that outsmarted American organisations.

CHAPTER 7

FUNDAMENTAL CHANGE MANAGEMENT THEORIES

Integrating theory and practice in the business process is vital It provides the knowledge base and expertise to develop and apply professional skills and better understanding of the problems.

I took up my first job in a retail bank after an undergraduate degree in Physics. All I knew about the concept of posting was the act of posting a letter in the mailbox. The accounting jargon was Greek and Latin to me. I got confused when my boss told me to post the vouchers, and I promptly put them in an envelope and posted them in the postal department's letterbox on my way back home. The following day, I nearly got fired because the bank manager and staff were frantically searching for the missing checks throughout the day. In the bank, tallying the cash book daily is a mandatory and they could see a huge gap in the credit and debit. The moment of truth was making me understand the need for conceptual clarity.

When I was a young boy, my father described how to ride a new bicycle. After carefully listening to all the steps, I tried cycling independently only to fall down repeatedly. I realised that theory wouldn't get you far, but practice is key to success. The same analogy is suitable for implementing massive change in organisations.

In his article, Van De Ven and Poole outlined a comprehensive picture of various theories on organisational change. He categorised multiple views into a set of four hypotheses, which are:

1. Life cycle theories.
2. Teleological theories.

3. Dialectical theories.
4. Evolutionary theories.

Life Cycle Theory

Change management literature will contain the life cycle theory as a common explanation. It is another way to explain organisation development as an entity from birth to death, just as a living organism. So, what is an entity? For our purpose, we can define an entity as a workgroup or an entire organisation. Organisations follow the evolutionary stages of birth, growth, maturity, decline and death.

The death of an organisation happens when it cannot respond to demands made by its surroundings. Therefore, the question is inevitable: if its life cycle pattern is similar to humans, what is the average lifespan of a typical organisation?

Business organisations have grown and matured to become high-performing organisations amidst even the most turbulent times when they remained flexible and adaptive. Life cycle theory is of the firm view that change is imminent. Any developing entity has a core form, logic, programme, or code regulating transition and moving the entity.

To quote Ven and Poole, "External environmental events and processes can influence how the entity expresses itself, but are always mediated by the intrinsic logic, rules, or programmes that govern the entity's development."

Characteristics of a Life Cycle Theory

As per this model, the change events progress in a single sequence of stages or phases and retain characteristics of the earlier stage during the subsequent ones.

Every pre-defined end-state requires a previous sequence of events that contribute a bit to the outcome.

The American sociologist, Robert Nisbet, worked on the philosophy of developmentalism and stated, "Organisation development is driven by some genetic code or pre-figured programme within the developing entity."

The life cycle theory helps to explain the development of institutional rules or programmes that require developmental activities to progress in a defined sequence.

Whenever we propagate new ideas, members have to go through training. Those aligned with the new ideas embark on learning newer ways in the organisation and advocate of the high-level sponsor.

Modification Phase

After the first initiation stage, there can be a lack of acceptance from three sources. There exists individual or interpersonal lack of support, which can be manifested in open hostility, difficulty in learning new terminology, skills and values, altering boss and subordinate relationships.

Organisational reluctance is exhibited through authority, lack of responsibility, pattern, decision hurdles in budgetary allocations, training and process changes.

The environmental level reluctance is shown in the form of government regulation or competitive pressure.

Out of such demands, multiple versions come out through consulting and bargaining amongst forces.

Maturity Phase

This phase emerged when the changes introduced become the way of work-life and organisation's routine or when the new change initiative programme is fused with the existing organisational processes.

Soon, changes begin to lose newness and special status as a new management tool in the organisation process. It is even the end of life or the terminal phase of change in one sense. But the initiative can fail as well, and fatality can occur at any stage on the missionary-maturity continuum.

A direct link between culture and the rate of adoption of changes is a proven fact.

A survey covering 2,200 global participants in 2013, revealed it is effective culture management that can deliver success. The success rate is correlated with culture change and the need for a culture change along with planned transformation is proven. In culture management there is a gap between the companies' view of culture, and the way they manage. Only 50 per cent of respondents felt that companies are managing culture, and more than half felt that major cultural reform was needed.

Change processes are not always overt, formal actions may be subtle and symbolic; it initiates symbolic acts in the organisation to preserve existing cultural values while creating some modification or changes to keep with time. Symbols are a means of simplifying communication. However, they express more than what is apparent.

"The physical symbol system view is that intelligence is nothing more than the ability to process symbols"- Wikipedia

The view is that the conception or manipulation of symbols impacts a life; it can restructure beliefs and expectations because the meaning becomes clear in day-to-day experience in the organisation; many of the routine acts in the organisation revolve around continuing the status quo.

Teleological Theories.

The term 'technology' has its origin in the Greek word elos, meaning 'end'; and logos, meaning 'science', the theory of morality, which states that duty or moral obligation from what is suitable as an end to achieve.

Chaos and Complexity

Chaos theory or complexity theory is the theory of nonlinear dynamics or dynamical systems theory; chaos theory attempts to explain the change of simple techniques that may happen suddenly, even in unexpected or irregular ways. The complexity theory focuses on interwoven systems with parts interacting, which often give rise to random order.

Chaos theory analyses the behaviour of dynamic systems, especially those which are highly sensitive to first conditions. It commonly refers to this response as the butterfly effect. Minor alterations in the first stage resulted in conflicting outcomes for dynamical systems, making the long-term prediction impossible.

Mutual Causality

Causes and effects are related to changes, events, or processes. Mutual causality is about the observation of organisations as complex systems and concludes that changes in these systems do not follow a straight path. Still, they chart a rounded pattern of interaction. Mutual causality gives a more complex view than a simplistic view of change. Mutual causality is when A and B may be "co-defined because of belonging to the same system of circular relations".

This concept is helpful in change management and understanding system dynamics. Mutual causality indicates that no single item can cause change. However, minor changes can bring significant effects just as the tiny water drops that collect in small cracks freeze to enlarge the crack, enabling more water to collect and freeze, which ultimately breaks the solid rock itself. The fish tank forms algae, and when the fish eats, it makes the tank cleaner.

To change organisationally, there are five essential steps:

(i) An improved structure of the organisation, with the least hierarchy and control system to absorb changes.
(ii) Relearning the art of managing when changing contexts.
(iii) Reskilling to initiate minor changes to create a more significant outcome.
(iv) Acceptance of transformation and emergent order as a natural process.
(v) Being open to new assessments that can facilitate processes of self-organisation.

Integrative Thinking is a Four-step Process

The first step (compliance) seeks to define the relevant aspects of a problem.

The second step (capability) seeks to determine the relationships between related and unrelated parts of the problem.

The third step is architecting or creating a model that frameworks the relationships defined in the previous two steps.

The fourth step is the resolution — an action that outlines the decisions and how one reaches them. The process is identical with the feedback twist in which every step links forward to the next step and back to the previous step.

Change unfolds through circular patterns of interaction and how organisations evolve or disappear to deliberate systematically about the context. So, what does this all mean? "The mutual causality is the on the premise that systems are complex and changes in these systems do not happen linearly but in circular patterns of interaction."

Therefore, try to perceive the change in circles rather than in lines. The linear way of looking at change is mechanical causality; the linear way is to deliberate rationally and logically, applying rules and believing that everything has an end. Mutual causality is much richer and more complex than this simplistic view on change.

Dialectical Theories of Change

Dialectical philosophy has been used in the past 2,000 years ago, during the days of Aristotle and Plato. The dialectical way is a philosophical way of arguing, involving contradicting processes between opposing sides.

The word dialectic has inherent implications by contradiction towards the relationship. First, the idea or thesis is born, and the contra view emerges as a reaction followed by the final synthesis leading to resolution. In the modern era, dialectic is used to describe movements towards truthfulness and change.

When you wish to achieve objectivity amidst truth, this method is robust. Van De Ven, said "dialectical theory assumes, organisational entity exists in the pluralistic world of colliding events, forces or contradictory values that compete for domination."

CHAPTER 8

CHANGE MANAGEMENT AND LEADERSHIP ISSUES

What is Leadership Effectiveness?

Enterprise-wide change happens when the leadership is effective. Leadership effectiveness is the capability to infuse and inspire a shared vision of a positive picture of the anticipated state that all stakeholders could collectively and willingly create. The leaders need to be architects and not engineers or managers. The traditional leadership style in most cases, is one with a problem-solving mindset. Change leadership differs in creating the vivid grand picture of the future in everyone's mind, while also inspiring them.

They understand that effectiveness is a function of the leader's personality, the follower's maturity and the situation. It is not about two styles or three styles of the leader's ability. It is about a leader's personal charisma.

Gandhi was not a born leader, but he was admired by millions of people because he walked the talk with simple living and high thinking. Charisma was a weapon that he used in every crisis that he faced under the British regime.

Facing the Visioning Challenge

Erik Weihenmayer was fully blind but climbed Mt Everest in 2001, proving "who dares wins". "It is not that there are difficulties; we do not dare. But, because we do not dare, that they are difficult," said Seneca, the Roman philosopher, in 16 BC.

Higher Level of Thinking

Where do great leaders operate in terms of thought processes? Transformational leaders work at a much different level of thinking and constantly find out what is difficult and seek to resolve what others may label impossible. Few moves they make may appear beyond the imagination of others, unbelievable and look complex, but for these leaders seeking change, the steps seem to be easy. They continually ask, "If our best brains and thinking got us here, will it let us know that the problems confronting today cannot be solved by the same level of thinking when we created them."

The change seekers challenge the imagination. Albert Einstein said, "We need to find solutions outside the framework of the days. Imagination is more important than knowledge." If we look at the history and evolution of human development, we see that it has been driven either by the power of positive vision or lack of imagination.

Changes were brought by visionaries who dreamt of better future states, as they created a vivid picture in their mind. They opined that the future was not an outcome of choice among alternative paths offered by the present, but a place to be created, first in mind, with determination and externally, through the action.

"For the leaders, the future is not the place to go, but the destination created in the mind for which no path has been laid out, but people and leaders' layout together," said John Schaar.

Vision limits the level of ability to achieve, as anyone can achieve only their imagination. We maintain that vision limits what we can do. The actual limits for creative thoughts are the ones that the mind can accept.

Thomas Edison failed 10,000 times with his experiment before he succeeded with the bulb. Abraham Lincoln had to face defeat eight times in local elections till he became President of the United States.

Challenges in Creating the Shared Values

Whether it's the business, family or children, 'founders' syndrome' always manifests at all levels. Most founders emphatically always state, "I don't trust anyone else to do it." At some point in any organisation's life, the founder is forced to decide and hand over the responsibility. Still, the most pressing worry of the founders has been the continuation of those values they espoused. The topmost concern for the founder is the fear of dilution of values that can prove detrimental to the organisation's uniqueness. So how does the new leader address value erosion problems even if in terms of deviation from the norm or changing the norm itself? The leader's challenge is to validate differing perceptions of what is right or wrong.

The old statement is, "When you have a hammer, everything looks like a nail."

When an organisation faces a severe problem, the perception of the causes differs so much based on the perceiver's role in the organisation. For example,

A manager's perception: A few employees are the root cause of the entire problem.

Employees' perception: Management causes everything.

CEO's perception: Everything is caused by capability problem. Resources are a universal constraint, will there be enough?.

Clients' Perception: Everything is an execution and delivery problem.

Executive Perception: Existing resources are not effectively being used? How resourceful are we?

The doubt often leads to a knee-jerk reaction, "this way and only way. No change is possible,"

An exciting new future creation involves three steps:

(i) Articulating mentally the expected future state that is needed.
(ii) Thorough understanding of the current state and capabilities.
(iii) Knowing what is not happening.

Leaders need to raise a few crucial conversations before introducing changes, however small or big the change is. When these conversations happen the stakes are high, emotions running strong, and opinions differ.

Clarity and consensus are crucial to the success of changes.

The urgency to change is often determined by the CEO's questions, as follows:

"Do we share a vision in our organisation?"

"Is there a personal vision that is aligned with the company's vision?"

"Can everyone relate and identify with the shared vision of the organisation?"

"If there is no alignment, why?"

The Conventional Approach to Strategy Development

Assess where one is at present and where one wants to go. When one has done that, ask- how does one get there? Unfortunately, this approach does not produce an innovative and futuristic strategy.

Change of the Norms, Standards, and Rules

Organisational culture is the shared beliefs and values which guide the thoughts and behaviour styles of its members. Norm refers to attitudes and behaviour that are acceptable and also rules of conduct. Defining explicit behaviour regulations for the general orderly conduct in the organisation and governing standards will achieve improvement and help in comparative evaluations.

Organisations need to focus on the following to run smoothly.

Leadership drives change initiatives in the culture's context and the norms, and these have influencing power. One has to identify existing standard practices that are not productive, thus:

1. Situation analysis is often deployed to find out the conditions prevailing inside and outside organisations.
2. One needs to create a "vision" of the future expectation.
3. The strategies are developed at four levels based on those findings, whether incremental change or generic.

Grand Strategy

The grand strategy defines everything and asks, why go to war? Who are the bitterest competition and the enemy if the goal is to leapfrog market share and become a category killer? Who is the competition, and who are allies? What is if mission fails what price to pay?

Just as declaring war may take time, grand strategy takes time. It took two years to declare war for Germany after they invaded parts of Europe.

Few leaders dream big to bring change in the mindset of the entire organisation. Martin Luther King or Gandhi did not start their actions to lead with business leader's attitudes.

Enterprise-wide strategy is a long-term plan to execute the action, through high-impact decisions, to realise the vision.

Key features include marketing decisions, diversifications, mergers, strategic alliances and joint ventures. All additional steps require unprecedented actions or decisions which contribute to the changes and are long-lasting.

Divisional Strategy

With every long-term plan comes the short-term tactical programmes that focus on actions and decisions that enable the long-term goals to become a reality. The more efficient we are, the more difficult it is to take steps that defy the rule or set a precedent to change the current scene and construct a new future.

Shared Vision

Shared understanding is a collective context in an organisational setting, and people propose, "What do we wish to achieve or create?" "What is the role of shared vision?"

Emphasis is on sharing the spirit of futuristic thinking and not on the vision. This is easy for people to visualise the future state propagated by leaders who create a collective vision. Shared vision emerges from the alignment of personal perceptions with that of the organisation.

An individual's own deepest drives create the vision. Shared vision comes from a natural affection towards a unique esoteric future.

Vision cannot be altered or fine-tuned based on events, as one cannot think that "we want what we can have, given the current condition."

An alternative way of thinking is provoking the self and other decision-makers, thus:

1. Where are we now, and is it the ideal condition?
2. Where do we want to go from where we are?
3. Why is there a difference between where we are and where we want to be?
4. To achieve the goal, what needs to change?
5. How do we get there?

An alternative way is to pursue a particular line of conversation with every affected party, thus:

1. What did we want to happen?
2. What is happening now?
3. Why is there a big difference?
4. What needs to change?
5. How do we nurture change and accountability?

Situation Analysis

The first step is the process of critically evaluating the internal and external conditions that affect an organisation, and that is done before a change initiative.

It provides the expertise to identify the current opportunities and challenges to the organisation its service, or product. A SWOT analysis is ideal to assess opportunities, and threats.

The next step is to examine the strategic objectives.

Shared Vision

The advantages of having a shared vision are beyond one person's dream. It helps in the following ways:

(i) Clarifies what is needed and empowers people to take the initiative.
(ii) Nurtures analytical thought process.
(iii) Encourages focus and creativity.
(iv) Highlights the need for change.
(v) Shared vision forces confrontation of the "status quo".

Shared visionaries ask: what do we want to happen or create?

They do not speak or even think of only what is feasible, given the present conditions. The critical question is, how immense should the vision be? It is not the bigness, and one should think about the care and concern the leader has.

The answer lies in the question, how deeply does one care?

Also, how much is one willing to change?

Every vision has a price. If stakeholders want something better and more significant, they have to pay the fee. The next question is how 'big' should the vision be?

Dreams have to be lofty, and the end-state shall be as good as the objectives were. The vision is the promise of what the organisation shall one day be. The leader's ideal is the prophecy of what the leadership shall at last unveil.

Vision building involves two levels of expectation setting. What should be and what should one aim to be?

'Floor setting' is an important way to visualise. It describes what the change organisation should be at this level in the next few years. We define it as 'go for ceiling'; the stretch level is what one truly wanted, no matter what the current status is. For example, we should be the category killer in data and analytic segments in the next three years with rare solutions in two specific verticals.

The ceiling- A sample reaction statement, aka, "we should be the super-category killer in the BI-data analytic segment".

To change something, established methods have to end, which happens only by challenging the status quo.

The eagle's life provides the better example of the pain the transformation brings in. An eagle can live 70 years, but has to make hard decisions when it reaches 40 years. It can no longer catch the prey as its nails have grown longer. The beak is bent, making it difficult to tear the food when the feathers are heavy. It finds flying to great heights an impossible task and that means its survival is at stake.

The choice is between fading away to death or changing.

The change involves the tedious process of rebuilding the capability and getting rid of the old ways. Finally, it chooses to go to the mountaintop, where it breaks its talons and the beak. It waits till the new ones grow. Once the new nails grow, it plucks all old feathers and waits till new ones grow. It takes the flight of rebirth and lives another 30 years.

Organisations and individuals behave like the eagle with forced choices when faced with a complicated condition. The changes have to be brought in the way of thinking, acting and doing, and this requires innate drive, strength and determination to carry out the difference. That is how the escape to the future can become a reality. Organisations and the people have to painfully discard past practices and preserve a few good ones to pursue future goals. The eagle has many lessons for us. It always loves to fly at a great height and uses its strength of vision to stay focused on its goal of catching its prey, however far. It soars above the cloud during the storm-achievers love challenges and relish them. The female eagle tests the commitment constantly by challenging it before allows mating. Organisations need to have committed people to create that shared vision. The safe nest built by the male eagle and the nudge by mother to fly out of the nest indicates that one must be prepared for challenges anytime. After the chicks come out of the nest, the male train the next generation for the future.

Challenges of Fixated Mental Models

Is it possible to decode the way human beings see and comprehend the world? Cognitive science and Human-Computer Interface (HCI) have tried to answer mental models based on a search to set up commonalities among how humans and computers understand the world. When we see and interpret the cues from outside, does our brain apply the logic? Studies do not support the premise.

The limitation is associated with isolating, studying, and validating the mental models. Individual's behaviour, when confronted with new ideas, has been studied with a comparable knowledge base. This approach makes attempts to isolate complex knowledge and study mental models, cues, and interrelationships. However, study techniques and results in this area have been questioned because mental models are not robust and stable. Furthermore, the studies have been highly subjective. Many studies could not map specific elements of a stimulus or cues relevant during the evolution of a mental model.

Impediments that arise while implementing change in organisations are because of the status quo mindset of people. The wrong sense of security and comfort contributes to ease and lowers the motivation to face the risk. Therefore, the trend is to stick to the tested and accepted behaviour and nurture the existing order, which becomes easier.

"Presumption begins in ignorance and ends in ruin,"

Gerstner of IBM said. "In anything other than a protected industry, longevity is the capacity to change, not to stay with what you've got."

Too many business organisations build up internal commitment based on their existing business conditions, which creates the problem for changes. It's difficult to "eat your seed corn," go into other activities or radically change a few things that are vital to what is being done. The pricing, and distribution channels or the communication system are not easy to change. Managers and decision-makers find it comfortable to keep doing the same thing which brought them success. The status quo people classify the way they're successful and write guidebooks and create manuals.

Management leaders focus on culture of sustenance model until threatened by external change; the change is discontinuous all too often. It requires force often from outside to push for change. Andy Grove put it well when he said, "Only the paranoid survives."

Often the Mental Models are Overconfidence, Bias, Skill Vs Luck

In an organisational context, falling in line and continuing with the status quo mantra works on every new hire, right from day one.

However antiquated, limiting and obstructive, the so-called 'norm' is preached, a safe course for those who spent long years doing the same job. I recall the early days of my career, when I worked in a bank. That was my first job as a junior banking assistant after prolonged unemployment. I was posted to a branch office near the city of Bombay. The unit had three staff viz., the cashier, a peon and me. There was hardly any transaction in a day as it was a remote rural branch in a tiny village. I had to fill up two hours of overtime as told by the cashier, who was the union representative. When I replied that I did not have enough work, I was told that I was part of the union contract norm and should follow the status quo and not challenge it.

We all live a life driven and bound by established societal and cultural norms with countless prescribed and defined conditions.

The reason for falling in line with status quo ideals is the brain's evolutionary design to resist changes in behaviour that may cause the risk of being isolated. Breaking away from the established norm means facing uncertainty, which leads to falling into line with widespread and commonly accepted standards.

Conformance is the easiest choice for any normal human being to avoid stress.

The condition is perpetuated through group members through the perpetuation process by everyone around who acts out the status quo. They become hidden forces of perpetuation in preserving the existing stability. Pressure is exerted on non-conforming members to conform, and those confronted with the fear of an unknown future try to maintain the current state. Three typical status quo ways of thinking stir up frustration and dissatisfaction, especially for change initiators and implementers:

Syndrome #1

Anyone who refuses to follow the established norms and adhere to the status quo are senseless. Any change is met with roadblocks.

The syndrome is "If the sentiment is the right thing to do, it's better to follow that belief and do the same."

Syndrome #2

This mental makeup forces one to exhibit the behaviour of normalcy even if the current methods are not pain-free.

Instead of change, even for positive benefits at a future date, it advises one to keep doing the same thing and be happy. Everyone is accustomed to following the regular drill, and is told that it's better to have an attitude of "this is the way we always do things."

Syndrome #3

A firm belief is that those who do not adapt and instead, change away from the norm may be extremist and not be encouraged. It complies with the majority with the path of least resistance.

"Challenging the status quo culture" itself is a leadership task and requires extraordinary leadership skills. Moreover, such transformation requires taking steps to overcome the resistance power arising out of the collective mindset.

To break away from the past, leadership has to put in extraordinary force. But unfortunately, dynamic bindings block the way to exercise freedom of choice.

The conscious choice to pluck the old feathers and break the ageing nails is not a pain-free choice, and if solid, committed leadership is absent, the option to adopt the change becomes even harder to initiate.

Disruption of the Status Quo

It is difficult to disrupt the status quo, especially when employee attitudes are hardened. However, there can be no better illustration than the following story of monkeys and bananas.

Five monkeys were put in a cage with swings, tyres and toys, with a few bananas kept hanging from a hook at the top of a ladder. Seeing the bananas, one monkey climbed up and went for the bananas; suddenly, a bucket of cold water fell on the monkey. The action completely rattled the monkey, and it climbed down immediately. Another monkey now tried to get at the bananas; it got a cold shower too. Soon, all the monkeys met with the same fate of freezing water, one by one. The monkeys gave up trying and sat huddled in one corner while the bananas started rotting. One monkey now was replaced with a new monkey, and the new monkey, with fresh energy went for the bananas. This time, there was no cold shower. Yet before he could touch the bananas, the old monkeys beat up the new monkey and tore him down.

Quickly, he gave up trying and climbed down to settle with the older monkeys in the corner; the second monkey was now replaced, and once again a new monkey went for the bananas. Soon the monkeys, including the last, returned to attack the newer one. In this way, all the original monkeys were replaced and no one succeeded at getting a banana. Each time a monkey would go for the bananas, it was attacked by the other monkeys, though none of the monkeys had faced the pain of a cold shower.

It is typical behaviour and a part of the organisation culture. The senior employees, accustomed to well-established ways, resist change, and newer employees get pulled down whenever they make any fresh attempt. Cultural differences are a complicated and time-consuming process to change.

Deal With Resistance to Change

Resistance to change is exhibited individually or collectively when people perceive that a change threatens their interest. Even though the perceived threat may not be accurate or large enough to permit resistance, resistance may be motivated or driven by peer or leadership influence. A live example of peer and leadership influence is as follows. In India, a public company was part of a reputed US-based global corporation. It manufactured borosilicate glass products and held a near-monopoly share in laboratory ware. However, the high manufacturing cost prompted the management to introduce a Total Quality Management Plan to eliminate waste and bring down the cost. The glass manufacturing plant ran 24/7, 365 days, as a continuous process plant. Glass melting and forming required skilled labour. A few of the specialty products were mouth blown. Working conditions in the factory were hazardous.

The skill was learnt on the job over the years. The primary raw materials for melting the glass were silica, borax, and the broken glass called cullet. In addition, the test tube manufacturing division made test tubes using glass tubes. The 1,500 full-time workers in the factory were highly unionised and had five labour unions.

It was common for any Indian manufacturing company to have multiple trade unions affiliated with different and opposing political ideologies.

However, the labour laws in India (Indian Trade Union Act 1926) have provision for legally organised collective bargaining channels through a recognised trade union that has majority membership. Therefore, the management had recognised one union with majority members for bargaining.

As part of the global quality policy, the Indian subsidy company got a mandate to introduce the TQM, and the factory personnel manager had the responsibility for implementing the change.

The project plan included a massive training of illiterate but highly skilled workers. As it was a completely novel idea, we carried out the readiness assessment, and it was revealed that the entire project would not even take off unless there was sufficient education.

The learning curriculum was prepared in the local language, which consisted of basic knowledge on the advantages of product quality. For the first time in the 75-year-old history of the company, the workers were invited to attend classroom training in a simple language. They were sharing the seats with supervisors, which had a high impact.

The initiative was well-received, and it excited the workers, and every worker felt good.

Phil Crosby's quality model on eliminating waste (EFW, or Error Free Work) reducing the cost of quality (COQ) was taught, which caught the workers' imagination. Before starting the TQM initiatives, the productivity targets, were based on make-norms for each shift.

Every worker in each 8-hour shift had a target to make a defined number of pieces, and they would place the test tubes they made in a box along the aisles.

The shift supervisor would log-in the number of pieces made in a particular shift and submitted the production report for the change. The quality department inspected the test tubes made, checked for defects, and finally, all selected test tubes went into the pack.

Because of the inter-union rivalry, the test tubes stored in bins on the aisle were broken by rival union members on the shift. The high breakage was contributing to the cost of quality (COQ). So much so, that the quality control methods of inspection at the end added to the poor selection. The make to select ratio was 60 per cent, leaving 40 per cent as rejects.

The TQM aimed to lower the cost of quality. Their quality plan would have improved the select ratio rather than attempting to meet or exceed the production norms. The approach involved a "work smarter than harder" approach.

There was a high potential to achieve this goal by bringing few changes in work processes. The workers were first trained in their language on the concept of cost of quality and QCC (Quality Control Circles).

The idea of QCC that originated in Japan, cultivates the involvement of small groups from the same work to solve quality issues by identifying improvements.

They deploy measure and display techniques to monitor the progress and have proven effective in Japanese companies.

It is the Japanese way of involved / collaborative quality management. In the daily stand-up meetings of QCC, the workers came with suggestions that would improve the selectivity. As an experiment, these process improvement suggestions were tried out in three shifts. The results were astonishing as the selection went up to 85 per cent and the workers were delighted to see their ideas working.

The ideas included placing the bins at a height closer to production lathes. As a result, the breakage is minimised; placing padded cardboard on top of each layer of test tubes in the storage bins minimised waste. In addition, they removed the containers after they were filled by every worker to a safer place, unlike the earlier process of leaving the bins on the aisle, which resulted in people tripping over the container, increasing breakage.

All these steps reduced the breakage considerably.

The 'measure display' technique was adopted to give the workers the QCC visibility of their accomplishments. In addition, the sight of more goods going into the pack gave emotional satisfaction leading to a sense of fulfilment. Until then, the unions were not even looking at this as an issue. They felt that the new personnel manager was sincere in educating and bringing relief to the illiterate union members by teaching them to work smarter than harder. They even agreed with the manager that the workers got more rest time, and the quality of work-life had improved as the workers spent less time on the fire lathes and still met their production target.

The workers got to learn new ideas, which they never articulated. Even though many were illiterate, the HR manager persuaded the top management to sponsor the team for a regional QCC conference to present their work. This unique experience was the most rewarding experience for the workers who felt respected.

The management now felt that the TQM initiative was paying off and wanted to formalise this as a plant-wide standard process and initiate the talk with union. Any change in production norms required a formal agreement with the union.

A prolonged negotiation with the union lasted six months, and the management could not agree on anything. The union leaders' perception was that the company stood to profit in changing any process, and the union wanted the share of gains through more production bonuses. The incentive demand included a stiff increase in the percentage as high as 75 per cent. The mood shifted from disagreement to resistance, anger and finally led to a showdown. The union even wanted the TQM programme to stop. The union leader influenced the same workers who were excited and convinced about the advantage of the entire idea opposing the whole initiative. As a result, the TQM programme ground to a halt.

The trade union's stance was: "We have the power to obstruct the change", and why not use that power to demonstrate the strength over the rival trade unions. They opposed the change because the union leaders accepted, they showed one-upmanship.

Union leaders always use their position power and do whatever it takes to prevent the change by refusing to support it even if the change outcome is positive.

In this case, the programme got underway after a prolonged negotiation and written agreement in the production norms that shifted from make-norms to pack norms. It was an excellent test of the persistent attempts of the senior sponsor of change. The leadership attitude was: "Those who oppose the change be treated with understanding, but in a firm but decisive way."

Tactics for Changing Mindsets

While dealing with resistance, the sponsors can resort to many of the tactics. One can draw inspiration from *Mahabharata*, the Indian classical mythology for handling any crisis. Chanakya, the brilliant coach and teacher and strategist, recommended seven strategies to the great king Chandragupta Maurya in dealing with his neighbouring powers.

The four levels, saāma, dhāna, danda and bheda, are effective methods of persuasion used by Hindu Kshatriyas (the warrior caste) and the kings to rule. A methodology to approach a problem starts with conciliation or gentle persuasion (saāma means respect). Hindu Vedic rules express that one needs to try rewards, incentives, or even bribes (dhāna, or gift, bribery).

If that does not change the status quo, one should create division among the people who disrupt (bheda or division).

Finally, one can use force (danda or punishment) to resolve the problem when the previous three fail.

Besides, the illusions or deceit (maya), deliberately ignoring the disruptors (upeksha), use of jugglery (indrajālā) are the other three suggested methods to resolve any problem.

Facilitation

A slow but most effective way to change mindset is to help people align their own individual goals with the change. When people are enabled and encouraged, they will be happier to work with change. Furthermore, this method allows all those struggling to adjust to the new situation and achieve the goals. In the above example, initial success was because of the facilitation without which the attempt to change failed ab initio.

Negotiation

When persuasion does not produce results, the best way is to negotiate and understand. Quid pro quo helps, as cited in the previous case. Usually, the unions place the most challenging demands first and make small concessions. The key is patience, which I learned in one contract negotiation meeting that stretched over four months and 35 days.

The trade unions are always willing to negotiate, and this often produces win/win deals. Managements guess a way to share the gains without which the change initiatives are not possible. Mutually acceptable solutions work for both parties in negotiated settlements.

Manipulation

A method of influence over others that uses hidden deception or psychological pressure to change the behaviour is usually manipulation. The target is kept under the power of the manipulator. In this modern era, political parties widely use social media to manipulate opinion through deceptive information.

Ethically, this is a questionable tactic but can be deployed if the outcome is positive. As a short-term gimmick, this may work when other methods fail.

The Science of Social Influence

Let me list a few experiments which demonstrate manipulation and change of behaviour. An experiment was once set up where a blind person would touch a shopper behind them to scare them. When the shocked person turned around and found out that their assumed attacker was a blind man who wanted to ask the time, they went through deflection and relief. The targets were requested to buy donation postcards for a charitable cause. The person who experienced the "fear and relief" was in favour than the control group, which wasn't manipulated.

This "fear and relief" manipulation technique is widely adopted in the common bad cop, good cop routine in crime investigation. While interrogating suspects, one cop will scare the suspect while another pretends to save them. The suspect is more willing to talk after this manipulation.

We are also victims of manipulation in our daily life. For example, the manipulation with fear tactics is rampant in advertisements on TV commercials, and the insurance salesperson injects fear. In addition, bad bosses manipulate subordinates by hinting that their job is in danger.

Employees manipulate bosses to make them believe that they are working hard, even when they are doing nothing productive. Judicious use of manipulation techniques may be helpful in breaking the tough resistors in change management. In one of our projects, five senior data warehousing professionals would not accept the idea of elevating themselves to align with the change goals. The manipulation was done with the client's help, where they worked to inject fear that the company may not get their contract renewed if these consultants did not pick up new skills. This manipulation worked wonders.

Training

The knowledge part brought into the equation for the change management methodology addresses the why issue and builds confidence to face the challenges. When one needs new skills to meet the changes, focused training helps to resolve the how questions.

A unique way of getting people's buy-in is to let people convince themselves about the reason for involvement.

Neuroscience and Change Management

Change leaders legitimately perceive that people in their organisation cannot benefit from change, and thus, resist change. Conflicting standpoints are inevitable in the underlying ways of approach by the change leaders in thinking and sensing and how the employees would perceive changes being introduced. While leaders see change as a logical business move driven by a need, employees see the same move as driven by hidden motives that may harm their jobs. A strong connection between fears, and how it affects the brain exists. Neurological responses of fear and anxiety get triggered by those facing change.

Anxiety affects the brain and is a warning sign to actions which are not normally contemplated. When a person's cognitive distortions, or irrational thought patterns, make him/her perceive everything as a threat anxiety is the result.

The amygdala- brain structure -is the cause for generating negative emotions. It becomes less active when one performs non-emotional tasks, which may be the best-suggested remedy for sadness as it is believed that keeping busy will help one feel better. A sense of fear, anxiety and protectiveness always accompany changes. Change leaders have to bear in mind that resistance to change is not always premeditated.

As humans, we're programmed and scripted to resist and make judgements before even attempting to change.

The human body and brain become 'wired' system and is on the lookout for potential threats that could arise from any direction. The threats could be imagined than real. Fear suspicion, frustration are always undesirable emotions leading to anxiety. If our thinking configurations are adapted to reinforcing negative feeling, every event in life becomes a threat, it becomes a vicious loop. Situational anxiety, as with change, needs to fight out, unlike other anxiety syndromes. The psychoanalytic describes anxiety as a conflict of 3 distinct, interacting agents in the psychic apparatus viz the id, ego, and superego (Sigmund Freud)

The change leadership must be sensitive to the impact on individuals and be prepared to get rid of anxiety. Living with anxiety is counterproductive in creating even the smallest first step of awareness.

People accept that life without change would be a life without growth, but change and consequent anxiety cause employees to break down when organisation leaders try to bend it till it breaks.

If sudden changes are introduced in established ways of working, anxiety levels go up and things go wrong. At that point, normal behaviour becomes a painful and slow process, and one may never get back to the same level of energy, passion and comfort.

Many ways are found to control people's emotions during change and reduce the anxiety of the fluid state during change. However, if many people are anxious, that invisible force will grind the rate of change to a halt. One strategy to manage this will be to assess the anxiety levels realistically and ascertain coping abilities at the individual and group level while not pushing through the change process faster.

One outcome of anxiety is the avoidance strategy.

Though for engineering the escape. speed is a prerequisite to getting change actions moving through the attention, awareness and desire phases. It is critical to understand that different units in the organisation need enhanced capabilities to accelerate and move.

All people do not jump on the change bandwagon because an idea is novel or because everyone's doing it. Many people may have to be helped with getting through the attention and awareness phase before developing the urge. It may be a good idea to introduce change as a strategy where stability and predictability are sure.

These "stability zones" will bring security and anchorage. Another solution is to build support networks that will get strength and affirmation to changing scenarios. Negative people can drain and increase the stress for others. Strategy for containing such influence in the organisation and anxiety exposure to a larger group of people has to be ready to identify and reduce unrelated stressors. The elimination of stress is next to impossible, but one can limit stress levels created by changes.

Value-driven Leadership

Company values are the essential beliefs upon which the business is conducted. They are the guiding principles; the organisation uses to manage its internal affairs and its relationship with all the stakeholders. If values drive decision -making, one can keep a sense of integrity, be sure of what is right, and approach decisions confidently and clearly.

Values make people feel good about themselves and the company.

They are to make one proud and represent what we support, even if the choice isn't popular.

If you don't have corporate values, what would you do? Will the business run? Yes. But the difference is between credible and non-credible images. Credible organisations run on value-driven leadership while hiring. They value control and direct the right hires, and that is crucial for a business to last long.

Sam Walton was so clear on values that he would fire instantly any executive for value violation if he came to know. Respect for the individual and being customer-centric were the topmost values of Walmart from the beginning.

Sam Walton would say, "There is only one boss, the customer, and he can fire everybody in the company from the chairman onwards by spending his money somewhere else."

Clarifying to people what values a company stands for and what values its employees espouse are important. Finding answers to the questions is challenging and worth pursuing. Every organisation's leadership makes values either implicit or explicit through a statement that is presented as a guideline and a binding commitment. They weave the facet of their business into one set of common principles.

These become the deeply ingrained principle and weaving fabric that guides employees' behaviour and company's decisions of credible organisations.

The value-driven actions are the behaviour they expect the employees to live by in day-to-day conduct, and that the employees expect of their leaders. Without values, the company will be like a body without a soul.

Unfortunately, not every company leadership agrees with this philosophy and many leaders think values can be restrictive beyond comprehension and can become a matter of varied interpretation.

The value statements are, at their best, exact reflections of what the company believes in, and the management and employees are willing to live. Core value statements play an active role in standardising business practices and foster confidence and happiness in the employees who work with the values in day-to-day actions.

The most critical part in building the long-lasting organisations is the intensity to which their values drive leaders. Moreover, the role they play in galvanising and influencing followers on their perception and behaviour is reinforcing.

Leaders have to remember that value-driven conduct alone has a lasting impact and can contribute to every step towards institution building.

Schwartz's influential theory of the structure of values indicates 10 universal value dimensions, such as benevolence, achievement, and tradition, which underlie all values. In addition, businesses espouse values on performance or quality, efficiency or profitability.

These values affect the dimension of achievement. Many organisations advocate values that emphasise employees' welfare needs which includes respect, empowerment, and the right to take part or influence the decisions. The value erosion, if ignored or allowed, can immensely and permanently damage the organisation.

Numerous cases happened where value erosion was the primary reason for the disaster, like Enron, Satyam, etc.

There was a Japanese company that made electronic consumer products. The factory's quality head would himself sign a guarantee card that read, "We have taken utmost care to make a defect-free product. In case you are not satisfied with any of the features, please return this card, and we will replace it free of cost."

The company would replace but the head of quality would go on a public platform and apologise to the audience openly, even if the company had received only one postcard in that year. Quality is a rock-solid value in all Japanese companies.

Build-A-Bear Workshop is an American toy retailer founded in 1997 in Overland, Missouri. Besides selling teddy they sell other stuffed animals too. They are innovative and take the teddy bear concept toys seriously; "bear-isms" is the central point of the culture. They operate over 400 stores globally and sell billions of toys.

The call their corporate headquarters as "bear quarters" located in St Louis and the company's six core values that are posted at all retail stores. Instead, within the company, these values are chief tools for bringing employees together across each business level.

New leadership aims to change everything in a takeover or turnaround but that was not the case with Build-A-Bear. Instead, the CEO protected the core values and encouraged people to do the same as if they were their life's values tied to the company values.

LL Beans, an American retailing mail order e-commerce Company since 1912, has over 2 billion in sales. Their golden rule is "Sell good merchandise at a reasonable profit, treat your customers as human beings, and they will always come back for more". The message was posted prominently in its retail stores and the manufacturing and shipping facilities, reminding everyone of their values. The statements are more than suggestive of a way of life and the way to conduct business for 6,000 plus employees. For example, LL Bean's trademark satisfaction guarantee includes a statement about the pride, the boot-makers have. A few years back, no one would have thought of starting an online shoe buying as a multimillion-dollar business. Yet, Zappos, an online shoe store based out of Las Vegas, changed the way people buy shoes and succeeded to make a trade worth 1 billion in nine years. Founded in 1999 in Las Vegas, Nevada, the company built its business by espousing 10 core values that unified employees and loyal customers.

Its Ten Core Values:

1. Deliver WOW through the service.
2. Embrace and drive change.
3. Create fun and a little weirdness
4. Be adventurous, creative, and open-minded.
5. Pursue growth and learning.
6. Build open and honest relationships with communication.
7. Build a positive team and family spirit.
8. Do more with less.
9. Be passionate and determined.
10. Be humble.

When Amazon bid to take over, the founders were not keen to go with the deal because of their value concern of "do more with less". The typical value of being customer-centric sets a fine example of being value-driven.

However, other examples of value erosion are plenty.

When Lehman Brothers collapsed, the comment on the mucin was an insult to Lehman Brothers CEO Richard S

Fuld Jr; it read, "So long, and thanks for all the fish". *The Hitchhiker's Guide to the Galaxy*, authored by Douglas Adams, originated in 1978 as a BBC radio comedy before he went on to develop five books. *So long, thank you, for the fish* is, in fact, the fourth book in the *Hitchhiker's Guide to the Galaxy* series.

Geoffrey Raymond famous for Wall Street CEOs' paintings created a portrait titled 'The Annotated Fuld', with the support of employees of Lehman Brothers.

These employees left the company and swore never to return. After completing the painting, Raymond asked the departing employees to express their sentiments on the collapse and their old boss, who had sacrificed the values to stay in power.

The portrait illustrated how Lehman's employees wanted posterity to remember the leader for perpetrating the worst business disasters in the history of Wall Street.

On the third floor of the Lehman building, people created a 100-foot-long wall naming it "Wall of Shame". It had insults scribbled on it about the leaders of Lehman Brothers. Fuld and Chief Operating Officer Joseph M Gregory was called "dumb and dumber".

The agitated employees did not spare even the board members. They considered the members to have been silent spectators and therefore, portrayed them as pensioners with the caption "voting in Braille only". The US secretary of the treasury was depicted to be sitting on Fuld's head, with the line, "We have a huge brand with treasury". These men who were in leadership roles with unbridled power, allowed value erosion, and that impacted an entire generation of people. Such a change left wounds with deep scars.

The impact the value erosion creates on organisations is enormous, and it throws up a tremendous challenge for the new generation, especially the leaders of an entire generation.

Systems Thinking

Systems thinking is the most significant breakthrough in how to understand and guide change in organisations. Peter Senge, in his work *The Fifth Discipline* had elaborated this concept as one of the five main principles. An organisation is a social system, and we need to understand the interdependence of sub-objects and their attributes. Systems thinking is a holistic view from which one can see a universe, an interrelated relationship of elements, focusing only on a single or a few details. We see events in the larger context of a pattern that is unfolding. Systems thinking is a perspective of seeing and understanding the totality in its entirety and not as collection of individual parts.

An entirety view is to see it as a web of interconnections that creates patterns. A system is an organised collection of units or subsystems that are highly integrated to accomplish an overall goal. The system has various inputs, which go through a process to produce expected gains, which carry out the comprehensive plan.

A system consists of many smaller systems or subsystems. Many times, organisations are confronted with this question. "Why does effectiveness keep declining despite so many corporate-sponsored improvement projects?" The answer is simple. It is a lack of systemic view. These sporadic attempts are constructed and designed to kill only the bushfire, while it may be the wildfire that needs attention.

As part of the learning culture, systems thinking can enable managers to deliberate differently and make sense of complex data and information and identification of solutions.

Status Quo Mental Model

Why is changing established business practices always difficult? It is difficult because the human brain wants to encourage the status quo and avoid anxiety and disturbance with even a slight change. For example, in 2016, in New Delhi, the capital of India, a maverick leader of the local government came up with a change in traffic rules that permitted only the odd-even number plate cars to be on the road alternatively to combat air pollution. Imagine how this change in old habits can be made to work amidst massive objections and counter objections in a city where no rule is followed. Yet, they imposed the rule, and it required one leader with a strong will to take the bull by the horn in the community's overall interest. Nevertheless, people saw overall payoff, and the experiment at least got a head start.

Many attempts to change people's sensitivity to environmental protection by banning polythene carry bags in Mumbai failed repeatedly. However, each year, the government spends billions of rupees in removing the plastics. The only reason is lack of will and conviction.

The status quo mindset is a mental model; people have in organisations and it becomes the major obstacle during change initiatives.

Mental models are beliefs, ideas, images, and verbal descriptions that we consciously or unconsciously form through our experiences; they guide our thoughts and actions, and predispose our behaviour in specific ways. Mental models give internal strength in a world of continuous change. Still, they limit our outlook on new facts or ideas that challenge our deeply anchored belief: the characteristic is incomplete.

The mental model differs from others of the same concept or subject, no matter how common. And we set up a mental model from the knowledge that comes from prior experience, however brief the experience may be.

Mental models can be pretty unstable and can change and are liable to alter in newer circumstances. When our mental models are in contrast with others, we view the mindset of others as flawed, and our view remains valid until the data to the contrary confronts us.

Many examples of flawed mental models that were mistaken for the truth can be cited. For instance, computers could weigh only 1.5 tonnes, and data processing is a fad that was a standard mental model recently. Even a Yale University professor believed that overnight delivery service was an impossible novel idea when a paper was presented by his student Fred Smith, who established FedEx.

Mental models are firmed up and reinforced by subsequent events, and the tendency to rationalise the current belief concretised the thought process. Organisations have conflicting interests and groups internally fighting for priority.

Change occurs when these negative values, forces, or events gain enough power to confront and engage the status quo. Thus, the dialectical process enables one to analyse stability and change.

If performed, readiness assessment and analysis can assess the targeted change users' mental model and influence readiness to change their beliefs.

Several techniques are used for capturing mental models, opinions and perceptions. Collecting data, organising and use the analysed results to guide the design of change initiatives at every step from awareness to planned levels are a few steps.

Task Analysis

Task analysis is one process of identifying and understanding user-level tasks and goals, the strategies they used to perform the charges, and the current tools. In addition, the analysis includes any problems they experience and the changes they expect to see in their tasks and tools. Tasks include those automated processes and manually performed ones. Task analysis activities are grouped into five categories: time recording, prioritisation, monitoring, analysis and optimisation.

Task analysis combines the methodologies of task management, risk management, and time management. These are: BPM or Business Process Management, CRM or Customer Relationship Management, ERP or Enterprise Resource Planning and BI or Business Intelligence.

Cognitive Task Analysis (CTA) is a family of psychological research methods for uncovering and representing what people know and how they reason. They are mainly used in the analysis of decision-making of experts and the development and evolution of mental models. It is a fundamental methodology in the assessment and changing by reducing manual error.

Feedback Surveys and Questionnaires

Researchers use surveys and questionnaires commonly for collecting demographic and opinion data of change users' backgrounds and levels of alignment. Survey research is the most critical area of measurement in applied social research. The broad scope of survey research encompasses any measurement procedures that involve asking questions of respondents.

A "survey" can vary from a short paper-and-pencil feedback form to an intensive one-on-one in-depth interview. However, many issues are associated with this traditional methodology.

The modern, easy-to-use, low-cost method is an online survey.

Tools to Use

A popular tool is Survey Monkey, which has a customised questionnaire design that can automatically design and mail the questionnaire to select the target group. Compared to customised traditional methods, the tool can even collate and tabulate data and save time in data collation and analysis.

Focus Group Techniques

This non-directive approach has been in place since the twenties and increased in appeal in the 1930s and 1940s as many sociologists used alternative interviewing methods to the traditional closed response choice questionnaire method.

Focus group interviews are informal techniques used for planning or evaluating a system design. The methodology involves a focus group where a moderator is questioning a group of users.

They interview individuals on a one-on-one basis. This method is valuable for questioning users on work or their opinion on the impact of changes in the system. For example, interviewers may ask users to describe a typical day or task before asking why they change said daily task, mainly when events occur.

Interviews or focus groups may include asking users to evaluate simple design features of a system design. When analysing data from focus groups and interviews, it is important to identify response patterns rather than overemphasise any user's comments. Focus groups and interviews collect self-reported data.

This may be problematic because users often do not accurately recollect or remember or describe what they did.

Contextual Inquiry

The method is an observe and record technique at the user's worksite and is used because the user is the closest to the work environment and can accurately report the effect of changes.

In contextual inquiry, evaluators observe and record a user's actions as they engage in a typical task in a workday. In this method, a great deal of information can be gathered on the user's environment, workflow, business processes, and use of technology.

The contextual inquiry is a specific form of an interview for gathering field data from actual users. One interviewer usually does it to one interviewee. The objective is to gather as much data as possible from the interviews for detailed analysis. The respondents are interviewed in their context while doing their tasks, with as little interference from the interviewer as possible.

Data is gathered during interviews and with no analysis and record of interview results in raw data. Inquiry consists of observing users in their work settings and their interactions with colleagues without time loss.

This enquiry can generate inappropriate data, as the observed users have distractions during a typical workday. Therefore, the *Usability Body of Knowledge* defines a contextual inquiry thus: "A semi-structured interview method to obtain information about the context of use, where users are first given a set of standard questions and observed and questioned while they work in their environments."

The critical differentiator between contextual inquiry and other user research methods is that contextual inquiry occurs in a particular context. It's not an interview and is not even an observation. Instead, it involves observing people performing their tasks and talking about what they are doing while working.

Participatory Design

Participatory design is also called collaborative design. It is an approach to co-design by actively involving stakeholders (e.g., employees, partners, customers, citizens, end-users) in the design process to help secure the change results meet the ultimate aim of change and have the defined expected outcome.

Participatory design is an approach that focuses on processes and procedures of design, involving a community of users.

This approach has the political advantage of user empowerment and democratisation. In initiating significant organisational change, such a co-creating method works effectively to enhance ownership.

Concept Testing

When initiating an enterpisewide and large-scale change programme, getting it right first with the launch to generate the escape velocity is needed.

Concept testing methodology is used before a new idea, product or service is launched full scale. The same concept can be deployed before mass marketing of concrete, tangible change ideas, and it can save disappointment and time and money. While working on a transformation concept, change communication campaigns, getting feedback from the target audiences in advance pays rich dividends.

Concept testing can vary from quick and straightforward dipstick tests to prolonged interactive and sophisticated processes. Here are a few thoughts to help with the pros and cons of getting it right.

First, the decision process assessment. During this, the change leaders and influencers communicate the change ideas, and this method identifies information sources change or decision.

This approach allows comparing an impacted person's intention to use or not to use a new change idea, depth of intention to adapt and potential at different speeds of implementation levels and scale of progress. In addition, concept testing is a helpful quality check between the idea and the actual programme. A variety of approaches are available for concept testing.

All methods involve a group of potential users rating one or more of the change programme ideas — concept statements — in which each concept is presented, focusing specifically on user needs or gains.

For example, this approach was used to test the water when embarking upon a companywide ISO–Quality Standard implementation. It came out that the R&D group was opposed to any documented quality systems. Because of their fear that their product development secrets would be open, they would not be confidential anymore. The change management leadership kept the R&D out of the certification.

Transformational Leadership

Just as taking intelligent risks, challenging the status quo is the sole responsibility of leadership. Therefore, it is a business leadership trait. Through transformational leadership skills, the organisation converts managers who are committed and willing to initiate large-scale changes and transform the behaviour of the workforce.

In addition, the transformational style leads to lasting changes by process improvement or breakthrough innovations.

Of all the leadership styles, the transformational leadership style is the proper style to inspire followers to change for the better. Much research shows that employees will risk challenging the status quo only when the relationship with their leader is robust and trustful and when they understand and assimilate the positive outcomes of change on the individual's job and the organisation.

The transformational leadership style always has a profound impact on team members. Teams led by transformational leaders display higher levels of performance and satisfaction than teams led by a traditional, task-oriented leader.

Surveys after surveys of employees' attitudes worldwide have focused on leadership characteristics and behaviour that enable creating a high-performing culture. The best measure of leadership quality is from the success of people. In high performing work culture, followers see the leader as mission-centric and result-oriented at all times to the job on hand.

The leader with clarity understands that the test of leadership is to accomplish the mission through people being led. The *Bhagavad Gita* says, "Whatever action a great man performs, common people follow. And whatever standards he sets by exemplary acts, all the world pursues."

Exemplary leaders distinguish not by managing resources and tasks but by attracting highly charged followers.

CHAPTER 9

VISIONING AND VISUALISING

Vision building begins with the superior ability to architect what to do in realising the future state, combining creativity and imagination. Archetypal leaders develop this ability to foresee the future and deliver the end-state. One can dream with a vivid imagination and create a beautiful image of the future, but the realisation of those future states can measure the effectiveness by the result.

A New York cab driver and a priest died on the same day and reached the pearly gates. The priest was sure that he would go to heaven, as he had been helping people to see God through his sermons. It reconciled the cabbie to the idea of going to hell as he always drove recklessly and cursed everyone on the road.

Once the gates opened, they pushed the priest into hell hole and the cabbie to heaven. Surprised by the reversal of fortune, the priest requested to know the reason.

The priest realised that the difference was in being "effective" on the job. Though the priest preached all his sermons, people slept through them. When the New York cabbie was driving, people screamed for their lives, prayed with all their devotion, and remembered to thank God.

The moral is clear.

Mahabharata is about the story of the war between Pandavas and Kauravas and there are invaluable lessons of life.

Arjuna one of the chief characters had developed excellent battle skills combined with sharp thinking. His Guru Dronacharya taught him the art of war fare.

Arjuna's rival Duryodhana had blamed common guru of unduly favouring and partial to Arjuna and ignoring him and his forces.

To prove his neutrality, Dronacharya put each student through a simple test of piercing with single arrow, the eye of the wooden bird which he placed on tree branch. He asked each one of the students "What do you see there?"

Everyone mentioned seeing the tree, branches, bird, leaves, etc. When it was Arjuna's turn, he stated: "I can only see the eye of the bird." All had set their eyes on everything, but Arjuna had set his eyes only on his target, the eye of the bird.

Arjuna's reply was reflected his abilities to streamline all his focus towards the goal.

While others failed to separate their goal from the distractions in their path, Arjuna was able to ignore unimportant things and had his eyes only on the target. In life, there are so many extraneous things that consume our energy on a day-to-day basis. We should always put the chaos aside and concentrate on things that matter. Arjuna was just like the other students. What set him apart was his will power. Distractions are always going to be there in some form. It takes will power not to get indulged. Determination is the key. Combine the concentration with determination and will power. Be your own Arjuna!

The moral is that outstanding leaders have the right vision and focus on the goal with missionary zeal.

Conscripting

Mustering the support of people to take part in a change is termed conscripting. For any change initiative to progress, people have to subscribe to the reasons advocated. People rally around the grounds and join the move when they have developed internal conviction. Most CEOs, because of their dealings, negate people's loyalty as an insignificant change. The managers safeguard others' loyalty by being genuine in transactions and establish conscripting or collection of supporters. Conscripting support does not come automatically because the leader wants it. Over years, it is constructed brick by brick by a leader's track record and the truthfulness of dealings that people have experienced. People will enlist if the leader's reason for the change appears genuine.

Empowering

A fine example of enablement is given in the following story. Marc Benioff of the Salesforce made no secret of how Larry Ellison and Steve Jobs had mentored him when he worked at Oracle and Apple. In his book, *Behind the Cloud*, he writes about how Ellison would advise him, "Always have a vision, be passionate, and act confident, even when you're not."

Benioff acknowledged how Steve Jobs had given him more help and advice than anyone, in an interview with Bloomberg. Whenever he was troubled and distracted from his grand vision, he could approach Steve, who showed him the future.

The inventor of PC, Ed Roberts would acknowledge Bill Gates and Paul Allen of Microsoft as enablers. Roberts hired Gates and Allen to work for him, and helped to bring Microsoft to light. Gates and Allen were inspired and enabled to create Microsoft after Roberts' personal computer, the Altair 8800.

After the death of Roberts, Microsoft founders Bill Gates and Paul Allen stated how Ed was willing to take risks on the two young people because of their interest in computers. He recollected the day when the first untested software worked on Altair. Benioff and Ed were genuine leaders who helped their people rise to their fullest potential.

Uplifting

Admirable and visionary leaders have a firm belief in the team and trust that the team members will deliver their best; they inspire people and empower them all the time. Whenever one tries to disrupt the status quo and liberate the organisation from the pull power of the past, the leader's vision reinforces the benefits of changes for the common good. Remember how Martin Luther King said, "I have a dream that my four little children will one day live in a nation where they will not be judged by the colour of their skin but by the content of their character. I have a dream today!" Martin Luther King inspired many young people who were subjected to discrimination.

Here are a few examples of exemplary leadership:

Lou Gerstner of IBM led IBM through a historic turnaround by restructuring, reinvigorating in 1993, when he took over IBM.

Mark Russell Benioff established Salesforce, an enterprise cloud computing company that is publicly owned. Russell Benioff (born 25 September 1964) is an entrepreneur with a net worth of USD 6.5 billion as of July 2019. Benioff's core values reflect his leadership style, personal philosophy, and management approach. In addition, he is known for his social activism and is the most outspoken business leader in promoting equality in the workplace and the community.

Organisational change calls for bold and confident leadership which can take calculated risks and lead change initiatives.

Demonstrating courageous leadership is necessary when trying to change. Whether it's by confrontation with people holding a challenging conversation or convincing tactics, the leadership must adopt all styles. Often one may have no convincing answer to many questions while deciding to change the task.

It's precisely the assuring leadership behaviour that creates trust and sets the change process in motion by encouraging and conscripting people to support.

Courageous leaders are not shy to confront and challenge obstructionists. They are not reluctant to encourage and accept honest feedback, knowing well that people give frank feedback. Brave leaders would not mind saying what needs to be said, even if the words are bitter. They are not opposed to being questioned, and they make complex decisions during change.

There was a life-changing incident in my career, which proved to me the point of quality in leadership. I was the personnel manager in a highly hazardous glass manufacturing plant. My daily routine started with meeting my boss in the morning when he arrived at work. Unfortunately, he was always late, and I had to wait. I had a list of all unresolved issues, expecting him to guide me to solve them. Instead, after listening to all the problems, he would tell me to solve the problem and never told me what to do.

It frustrated me, and I stopped going to him with issues. A few months later, he sarcastically enquired about the daily problems and even patted my back. This was a golden moment to tell the boss how unhelpful his attitude had been and how I had solved problems independently. I told him, "I found my way and solved many issues and left a few unsolved". The boss smiled and said that he had deliberately done this because he had firmly believed in my capability, and wanted to raise the bar of performance and empower me.

Had he given me ready-made answers, I would have implemented those with no original view. But, instead, he quoted the Chinese proverb: "Give a man fish, you cure the hunger for the day; teach a man how to fish, you cure the hunger for life."

My hatred for the boss turned into genuine admiration for the ablest boss and leader I'd ever have had. All my life I followed the empowering and encouraging routes with the team I worked with, and met with remarkable success.

CHAPTER 10

ONE STEP AT A TIME

When dealing with people's attitude change and die-hard habits and biases, it becomes next to inconceivable to progress with speed. However, change requires reaching the escape velocity sooner than later; it may be worthwhile, to convert one group consisting of radical people. The following story illustrates the concept.

There was a royal prince, and he had an illusion that he was not human but a turkey. So, he behaved like a turkey and always sat naked under the dining table for food. He would peck at breadcrumbs and eat like a turkey.

The king was sad, and he ordered the royal physicians to try every method to cure the prince, but they failed.

One day, a sage came to the palace, and he took pity on the prince and promised to cure him. So, the king hired the sage to try healing. However, to everyone's surprise, the sage wanted to be left in the same room where the prince was; he also stripped and slipped under the table where the prince was sitting.

The prince was surprised to see the sage and questioned, "Who are you, and what are you doing here?" The sage replied, "I am also a turkey, just as you are", and he started pecking at the breadcrumbs along with the prince, as a bird would do. After few days together one day the sage called for a shirt and he put that on. This surprised the curious prince and he enquired, "Why are you wearing the shirt?" The sage looked at the prince and said, "Why do you think that a turkey can't wear a shirt? You can do it and still stay a turkey." He wore the shirt after a few days. Next, the sage requested a pair of trousers; he put them on, and told the curious prince, "You can wear pants and still be a turkey." The prince agreed and put the trousers on.

Both the sage and prince continued in this manner, and their friendship rose to the best level, and the prince would listen to the sage. Soon, the sage ordered regular food on the dinner table. The sage told the prince, "You will not stop being a turkey by sitting and eating on the table. In fact, you may find it comfortable; you can still be a turkey." The prince thought deeply and accepted the idea. As per the sage's suggestion, he got up and walked like a normal human being and behaved humanly. This fable illustrates the psychology behind the dynamics of change.

The sage tried to change a person but was not in haste. He transformed the prince by taking one step at a time and by making positive strokes with empathy. He built the change progress step by step while remaining focused on the goal.

Change is a Paradigm Shift

Is it a fact that the goldfish has a slender memory that lasts three seconds long? It might be not true, but let us, for a moment, imagine it to be true. With such a memory, the fish would continually rediscover the world around it. It would have no operating guidelines to help it navigate the world and no mental maps. Without personal paradigms, we would all be the goldfish. Though the small bowl of water is the world, the fish is forever rediscovering.

Paradigms enable us to interpret, define, and engage meaningfully with the world. Without paradigms, we would be constantly struggling to decide and explain what we see, and do. Instead, our paradigms help us move through our lives effortlessly. Thus, paradigms or mental maps act as a personal frame of reference we have.

We all carry our prejudices and biases. The experience of the world, particularly over some period, builds core beliefs and the paradigm of life. The earliest learnings hardly ever change.

We seek support from people with similar ideologies to avoid change because any contradictory idea disturbs the normal conduct of the brain's behaviour. Human inclination is to find people or groups to affiliate to reinforcing the existing beliefs, countering even undeniable logic.

David McRaney, the author of *You Are Not So Smart*, calls it the illusion of asymmetric insight.

The illusion of asymmetric understanding gives rise to the mindset that one knows others better than oneself.

People discard any conflicting information and resist because of a w notion of being more informed and correct.

Do Paradigms Shift?

Thomas Kuhn, a trained physicist, became a historian at Harvard University and later became a philosopher. In his influential book *The Structure of Scientific Revolutions*, he cited the paradigm shift as a change in the basic theories and experimental practices within the ruling theory of science. It is a radical change from one way to another form. In a lighter vein, here is an example of how a paradigm shift happens in actual life.

There was a man who was hardcore atheist. His paradigm was non-existence of God. He was once fishing in a vast lake which he usually did. He was fishing in the lake for an hour, and failed to realise that the boat in which he had set sailed had drifted towards the middle of the lake.

It was a cold and dark winter night, and also the night of the new moon. As time went by, his boat went far away from the shores. Soon, he was in deep waters in the middle of the lake. Rain started falling, and the black clouds darkened the sky; the wind was now blowing faster. It was dramatically life-threatening. Suddenly there was a thunderstorm, and rain started lashing, and the boat was wobbling.

The man got terrified and thought of looming death and had no clue as to what to do. He had not carried a life jacket and did not even know how to swim.

The man was an atheist, and he could only consider seeking God's help by praying. He called out for the first time in his life, "Oh God, save me." Suddenly, a bright light appeared, and God appeared before the man.

Before acceding to his request, God asked the man for a reason for not having remembered Him throughout his life and only remembering Him now, when faced with imminent death.

He began to believe in God, because he could see Him with his own eyes. He had no reason even to call Him, leave alone remember Him in the past, as he had never had life-threatening moments. It is not that you need life threatening moments for paradigm shift but if one is pushed to the limit, he may change the belief system.

Paradigms shift when one's belief system gets challenged.

Paradigms can shift based on factual data and information convenient to an unsuspecting target audience.

This is the story of a young father travelling in a Mumbai suburban local train on a weeknight. He was travelling with his children at 1 am on the last train from Churchgate station in south Mumbai. All the small retail shop owners who had closed their shops were also on that train, heading home. As soon as they entered the train, they grabbed the seat and closed their eyes.

The man entered the train with three small kids at Bombay Central station, and as soon as the train started, the children started jumping and playing, which disturbed the sleeping passengers. After a few minutes of patience, the passengers got angry and yelled at the man to control the children.

More stations went by, and the children wouldn't stop playing. Finally, the passengers were restless and scolded the man to stop the children from playing. The man, who had been keeping quiet so far, opened his mouth and told the co-passengers that he realised well that the children were playful. He told the stunned crowd about his inability to stop the children from playing because his wife and the children's mother had died in hospital, and he did not know how to convey that to the children. Because they were children, they did not understand the impact of the tragedy. Once the passengers heard this, there was complete silence, and the same people who had been hostile were full of sympathy. A few minutes later, some of them offered to help the man and started playing with the children. This is an obvious case of paradigm shift. The moral of the story is, paradigm's a shift, but we do not need life-threatening events to shift the paradigms. Instead, there needs to be a compelling reason for people to believe in something that one does not consider accurate.

CHAPTER 11

ASSESSING AND ENHANCING READINESS FOR CHANGE

The measurement of success of change programmes is on delivery of tangible value, which means focusing from the beginning and consistently delivering on defined metrics. The measurement methods and processes must assess and track change progress as described in the business case for change.

Assessment bases value delivery on the post-implementation impact on the cost reduction and capability improvement initiatives. One can secure through evaluation of business processes or procedures delivery of the expected benefits.

Answering Key Questions and Managing the Impact of Actions:

What is the best way to track, report and realise the output intended? Here are some guidelines:

(i) Document programme-specific change metrics.
(ii) Deploy measurement tools to collect data, analyse results and take corrective action where necessary.
(iii) Provide vital management information on the change programme progress and if on track.
(iv) Take an early action to minimise transition risk.
(v) See value chain linking interventions, transition, and realisation of business improvements.
(vi) Benchmark current change with past and future programmes, support the best practice approach. (However, it carries risks if it carries no readiness assessment.)

(vii) Quantify data for measuring capability to speed up the progress of change.

Management often lacks the critical risk management mechanism, and corrective action may be too little or too late.

The business readiness measure is the organisation's preparedness to absorb the transition to a future state. It involves ensuring transition arrangements are complete, and the criteria and checklists are ready.

The advantage of identifying and resolving issues well in advance engages leadership, solidifies ownership, and equips the organisation for the transition.

If an organisation has no proper readiness before going live, it will invite enhanced risk and costs associated with disruption. The Business Readiness Plan lays out the project's strategy to track and measure if one prepares all the units and people for a successful go-live of the renewed capabilities and whether the organisation is ready to support the changes after going live.

The major challenge before changes leaders is dealing with the human dynamics from initiation to closure. We can define change readiness as the degree of psychological and behavioural willingness of people to act and make the change permanent.

Change readiness maturity involves moving people gradually from an existing level to a better level to speed up change

1. Ability to embrace change, aka, trainable skill.
2. Willingness to embrace change, aka, individual and collective attitudes.

Readiness maturity must be assessed in terms of both these dimensions. The following grid shows the strategy to tackle each group:

	G	M1	M2	M3	M4
	2	G2	G2	G2	G2
	G	M1	M2	M3	M4
	1	G1	G1	G1	G1
		M1	M2	M3	M4

Willingness

Ability

M1G1 - Level 1: Low willingness-Low ability-Low maturity.

M2G 1 - Level 2: Average on ability-Low on willingness-Low maturity.

M1G2 - Level 3: Low on ability-Above average on the willingness.

M2G2 - Level 4: Average on ability-Above average on the willingness.

M3G1 - Level 5: High ability-High willingness.

M4G1 - Level 6: Above average to high ability-Low willingness.

M3G2 - Level 7: High ability-Average to high willingness.

M4G2 - Level 8: High ability-High willingness.

Strategy for Enhancing the Maturity of Groups

L1-Training and communication-Resistors.

L2-Training-Communication-Laggards.

L3-Communication-Early adopters.

L4-Communication-Early majority.

L5-Training-Sceptical communication guardians.

L6-Training-Communication-Confirmed traditionalists.

L7-Communication-Late majority.

L8-Communication-Influencers.

The measure of readiness to change can range from the intensity of the need and motivation for change to involvement in implementing changes at the individual and organisational levels.At an individual level, readiness consists of the felt or created benefit with a powerful urge to take part in changes of the organisation.

Organisational level readiness will mean members' collective struggle to change and share the vision to deploy the combined ability to accomplish change efficacy. Change effectiveness is the members' common beliefs in their mutual abilities to execute the courses of action.

Change is needed, even if it involves doing a complete overhaul of ineffective, unhealthy business practices, habits, and systems impediments.

For example, even in this day of advanced IT systems, many large banks, even in America, have computer systems based on COBOL and FORTRAN and are reluctant to change. But, if the organisations run world-wide business policies, processes, and procedures on their legacy systems, it is inconceivable to abandon them.

Significant system changes need a switch not only of code but of supporting tools (e.g., compilers and editors), development processes (testing and version control), and personnel. Thus, a significant change is a combination of discarding the existing system, completely revamping existing parts, writing new policies, and purchasing different aspects from external vendors.

If the change requires abandoning the existing system and buying or developing a new system, the project is termed as a complete redevelopment and cannot be easily done. If the change is by modifying the current system, the project is re-engineering the project. Rewriting and re-engineering are thus two extremes along a spectrum of strategies for IT change. How much outdated they are (users and technical staff of legacy systems) the attitude towards new technology is one of resistance to change. It is a well-known people dynamic anywhere in the world. People are afraid of their expertise and professional experience with legacy systems may become redundant because of modernisation.

Surprisingly, resistance from technical staff is not an isolated problem; in fact, cultural resistance to adapt to new technology adds to the difficulties. Such a challenge is faced in legacy system modernisation.

The resistance from staff comes from emotional attachment to systems and because of working on it for many years. They know every condition and withhold the job secrets, as fear of job loss makes them resist sharing information.

How many people are available with COBOL / FORTRAN knowledge? Staffing of maintenance projects is difficult.

The proper attitude recognises the need for change, which presupposes the present systems to be far from effective. Organisational readiness for change is a function of the collective value of members' change readiness and how they view and take part favourably.

Not providing an effective unfreezing process before attempting a change induction and failing to analyse inclination issues can lead to abortive organisation change. Successful change starts with the first decision to introduce change.

Later, we highlight how attention and awareness help create interest and provide a motivational push in the new 10-step process.

Definition and Analysis of Change Readiness:

Readiness to change is having the ability and willingness to get involved and not to comply with directives. Readiness is much more than being a passive observer, and readiness level at individual and organisation must be kept in mind by change leadership.

Alignment is crucial, especially by the influencers and change leaders and champions.

Changes involve redefining individual and organisational readiness for change. Readiness is all about people's beliefs, attitudes, and motives when it comes to the extent of changes are needed and their perception of own capacity to make those changes.

Understanding perception of self-readiness and organisational readiness is a step-in readiness assessment. Change readiness involves getting people into a state of mind with a compelling urge to change, altering the existing mindset; it is the cognitive precursor to either resistance or support for the actual change. Undoing what we learnt is the first part of cycle of change.

Readiness preparedness for change in this way has implications:

First is the Compliance which is going along with a new initiative. Second, actively participate in industry-related activities: people may comply because they may agree with the proposed changes and see the personal value in the change. Third, they may comply because they have no power to oppose the proposed changes and risk the job; therefore, people may comply because of fear of job loss.

Finally, people may choose to participate and engage in a project activity designed to help everyone change. Making everyone attend a training programme is helpful before a project kicks off.

Readiness can be enhanced because it does exist as permanent element of individuals or systems. Readiness starting point varies depending on the external or internal circumstances, the type of change, or the characteristics of change adapters. An organisation's different units can be at varying degrees of readiness.

Change can progress with slow conditions of enthusiasm but behavioural science research indicates that the probability of success is reduced. Low willingness leads to low motivation to change and then to active resistance.

Methods for Assessing and Enhancing Change Readiness

A good deal of behaviour-based methods has been deployed for assessing readiness for change:

 (i) Surveys.
 (ii) Focus group discussions.
 (iii) Site interviews.
 (iv) Site visits and observation.
 (v) Group profiles, leading to a comprehensive team assessment.

Leader's Communication

The way leadership communicates change reasons decides the readiness of the organisation. Once the readiness assessment is carried out, steps are taken to tackle the areas of lack of interest. Any action step that can accelerate change readiness includes ensuring active participation in education, learning sessions and persuasive communications, explaining the need to change and the consequences of not changing.

Change management initiative requires a compelling reason and strong communication, besides project planning and strategy. While the reasons for change appear to be logical to the leadership, the employees may not experience the same intense need for change or may not visualise what is changing, leaving alone why the change is happening.

Here are a few usual reasons that are presented by the top leadership:

1. Customers' needs for the product or service have changed. Steuben did not even realise this change in consumer taste and preferences

2. The competition is eating into the market share and profits. Employees usually get confused with this explanation and will question, "If that is the case, what were the sales and marketing guys doing about competitive intelligence? Why did they present every quarter rosy quarter picture of sales in an all-hands meeting? What reason could be there for taking long time to figure out that market share is falling?"

3. The performance is below industry average in a growing market, and the change is required. Such an explanation reflects a desperate move.

4. The ship needs to change the course and make 30-degree turn before it hits the shore. People will perceive this explanation as change for the sake of change.

These messages may be perfectly rational, yet they cannot often impact employees because people cannot relate to the generic form of the message.

If change is inevitable for leadership, resistance to change is unavoidable despite all explanations. While opposition to change appears irrational to the leaders, it makes perfect sense to oppose change that disturbs routine and proven norms for those who are resisting.

Cues come from peer or leadership pressure from their trade union leaders who can instil the biggest fear of job loss, and of status or job security.

Human nature urges us not to make changes that would be perceived as causing difficulty to the existing condition in an organisational setting. This people will resist structural or technological changes because of fear their roles could be redundant or diluted.

From their perspective, change is a threat to their survival and their position in the organisation. Motivation and willingness to change are influenced by perceptions about change impact on their jobs. If the change is perceived to be beneficial, the resistance is lower.

Resistance is a natural human emotion displayed during change and must be dealt with. However, researchers claim that prior outlook is not influenced on the whole by an individual's level of resistance to change.

However, the depth to which the individual focuses on the short term will impact an individual's prior outlook.

Research has shown that the motivation to change may come from employees or managers sensing visible positive impacts personally. For example, impact at an individual-level career advancement, improvement in pay, benefits, etc., affect change acceptance. A manager's perception of the beneficial impact of change on the team or impact on the working group and how change affects smoother relationships and work climate accelerates change.

The organisation measures the impact of change on the shareholders' value, the market impact on the customer service, improved quality of service and more sales.

Society at large measures change impact by the organisations' enhanced ability to discharge social responsibility and standing as an excellent corporate citizen.

Can Readiness be Assessed?

Psychological readiness is a mental state that leads to obvious change in behaviour much later in the cycle of change; it can be measured using various behavioural science approaches.

Readiness Is a Cognitive Characteristic

Cognition means 'knowing'. Cognition is "the mental act or process by which knowledge is acquired". What counts in assessing readiness for change is people's beliefs at both the individual and collective levels. Readiness for change is tempered by people's perceptions of whether they or their colleagues have support, a well-defined mission and leadership, a goal-aligned work team, and the technical skill level needed to adopt a particular change.

The mere existence of skills is necessary but not sufficient for readiness to change, and mindset change depends on the trustworthiness of the change leader's attitude and communication.

Perceptions may relate either to a specific change being radical transformation or the organisation's phase shift, such as its offerings or line of business. Wipro was established in India during 1945 as a seller of vegetable oil but transformed into a multi-product and global IT service provider. This is a successful example of transformation.

Behavioural Science Knowledge Base

Change initiatives are consequences of perceptions of change leadership, and the environment and pressures from the environment alone do not prompt change. While initiating and implementing change, the felt urgency and energy required for change involve more emotional issues than rational ones.

People in organisations develop the energy to change when faced with adverse existing conditions, irrespective of whether the change affects one personally or the work.

The concept of readiness for change has its origin in social psychology, especially in work on the human dynamics of change among individuals and groups and the work done on resistance to change and resistance in overcoming it.

People's discerning capabilities lead to robust thought processes, and eventually lead to actions that produce required results.

An old Sanskrit philosophy is, "As the thought so the mind, as the mind so the man". Therefore, when thoughts shape the mindset that influences the behaviour, the feedback at every step towards progress of change-readiness and maturity will speed up the learning.

Conditions that affect readiness are, intent, environmental constraints, ability, anticipated outcomes, norms, self-standards, emotion, and self-efficacy. Intention and the other factors (assumed to influence intention) are cognitive components linked to the readiness for change.

Enhancing Change Readiness

The purpose of a change readiness assessment is to analyse the level of preparedness of the organisation's conditions, attitudes and resources at all levels. The complexity and extensiveness of the proposed change will determine the criticality of understanding and the depth in the readiness for change. Based on qualitative and quantitative assessments of preparedness, one can choose whether to introduce the change now or later.

The issue is not about 100 per cent readiness but the preparedness that will create the escape velocity. Change readiness involves having an adequate and conducive organisational climate, preparedness of resources to absorb, accelerating change, and clarifying the end goal status for the intended change. In addition, it is about members in the organisation having the ability to engage with the change and make it work.

Planning for Assessment: Social Marketing and Contextualising Readiness

The readiness for change is reflected in commitment at all levels of leadership.

Change readiness is multilevel and multifaceted. At the outset, readiness refers to the preparedness of minds and readiness to shape behaviour to act expectedly.

Preparations are, therefore, required in terms of willingness and ability. Also, the shaping of both attitudes and skills is necessary. Collective determinism to change by leadership and all those who are involved in driving change is must.

Every person involved in driving and leading change contributes a bit to rotate the change wheel in the right direction and is attracted to the force of shared vision. Change can happen if seen as a team effort by the leaders while architecting the plan. In any collective creation, the strength is determined by the weakest link. Therefore, importance must be given to picking the members of the project team carefully. Evidence indicates organisational members commit to implementing an organisational change because of three different degrees of alignment:

1. Everyone fully participates; they understand and perceive the value of change to be inevitable.
2. Experience the urge to take part; they perceive they have no choice and perceive change as imposed but with good intentions.

3. They ought to; they are obligated to the organisation and leadership and keep their job.

Those who fall in category 1, "I want to", are the ones with the highest motivation and commitment to drive and carry out the change. Therefore, they will be the ideal and safe bet to be in the transformation of leadership teams.

CHAPTER 12

THE CRUCIAL QUESTIONS

To initiate the change, the leaders must start crucial conversations with every one of the key people. That conversation involves responding harshly while answering the most challenging questions. People do not have complete information, and typically ask, "What is wrong with whatever is being done?"

This question often brings opposing views, as people are happy with the status quo. They rarely challenge it, especially if the revenue is rising. A blend of the words 'presence' and 'sensing' refers to the ability to sense and bring into the present one's highest future potential as an individual and as a group.

In one of the pre-kick-off meetings, the conversation began with these questions:

Are there enough competent people amongst us to take the company where we want it to go?

Naturally, this question evokes strong emotions if raised by the CEO, as people interpret this as a confrontation with a blot on their capability. Reactions include "why are we being asked this when we have brought this business to the present level?"

Is there enough steam for the team to gather speed to engineer the escape?

What people often cannot realise is that what brought them here, cannot take them there. When one takes large-scale global initiatives, the speed with which the change begins, raises the stakes. It requires a minimum threshold level of investment coupled with speed, which the present setup might not have experienced. That is why it involves high stakes.

145

Is there the right talent mix for discussing the level of new business model?

If the company has been around for two decades and has hired the best, groomed them for a specific market, one must remember that in the changed scenario, one is now looking at multidimensional competency. There can be enormous difficulties, which evoke strong sentiments. In addition, new skills can be challenging when the organisation itself has not supported a learning culture.

Propagation of the Vision

This task is making the vision inspiring and easy to relate by everyone. A vision is futuristic; not everyone can connect or align with it. Therefore, vision needs to be shared. Vision sharing empowers everyone to contribute and gain a sense of accomplishment. The task involves identifying the key people (G7, G8 levels of maturity) who will empower and conscript.

Conscription is also called draft, or compulsory enrolment for service in a country's armed forces. It has existed at least from the time of the Egyptian Old Kingdom (27th century BCE). There have been few modern version of universal conscription which is calling all those physically capable between certain ages. In addition, sharing enables elevating the role of crucial managers to draw on their full leadership capabilities along with that of the employees.

The task is to develop and put in place alternative systems and processes. That must support while reinforcing the vision and consistently reinforce the values of a radical approach. Propagating the change message must be through conversations laced with anecdotes. Mere information or request from top-down commands is not effective.

Reorganising is not an excellent way to start, even if felt that parts of the organisation do not have effective leadership or competency readiness.

Clarifying the vision along with the management's roles and systems that reinforce the vision is essential leadership task.

1. **Assembling a committed team:** Such a committed team of top-level managers while initiating change is most effective.

An entirely hand-picked new team is least effective during change, as people always look up to those old guards who are in tune with change.

The approach is to work with the existing managers to draw out people who swear by, share and support the vision. Recently, in an email communication with employees, Satya Nadella, the new CEO of Microsoft, spoke of how he wanted to "rediscover our soul," and pointedly stressed Microsoft's mission as not to deliver long-standing software products such as Windows or Office, but to develop technology to help people to better living and businesses to run more efficiently. That was a powerful message indicating adaptiveness.

2. **Non-reinforcing reward systems:** Employees resist change when they do not see any beneficial positive outcome because of change. Without a reward, motivation for people to support the change over the long term is absent.

    The implication is that organisational reward systems must be altered to support the management's change.

3. **Surprise and fear of the unknown:** Fewer the people who know the reasons for change and its impact on them, more fear is the outcome. In the absence of constant two-way communication with leadership, rumours fill the void and the anti-change squad sabotage the change.

4. **Peer pressure:** People resist change to protect the interests of a group. The employees were fighting change to protect their co-workers. Likewise, managers will resist change to protect their workgroup.

5. **Culture of mistrust:** Change cannot occur in a climate of distrust. Trust involves faith in the intentions of leaders and the behaviour of followers.

6. **Organisational politics:** Few people resist change as a political strategy to prove that the decision is wrong. They may resist showing that the person leading the change is not up to the task. They are committed to seeing the change attempts fail.

7. **Fear of failure:** large scale changes can cause employees to develop doubts in motive because of their capabilities to do at expected levels. As a result, the employees resist these changes

because they are worried that they cannot adapt to new work requirements.

8. **Lack of tact or poor timing**: Preparing a comprehensive change strategy to address the barriers is always a leadership challenge.

Effective Ways to Manage Resistance

Step 1: Creating two-way communication with employees on change initiatives, the expected outcome, and the progress at frequent intervals are crucial.

Key managers have to give employees frequent and regular updates at team meetings.

Step 2: Marketing the change plan and assessing how it affects business to each group. Explaining the change programme (a standard message) helps each group to understand how the new strategy will make their jobs better or easier. Everyone in the organisation must understand the goal of the latest change strategy.

Step 3: Invite a team member from every functional group to participate in meetings or give seminars for each group to market the strategy.

Step 4: Select a group of forces from critical positions to actively involved in managing implementation. Find one person from each group who is vocal. Select those in non-management positions as well.

Step 5: Develop critical deliverables for each department, organisational unit and person involved in implementing the change strategy. A deliverable is a final report or the output from implementing the new change strategy. Each group must tailor the deliverable to the goals of the group. For example, one deliverable can increase sales by 5 per cent, and another can lower quality costs by 25 per cent.

Step 6: Link successful implementation with rewards. Create at least four key milestones to measure success throughout the year. Report on performance and reward those people or groups that meet objectives.

CHAPTER 13

A NEW METHODOLOGY FOR CHANGE MANAGEMENT

The Foundation

The U methodology is highly powerful concept which proposes that, "The quality of the results we create in any social system is a function of the quality of awareness, attention, or consciousness that the participants in the system operate from."

The U theory of change management method specifies change-leadership as social innovation. U-process or U-procedure, which is also called a 'bathtub' was proposed by Otto Scharmer.

In 1968 The 'U Way' was developed by Dr Friedrich Glasl and Dirk Lemson of the NPI. (Netherlands. Pedagogical Institute). It has widely used tool in organisational and social development since that time. This new organisation change model presented here is a step-by-step method to implement change management. It is built around the psychology and behavioural approaches. The human behaviour models have a tremendous impact on the process to adapt to any change.

This approach has proven to be effective in accelerating change.

The 10-step Process Model

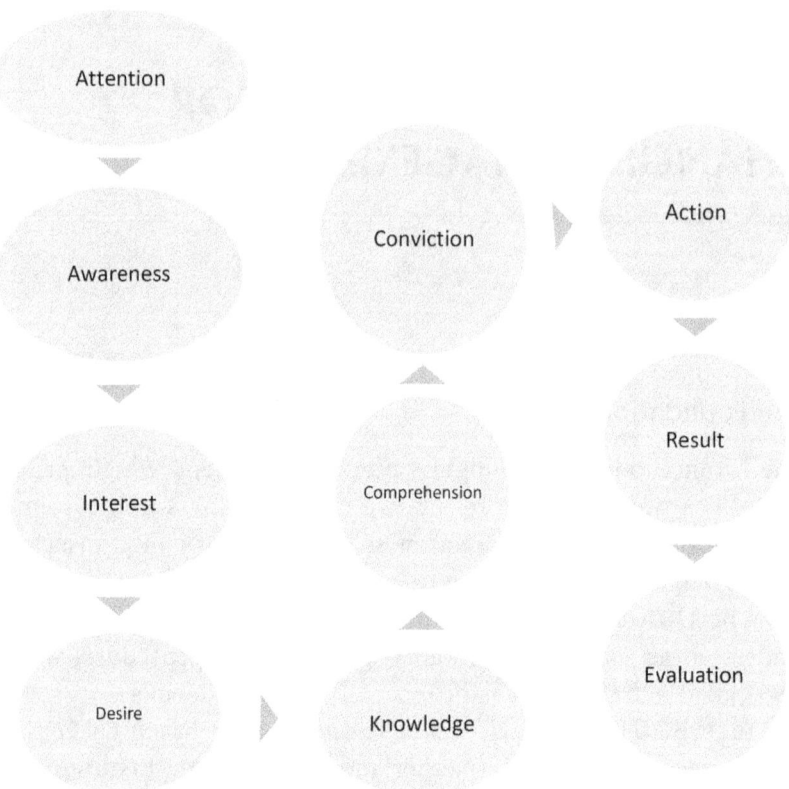

Step 1: Attention

Many of us, when we don't appear to listen when someone is speaking, are told, "You don't pay attention".

Did the speaker fail to arrest one's attention, or was the receiver not interested in the message?

Getting someone to pay attention is a deceptively simple task but rather difficult. Arresting attention is key to the change communication process if one wants people to listen to the message and subscribe to the change ideas. Unfortunately, the receivers are unwilling to pay attention unless the message has the right cue and the magnetic pull power to elicit the anticipated response.

Attention is cognitive process of receiving explicit information from outside and the way it gets response The surrounding noise, adversely affects or blurs the attention. Innumerable signals get through our eyes, ears, taste, smell, and touch sensations, impacting perceptual ability. How do we use these sensations to focus on one element that grabs attention and arouses curiosity?

Psychologist and philosopher William James said, "Attention is the taking possession by the mind, in clear and vivid form; of one out of several simultaneously possible objects or trains of thought, localisation, concentration, of consciousness are of its essence. It implies withdrawal from things to cope with others and is a condition which has a real opposite in the confused, dazed, scatter-brained state which in French is called distraction, and Zerstreutheit in German."

Attention is like a highlighter that we use to draw attentiveness to which we read and find appealing.

The highlighted section is expected to guide us to focus our interest in the specific thing.

Attention is useful for editing out unwanted information, sensations, and helps in the formation of mental maps relevant at that moment without wasting energy. Therefore, when attempting to convey the reasons for change, the message must grab the attention to enable everyone to proceed to the next process step of creating awareness.

"On an average, five times as many people read the headlines as they read the copy," said David Ogilvy, the father of advertising.

In surroundings full of noise, getting people to listen to what is being said is never easy. It takes more than good content or great visual appeal, or eye-catching design to make people even glance up. The most crucial step to take while communicating a change message is capturing attention.

David Ogilvy said, "I don't know the rules of grammar. If the aim is to persuade people to buy, one should use their language, the language they use every day, the language in which they deliberate."

It is similar to writing catchy headlines to grab the attention that appears on a daily newspaper's front page. During a change communication message sent out to initiate massive automation in finance, the CEO said, "You can keep doing your job and still do more of it in less time; even make more money. Every accountant ought to do for being an intelligent accountant." This punchline attracted the specific target audience's attention to read the entire message.

Emotions and attention processing are interconnected. Change implementers have to know this. But are emotional stimuli encoded automatically, and what does that imply? How does one select emotional triggers and do enhanced processing?

Brain initiates a two-stage process. First, "the emotional significance is evaluated pre-attentively by a subcortical circuit involving the amygdala; and gives emotionally significant stimuli to access selective attention."

Humans associate anxiety with impending negativity or danger or even with an unpleasant experience. For example, many air travellers would carry the anxiety and expect the plane to crash even at the slightest turbulence during a flight (aviophobia). Likewise, when the security of being in the comfort zone is disturbed, people are prone to be anxious. However, anxiety is not always the danger or risk. The positive attitude that something great is going on and that charting a new unknown course towards one's dreams may bring good change.

The amygdala is the cluster in the brain that handles the signals. For example, prompting the worst sends panic notes, which does not help people generally driven by anxiety and stress. Understanding how the amygdala processes events help to devise communication during change when stress-prone people ring the alarms, especially during the transition stage.

The amygdala pairs any perceptive signal-trigger with negative experiences embedded in the brain. For example, one person recollected many years later that he had witnessed as a child, a violent street protest where people were stabbing women and even children during the violent rally. Whenever he saw a mob, he would recollect his past. He had seen people belonging to a radical political party indulging in violence were wearing a saffron-coloured shirt.

The saffron colour is the typical trademark colour used by the Hindu religious fundamentalist party in India. Later in life, whenever that person saw many people wearing the saffron coloured shirt, it evoked panic and became the trigger for fear.

Before witnessing the adverse event, the saffron was another colour; now, it aroused anxiety and panic. Events in our childhood incidents that make a heavy impact, remain in memories with deep roots.

Every time one experiences substantial change, fear and anxiety are the inevitable outcomes. Only the degree varies. Change leaders must be sensitive to keep this amygdala effect in their minds while dealing with people's adverse reactions and resistance while implementing change. Attention catching is the first step in OCM communication and its effectiveness in the interface between emotion and attention.

Philosopher William James defines attention as "the taking possession by the mind, in clear and vivid form, of one out of what may seem several simultaneously possible objects or trains of thought." One needs to take focus away from one thing and face another. Tuning off noise is vital when a change message is competing with other distracting information. Change communicators have to be based on a compelling communications strategy and a plan to attract attention.

In initiating any change, a compelling reason for no result outcome is the closed minds of initiators. Therefore communicate that reason powerfully to catch the attention of everyone who is impacted and everyone who can positively influence the change process. To execute effectively, communicate directly using anecdotes and storytelling.

Do an abundant number of seminars. Use multiple channels. Repeat the message in every forum.

Summary

Arresting attention is the first step to get the target audience to move towards acceptance when change is being communicated. The importance is in designing the message to discuss "why" and "how". It does affect the change efforts on the people and organisation in positive ways.

Step 2: Awareness

Once the person pays attention, the next step is the awareness state or ability to comprehend, experience, or be conscious of happenings, using sensory patterns. Finally, it is the level of consciousness when the receiver confirms data without the implications of understanding.

Unlike humans, animals are partially or subconsciously aware. Awareness is an internal state; it is the visceral feeling or recognition of external events through sensory perception.

Awareness provides the ingredient to develop qualia (individual experience of subjective consciousness or experience) or unique ideas. Awareness is being conscious of something. How do you know that the message attracted every member of the target audience's attention?

Humans have been created equal but they differ when facing similar events. While a few react positively to the same message, others do not do better because the individual learning ability varies. Adding knowledge as progress begins with understanding the basic facts and building advanced way of learning.

Reflection, Inquiry and Advocacy: The threefold essential communication skills of reflection, inquiry, and advocacy are the ingredients for the most effective ingredient of change leadership.

Reflection is being aware about the state of mind; inquiry is arousing curiosity; advocacy is the ability to promote one's views clearly and honestly.

Advocacy without reflection and the intent of inquiry is ineffective. It is more likely to end in arguments over fixated stands.

Reflection begins with self-awareness. It usually slows down our thought process, while recognising our assumptions and biases.

Awareness means bringing one's attention into active present moment. After that comes introspection, looking in-depth at one's thought process. Inquiry is empathetic listening and engaging in conversation.

Finally, advocacy can be expressed in mutual exchange and not through misunderstandings or imposing one's views on others.

My leadership prescription is these three aspects.

If leaders succeed in creating organisational cultures due to the changing need, quality communication has to be based on a healthy balance of reflection, inquiry, and advocacy.

A leader's commitment to listening and curiosity provides powerful ground for **genuine leadership.**

Conversely, advocacy is ineffective without reflection; It defeats the purpose of investigation. It is likely ending would be arguments over fixated ideas. Contemplation begins with knowledge of oneself and usually slows the way we ponder, while recognising our beliefs or partialities.

Awareness means bringing attention to the current moment. Next is the introspection, which looks closely at the process of one's opinion formation. The dilemma is about listening, empathising and talking. This is where advocacy comes in, which helps one express one's points of views to others through mutual dialogue, keeping misunderstandings at bay.

Quality communications based on a good balance of reflection, inquiry and advocacy are the key to successful leadership in creating organisational cultures because of the changes. The commitment of a leader to listen and be curious provides a solid basis for genuine leadership.

Impact assessment can help the message reach far deeper than anticipated. However, when attention is to be drawn, continuous communication and powerful delivery of message is required. Any Business process re-engineering involves awareness as the first step according to Michael Hammer.

Summary

The difference in learning ability differs from person to person which impacts the way the message is absorbed. The current state and strength of awareness affect the power required to change understanding.

The person may either accept or deny the change message, depending on the earlier experiences with change.

Step 3: Interest

This is not something that we have or don't have which is cause for action. What we do, as we're looking at the subject with a will to own. Our interest itself will reveal more on the subject. Interest cannot be generated by falsification or faking Answering with, "Oh, that is very interesting!" is mainly perceived as fake when eye contact is absent. If we don't mean what we say, one can assume that our interest may be piqued or developed because something is more alluring. Eventually, we want to explore more to understand. Attention is an enabler of the sharpness of our mental faculties to get a better view.

What the mind absorbs is contingent upon entirely on the selective action of attention. During daily life, many impressions are streaming through the different sensory channels and those to which attention is directed. They take natural hold of the mind.

Attention-grabbing is not a momentary exercise; consistent and frequent attempts are required to keep the attention fixed on any unfamiliar subject vying to get one's attention. There are numerous ideas, embedded in our minds, which serve as building blocks to make up our subject knowledge. When other people's experiences mirror our own, they become particularly ingrained in the memory, rendering cognition easy and acceptable in future events.

People easily develop sense of taste for futuristic experiences, embrace them with ease and satisfaction. The ideas in any topic constitute an interest in permanent disposition of the mind. The intensity of apperception, or assimilation of others' ideas into a body of ideas one already possesses, is perceived as actual, conscious attention.

Developing interest is a highly individualistic attitude that incites action. The result is either pleasure or satisfaction. Attention generates curiosity towards the object of interest, enthusiasm, strong willingness while doing the task, to extract behavioural change.

Some expert psychologists describe interest as an expression of mind shown in action.

"Interest is a tendency to become absorbed in an experience and to continue it, while an aversion is a tendency to turn away from it to something else."

Interest is also classified as,

(i) Expressed interest, which may not last long.
(ii) Manifested interest, exhibited and seen by others.
(iii) Measured interest, the depth that can be evaluated using tools.

Professor Strong of Stanford University, California, developed a standardised checklist containing 400 separate items. The respondent is asked to indicate likes and dislikes on a three-point scale as a measure of interest.

A ludicrous event or any fancy idea that one may find difficult to comprehend or relate can surprise the mind. But unfortunately, the idea of changing appears to be shocking to many.

However strange the idea may be, it can awaken, at least temporarily, a keen interest. These experiences that evoke fear or anxiety, when they kindle interest, are explainable on the thesis that they associate interest with pleasure or pain.

All those items that arouse or sustain non-voluntary or spontaneous attention are attractive, while phenomena we attend with voluntary attention become uninteresting. We are inclined to be interested in subjects that are connected with and related to the chief occupations.

The change-related narrative in organisations must be robust; the reasons stated for the change should be compelling enough to evoke interest. No change imperatives must be highlighted; the outcome of change must be conveyed powerfully to echo what people said. One can kindle enough interest to propel the persons impacted by the change to act if people can connect with the reasons for change which is an anchor step in creating the interest.

Summary

Interest means developing a positive and favourable attitude towards the change issue while developing an intense need to act upon it. Interest is not what one owns or doesn't but is about action.

Step 4: Desire

Two central characters in the Hollywood movie *Silence of the Lambs*, speak as follows.

Hannibal Lecter: "First principles, Clarice, simplicity. Read Marcus Aurelius. Of each particular thing, ask, 'What is it in itself? What is its nature? What does he do, this man you seek?"

Clarice Starling: "He kills women." Hannibal Lecter: "No. That is incidental. What is the principal thing he does? What needs does he serve by killing?" Clarice Starling: "Anger, um, social acceptance, and, huh, sexual frustrations, sir."

Hannibal Lecter: "No! He covets. That is his nature; how do we begin to covet, Clarice? Do we seek things to covet? Make an effort to answer now."

Clarice Starling: "No. We just…"

Hannibal Lecter: "No. We begin by coveting what we see every day. Don't you feel eyes moving over your body, Clarice? Don't your eyes seek the things you want?"

The nature of human beings is to covet (yearning to possess something mainly belonging to others) what we need and desire. Desires can manifest in many forms. However, three basic desires are animalistic, and the more complex conditions of desires are spiritual. The need for food, shelter is a more basic as well as animalistic.

However, the basic desires are overcome, and desires for other higher-level things like knowledge, power, fame, wealth take over.

The motivations that come are physical, and are deeper which come from within our souls. As humans, we are constantly seeking to fulfil both forms of the drive. People express craving through emotions of 'longing' or in its extreme form as greed. In most large-scale frauds, an intense urge to amass wealth and fame through quick means are converted to greed, as with Enron, Barings Bank, and Satyam Infotech.

On the Friday after Thanksgiving, people in America crowd malls and department stores to grab products announced as on cheapest sales.

People call Black Friday and that is time when commercialisation and corporate greed are on full display in America. When we are motivated by an urge to possess, the crave becomes intense for those things; action is immediate to satisfy that urge at any cost.

Greed is not bad. On the positive side, the human wants and desire for things make life meaningful for many. Excessive greed is bad.

Many significant innovations, inventions or improvements came out of the deep drive of innovators to improve the quality of human life. A constant force of desire drives us to work longer hours to enhance the wealth, status and life. The famous CEO Jack Welch of GE was accused of receiving lavish perks, which were ridiculous even by the capitalistic standards. Welch was the epitome of an excessive display of capitalism and greed. Yet, GE Capital saved the jobs of 1,200 people who worked at Malden Mills.

Three of Malden Mills' leading factories burnt to the ground in 1955. The CEO, Aaron Feuerstein, vowed to rebuild the factory and pay wages to all workers. But unfortunately, the capitalistic world did not support noble ideas in business, and he had to face bankruptcy because of the huge borrowings. Jack Welch, famous for laying off workers, came to the rescue. Through his GE Capital he bailed out the company and the CEO Aaron by investing funds.

Desire has a vital role to play in the entire process of bringing a mindset change. Desire is the cornerstone of motivation for all actions. The subject of marketing defines desire as the deep-rooted appetite for an object of craving. The urge for product consumption is kindled and fuelled by solid advertising cues, which ignite even the buyers' non-existing needs.

By showcasing the product attractively and tempting to use the offering through samples and by appealing to consumer's mind for the betterment of lifestyle, an intense craving is created through marketing gimmicks.

Those who have lost hair want to grow back hair, thus, end up buying all the hair growth creams, oils, and other medications. Those girls who are dark-skinned in India are conditioned to look fair skinned and they develop a deep desire for fairness creams marketed under the brand name 'Fair and Lovely'. Its advertisement displays the transformation of darker-skinned women into paler versions.

All these are clear cases of opportunism and exploitation of human weakness because of greed.

However, if the potential user has a deep drive for the need satisfaction through a product, the advertising and the sales intensify and push the urge to take a step towards deciding and choosing.

If the potential buyer does not show thirst for the product or service, every effort is made to create the need. Marketing theorists call the desire "the third stage in the hierarchy of effects" when the buyers develop a conviction that the advertised product is what would quench their need. Any change will need a sound strategy to create an intense urge in people to embrace change. The step is to ensure that people's alignment and conscripting for the process.

Unless a powerful urge is created in a majority of the early adopters of change, the result will be delayed progress of the change programme.

The measure of success is the number of people who are impacted by the communication and have become eager to embrace change. Creating an intense urge to adopt a change need is proactive rather than managing resistance, which is reactive.

The role of the circle of influence is the idea from Steven Covey in his work Seven habits of highly effective people.

For people to adjust to new things that profoundly impact their job and career or even their life, people must get the right drive to accept the change, and any attempt by leaders to shrink the circle of concern will be the most productive endeavour.

Summary

Change requires exploiting the covet, which is developing a deep motivational push to change and accept the communication cues from their leadership. A robust initiative to create urgency addiction can accelerate change and help in developing a shared vision.

Step 5: Knowledge

The tenet of change management is "know the atom for knowing the universe." One must understand the basic concept to get the practice right, as nothing equals the power of robust knowledge.

"Information and knowledge is power. If you can control information, you can control people," said Tom Clancy.

We understand that theory and abstracts won't help as much as practical experience will. But are the two aspects distinct from one another? It is a common dilemma and seems to be big like the question, "Can a tornado exist from the wind?"

In dealing with change and managing change, first, we need to understand the basics thoroughly. No shortcut exists to initiate large-scale change; the leadership challenge is to thoroughly understand the concepts. Once that is done, it becomes easier to get the practice right.

A group of technical project managers in charge of a large team were made to define the concept of efficiency and effectiveness.

As one would have expected, nearly 90 per cent came out with a definition of efficiency as input-output ratio. It is the well-trained engineering mind which pushes the line of reasoning. None could state precisely the meaning of effectiveness.

One or two participants who had attended leadership seminars or read a few management books described effectiveness. They all handled the large-scale enterprise-wide implementation of Salesforce (a computer software for sales automation) and complained about people unwilling to change. We know by now they were only dealing with their engineering mindset to drive efficiency. Their attitude of dealing with people is oriented to mechanical efficiency. For change management, the need is to build new capability, and the mindset of managers must be to balance the yield with enhancing the capability of people. To realise this, the leader or managers must know the subject and not the tool. Let's look at the story of the golden goose.

Once, there was a farmer who was poor and suffered. He prayed hard every day trusting that God would help. One fine day God listened to his prayers and appeared before him. HE told him that he could get one goose that lays one golden egg every day but the condition was he has to be happy with one golden egg.

The farmer was happy. He got the golden egg which he took to the market and sold it and earned decent money every day. He could buy the food for the family.

Few years passed and he found that the size of the egg had become smaller and it looked like a pigeon egg. The farmer got greedy and thought that it would be easier if he got all the eggs at once and make more money. He tried to cut open the goose to take all the eggs and he lost the goose as well. He was trying to maximise the profit. The obsession to deal with efficiency in organisations destroys people's enthusiasm and drive.

Imagine if the farmer had changed the strategy and approach. What if he had fed one vitamin pill every day to the goose? As a result, the goose would have stayed healthy and laid bigger eggs for many more years. That would have been a simple way to enhance gains and been effective in improving productivity.

The answer to our actions is simple. If one is oriented to efficiency, changing that orientation and attitude becomes difficult. If the understanding of these two ideas is robust, the change initiators will focus on effectiveness, as change must happen in people's mindsets. Conceptual clarity by change leaders is required even to make people think of change.

The brand of learners includes experiential learners, which involves learning through practice. Psychologist David Kolb proposed the concept and others including John Dewey, Kurt Lewin, and Jean Piaget added. Kolb refers to this learning as "the process whereby knowledge is created through the transformation of experience. Knowledge results from the combinations of grasping and transforming the experience."

Cognitive theories revolve around many concepts, including problem-solving skills, memory retention, judgement skills, and learned material perception. However, these ideas depend on mental processes and ignore the role of subjective experience in the learning process.

Experiential learning is a holistic approach and focuses on how experiences, including cognition, environmental conditions, and emotions, influence the learning process. If learning is to be tested, a better method is putting it into practice. The practice is proof of learning effectiveness.

Application of learning is the actual power that is going to stay until another robust understanding is found. Another form of learning is inquiry-based learning. Those who enquire are in pursuit of the truth; being curious to enquire is cardinal for the refinement of knowledge. Finally, the utility of the self and others is when it takes shape, in outward expression through speaking to others.

One Tamil poet classified five breeds of students of learning.

The first category is the royal swan. It is an old fable. If you mix water and milk, the royal swan will suck the milk, leaving water behind. Though a myth, it is symbolic of the Hamsa's (hans /hams-a Hindi name for swan) association with wisdom. Wisdom enables us to select the useful and discard the useless.

It teaches us the discrimination of what is proper and what is not. So, the first category of learners is much like the royal swan. In OCM, this category is of the early adopters, and they have the most significant influence over others.

The second category is that of a cow. The cow grabs all the grass and with one or two bites, swallows everything. After that, it goes to rest under a tree, brings back the food to its mouth and chews nicely to enjoy it, while digesting as much as possible. The second category of learners, therefore, is like the cow. These learners are easy to train, and learn the vital aspects completely.

The third category is a parrot. These people merely repeat what was taught. They can be trained and motivated to change, but to expect a value addition is beyond their capacity.

Fourth is the goat. When a goat grazes, it nibbles here and there on the grass. Even after extended grazing, the goat will stay hungry. Such a category of students absorbs only superficial knowledge.

The fifth category is the mud pot with a hole at the bottom.

It cannot retain anything and no matter how hard it tries, it all goes to waste.

Convincing someone through communication to change will not have any effect on them. They are laggards with low attitudes and low willingness. Finally, learning and knowledge building are critical steps in the change methodology and process.

Summary

Knowledge is like loading the gun; the weapon is made powerful in executing the task. Both theoretical and practical knowledge are important.

Step 6: Comprehension

Once knowledge is acquired, comprehension happens in the minds of people with the eagerness to change. You can't comprehend what you don't even know. For example, if you want to buy a super Luxury Lexus ES 350, that costs at least USD 50,000, you will do everything possible to get as much knowledge of that car as possible, before you even visit the dealer.

After the dealer visit, you may go home, research everything about Lexus ES350 and convince yourself as to why that car is the right choice.

But unfortunately, people do not instantly make changes; they think of the benefits of effort vs rewards.

An example of an act of hearing and attempting to comprehend the meaning of everything spoken by another in dialogue, conversation or speech. Active listening is an important communication skill, which involves attentiveness. Active listening increases understandability.

Enabling understanding through active listening requires that the information is presented in understandable ways to anyone with proper subject knowledge and willingness.

Unfortunately, language comprehension is not as easy, as a combination of words does not mean the same thing. Expressions can often be interpreted in more than one way when communication is ambiguous.

For example, the exact words can lead to more than one interpretation based on the recipient. Finally, language, spoken words, active listening etc., play a role in learning and understanding.

Summary

Comprehension is creating a more profound urge in the minds to adapt to change. Encouraging people to indulge in active listening is one sure way to enhance comprehension.

Step 7: Conviction

Conviction develops a firm belief or faith in one that the thing is good for self-that faith will intensify the yearning to own it. When a person can analyse, the determination to develop a conviction about embracing, change happens. However, unless confidence is developed for embracing a change, it will have a positive impact and there will not be any action. Therefore, it is essential to have over 80 per cent of the target population in this category to begin with, when the change project is within a few months of its initiation.

Belief is born and takes shape when one has a solid and extensive reference base on those preferences for which one develops an intense emotional state. The data points give strength and surety of direction. The reference points accumulate from the prior experiences or facts and data used, or even one's imagination.

When strength is high, the serious form of the belief system is that the person stops accepting and even closes his mind to new ideas. Thus, the cause for resistance during change initiatives is predominantly coming out of the convictions. Change leaders can break this or interrupt this closed mind by developing personal rapport through direct communication that enables people to challenge their reference points.

Customary beliefs are always overshadowed by conviction because of the strong emotional attachment, and the person concludes that what they think is the truth; nothing can shake that belief. Therefore, people get agitated if made to challenge their convictions. For example, Hindu religious leaders believe that cow slaughter is a sin and anyone who kills a cow will go to hell. Any attempt to challenge this will cause angrier and violent reactions.

According to a few religious sects of Hinduism, a staunch conviction that if a wife jumps into the funeral fire of her dead husband, she would gain moksha, aka, liberation from sin.

This practice called Sati could only stop through legal bans, as nothing else could break old religious convictions.

The 2014 Nobel peace prize winner Kailash Satyarthi is a sterling example of a human who is convinced that children are the gift of God to humanity. According to him any sort of child exploitation must be stopped. He gave up his lucrative government job to become a social activist against child labour in India, and he had to pay a hefty price of a near-fatal attack many times by the land mafia. Yet, his conviction drives him even today to fight child labour and exploitation.

People with belief and with conviction are those who develop confidence, passion followed by action. Imagine entering Mumbai's biggest cricket stadium-Wankhede Stadium, with a capacity of 100,000 for a T20 cricket match. One is a crowd in the east stand. They stand is full of decibel noise. They come with drums, bugles and scream.

They all know little about the game of cricket. Their goal is to enjoy and have lots of fun. So, they clap, scream and blow the trumpets whenever a batter scores a run.

The crowd in the north stand seats that come at a much higher price. Many of them know rules of cricket.

They have their favourite team, which they support. The spectators' goal is to enjoy the game and celebrate their team's victory.

The expert crowd in the pavilion. That crowd consists of retired players, umpires, coaches who know cricket. They analyse the game and gain insight into the day's match. The two umpires in the middle ensure that the game is played as per rules. Their goal is to impose the rules and that the teams play in genuine game spirit in all fairness.

They are knowledgeable of all the laws. The team whose goal is to win and that has the strongest conviction of being the best, has greater chance of winning. The team which has the strongest conviction of their capability can win.

The teams do not behave like the spectators, who think that cricket is fun and an excellent game. They are in the stadium to see a game and enjoy and mentally take part. Compared to competitive sports organisations, especially during change, organisations need dynamic teams and players and not spectators. Changes in organisation need people with the passion for carrying the torch and bringing people together to influence conviction through contagious enthusiasm. What do we do when we do not know right from wrong?

We tune with people we trust to give us an idea, share their beliefs, or provide a solution.

If the person we look up to is an opinion leader, the influence is substantial.

Social psychologists who study the mob mentality explain the phenomenon. In such cases, people lose their self-awareness and shed their individual identity, identifying themselves with groups that create excitement. There was an incidence of mass suicide in southern India. People immolated themselves when their leader of a political party was arrested by the police. The entire mob frenzy started with one person attempting self-immolation during a street protest.

Summary

The strength of one's belief tests conviction. The change is possible with the sole conviction that the change is good.

Without conviction, the change may become temporary compliance.

Step 8: Action

Action is a movement being done once the decision to act is taken. Eliciting the action is possible if all the previous steps were taken. After making people pay attention and developing the need to gain knowledge, one will wish to take a few steps if a decision is made to act and realise the expected positive outcome. The action step is taken, hoping to solve a problem. Action is well-thought conscious activity or a set of activities that have meaning to the person in that change and action. We may even act with or without knowing the consequences, but the effects of not changing need to be made in change initiatives.

We are not dealing with knee-jerk reactions in change management because the process takes people gradually through all the steps to build a thoughtful action step. To make people take action, they must be inspired to do what is to be done and trust what is said and expected.

Transformational leaders have a responsibility to create a strong bonding by being empathetic.

A notable difference is between a semblance of action or pretence of action, and proper action. People pretend to take action by indulging in unproductive activities or rituals. They are not performing to produce the results because they lack conviction. While implementing change process steps as per this model for change, leaders have not cared to take people through comprehension and belief.

An action is possible in change, and only with conviction to change.

If people display gestures of change, the leaders must help set timelines to take steps for results. Enough time, if required, must be spent in creating the conviction in the process model to make sure that the change is for good. Mere activities do not produce results, and indulging in some action is not moving towards achieving planned and chosen results in engineering an escape and creating the threshold level of speed in change initiatives.

People don't buy what leaders do or want them to do; they buy the reasons. The motion phase can be used for capacity building; the leaders should not make everyone act. The goal is to make people go along with what the leaders believe in.

Dr Martin Luther did not get people to rally around in America because he was a great orator. He wasn't the only person in America who suffered in the pre-civil rights era in America. His ideas weren't always the best of the lot, either. But he had the gift to put across to people what he firmly stood for, and people who developed the conviction in what he preached took the cause and made it their own.

Gandhi did not tell the Indian public what to do to get independence. He only spoke inspirationally, citing his conviction that freedom is a birth right and many are emotionally connected with it.

The African leader, Kwame Nkrumah of Ghana, visited Gandhi in India during India's struggle for independence. Nkrumah returned to his country and fought for Ghana's independence, using Gandhi's ideals and principles of non-violence and boycott the British regime.

It took 10 Years of protests for Ghana to become the first African country to break free from British rule in 1957.

Not long after Ghana gained its independence, the remaining British colonies in Africa would tumble like dominoes. The decolonisation of Africa was the most peaceful process in history. Gandhi and his preaching were great influencers in the whole liberation process.

Nelson Mandela struggled throughout his life to the serve Africans as a human rights lawyer. He was a prisoner of conscience, an international ambassador of peace and the first democratically elected president of a free South Africa. Both Gandhi and Mandela were firm believers in non-violence.

Many people leaders had brought massive changes for social justice using the principles of non-violence of Mahatma Gandhi. Martin Luther King led the American civil rights movement. Nelson

Mandela brought an end to apartheid in South Africa. The Dalai Lama has been seeking a peaceful resolution in Tibet. Aung San Suu Kyi continues her fight for democracy in her native land Myanmar (Burma).

Mahatma Gandhi was dedicated and principle centred. Although ahimsa means 'no injury', Gandhi's use of the word encompassed universal love. To follow the doctrine of ahimsa means not to hurt or offend anyone, and not to harbour an uncharitable thought, even about the enemy. The one who follows ahimsa has no enemies.

"A man cannot practise ahimsa and be a coward."- Gandhi. These thoughts looked unrealistic to many people. Recently, someone shared an experience with one of my trainees. A question was once raised in the training sessions about handling people who constantly oppose your ideas. I had replied that one should help such people see reason. The trainee was not convinced. 15 Years later, the same person told when she met me, it had made little sense to her what i had told her, but later in life, she tried to practise that principle and got positive results; a model illustration of being driven by values.

Ethical considerations should permeate every action to make lasting changes. Any act that can be assessed in terms of morals and principles has a powerful impact in handling change because the sincerity of change outcome is in focus.

But unfortunately, it is incomprehensible to many team members.

Summary

A conviction follows action. Gandhi and Mandela acted for human liberty because of their deep-rooted conviction about human rights.

Step 9: Result

The result is an outcome and consequence of an action taken and could cause single or multiple effects. The effect and its impact could be instantly evidenced or could be found out after an analysis.

Space programmes are examples of high-risk initiatives, and the results are instant and catastrophic if a small calculation fails. The world witnessed it when 73 seconds into the flight, the space shuttle Challenger disintegrated, killing all seven astronauts on board. At fault was the O-ring seal on the right solid rocket booster. The outcome was that the entire space shuttle programme had to be suspended for 32 months by NASA. In 2016, 18 space programmes resulted in fatalities.

What happens with disastrous, unwanted results? The only way is to create a culture of accountability at every level.

"Accountability breeds timely response-ability," said Stephen R. Covey. "The best way to achieve the aspiring results is, to begin with, the end in mind."

Visualisation of the cathedral picture requires imagination —the ability to envision in mind and is based on the vivid power of creative imagination. It is beyond what our eye sees.

To create physically, we need to first develop our mind.

Leaders who initiate change visualise what the changed condition would be and enable other people to see the same picture- creating favourable conditions to shape the realisation of the results. Result orientation means to begin each day any task, or activity of the change programme with a clear vision of direction towards the destination and continue to take those steps.

Do we learn from failures? Unfortunately, we only know if one looks at the results and evaluates the cause.

Summary

Efforts with no results as envisioned are meaningless. The results determine the measure of both success and failure. A clear definition of the changed state and outcome is a must for change to happen.

Step 10: Evaluation

The Indian Space Research Organisation (ISRO) had set its eyes on soft-land a probe on the moon through the Chandrayaan (lunar spacecraft) missions, way back in 2008. Chandrayan 2 was the moon landing spacecraft launched in September 2019, but the lander lost communication at the last minute and failed to land on the lunar surface and crashed. It took three months to work out the location and the reasons for its crash. Attempts were made to locate the lander which analysed the moon's terrain and sent back data for 14 days. The glitch was unexpected since the software was functioning well throughout the trial period.

The moral is that one must "evaluate to learn from the failures' '. One must look at the results and evaluate what went wrong. If, even after deploying the best technology and using scientific precision, the results did not come for the lunar mission, we can say little about change projects that do not have even 10 percent of that precision planning.

For any change to occur, the organisation's leadership must act on their vision of an improved state, and identify several goals that must be reached to realise that vision. Change programmes are organised methods to improve the business performance; change programmes must be evaluated to decide if the programmes meet the goals.

Programme evaluation is collecting information and details of a programme to make necessary decisions. Change programme evaluation includes various forms of assessment, ranging from needs assessments, cost/benefit analysis, effectiveness, efficiency measure, goal-based, process, outcomes, etc.

The choice of the evaluation method depends on what is being experienced.

Myths around Programme Evaluation

It is an unwanted unproductive activity as it generates lots of data leading to useless or no conclusions.

Evaluation is proving the success or failure of a programme. But evaluation is also the act of getting continuous feedback to initiate corrective action.

It is a highly complex process and needs outside experts.

The following steps, if taken, give a reasonable probability of success.

The success of any change management programme depends on how well the programme enables people to focus on the shared vision and gather enough speed to work towards the ultimate purpose of change. The level of acceleration, if stated clearly, upfront, reduces the time that will be wasted later in clarifying or, at the worst, agitating on time.

Those rules for speeding up are:

1. I - Implement

Initiate steps for creating an adequate level of commitment. Just because the leaders gave employees a set of change programme objectives and told them what to do, they would not willingly execute it. But, beyond goals, commitment to achieving is an essential expectation. Employees are most likely to commit to doing this if they know, they find an answer to personal benefit and connect with the organisation's gains.

Not all employees are 'cathedral builders' and stone breakers too.

2. M - Milestone Measure

We need data to hold employees accountable and measurement mechanisms for ongoing performance measurement of the programme. They need sound managerial skills to bridge the gap when noticed.

3. P - Performance Assessment

Feedback will open the door for discussions and follow-up actions. The employees need proper feedback to improve in areas where performance is falling short of expectations. Setting expectations followed by quality feedback is the backbone to hold anyone accountable for results. Managers must take courage to tell one openly if the performance is not above expectation.

4. L - Link Reward to Consequences

Employees need to be aware of the consequences of achieving and not achieving the change objectives. Fear of failure most times holds people back from trying or doing strange ways which change programmes. When faced with road bumps, employees need proper coaching, mentoring to cross over smoothly.

5. E - Evaluate Effectiveness, Balance the Progress Productivity, and production capability determine

Often, while implementing change, reskilling becomes essential to establish enhanced production capability.

6. M - Maintain Speed

There have to be planned ways of accelerating progress, as the average human impulse is to slow things when dealing with any newer activity. As a result, they develop a false sense of satisfaction with the progress.

7. E - Enforce Set Process Standards

The five processes that ensure meaningful action and performance are problem-solving, communication, reasoning and testimony, representation, and connections, as in mathematics.

8. N - Never Lower the Bar

Lowering the standards slows the momentum. As a result, the entire process slows, and one may have to settle for process delays and substantial cost escalations.

9. T - Terminate Project

Project must be terminated if the cost consequences are overwhelming.

The formative evaluation takes place in the lead up to the project. The researchers often subject formative evaluation to qualitative methods of inquiry.

Need assessment determines who needs the change programme, how great the need is, and what might meet the demand.

Structured evaluation helps stakeholders define the programme, the target population and the outcomes.

Implementation evaluation monitors the integrity of the programme delivery. Process evaluation investigates the process of delivering the programme, including alternative delivery procedures. Only when change objectives are made clear, they can be subjected to the goal-based assessment. This can help to assess if the intended goals of a programme were attained. For example, in one change programme, the purpose was defined as follows. The change goals were set at: by the end of the first phase of the initiative.30 percent of the technical consultants must pass the test for being business and functional consultants. Outcome evaluation investigates whether the programme caused demonstrable effects on the specifically defined target. Impact evaluation is broader and assesses the overall or net effects of intended or unintended changes because of the programme.

Cost-effectiveness and cost-benefit analysis address questions of efficiency by standardising outcomes in terms of their monetary values.

An evaluation is a process of scrutinising the actual outcome after implementing a programme to establish whether the intended goals were reached as planned and strategies were implemented or carried out. In-process check is also a must as corrective action can be initiated. Evaluation does help decide on the continuance or otherwise of the programme or extension and refinement of steps.

Change impact analysis is defined by Bohner and Arnold as "identifying the potential consequences of a change, or estimating what needs to be modified to accomplish a change", focusing on scoping changes within the details of a design.

Traceability and dependency are elements in impact analysis to establish links between requirements, specifications, design elements, and tests. These relationships can be analysed to determine how to initiate change. Independency, linkages between parts, variables, logic, modules, etc., are assessed to determine the consequences of initiating change. Finally, outcome and impact evaluations are the stable steps to process evaluation.

Outcome evaluation measures the change that has occurred because of a change programme that was planned and initiated.

For example, process evaluation might confirm that 200 people have completed the OCM concepts training programme. In addition, an outcome evaluation could reveal how many of those who completed exhibited increased awareness, knowledge, and attitude change relevant to making progress on change implementation.

While the outcome evaluation can indicate the degree of changes that occurred, an impact evaluation assesses how a programme had affected the process of change on a broader scale. Impact measurement using an independent evaluator, with control groups, and measuring changes over extended periods can be reliable and accurate but consume time.

Summary

Evaluation is based on the success or failure criteria which must be ab initio defined. Recently, the Indian space research organisation planned their moon landing with significant fanfare. Even the prime minister was invited to witness the historic moment. But, unfortunately, during the last few minutes, the spacecraft lost contact. The chief of ISRO was found sobbing on the PM's shoulder. As per their evaluation, there was no room for 90 per cent success, and the mission had failed.

This new methodology is based on a few vital steps to make sure of the success of change implementation. However, if each step is architected, success is inevitable.

CHAPTER 14

ROLE OF LEADERSHIP ETHICS AND VALUES

During the implementation stage of any change programme, everything a leader or manager does and every exhibited behaviour will send a powerful signal about the company's leadership attitude toward change. If ethics and values temper the behaviour, the initiative will mobilise support quickly. Managers are often expected to be in the coaching role during a change initiative, and they are the most influential when the organisation is in a fluid state.

What they express, do and don't do, both on the job and off the job, radiates a message about the organisation's values and reveals what the leaders prioritise and how committed they are to the change.

Each manager involved in change must ask at every stage "What message am I sending through my actions? For example, suppose the manager calls for a steering committee meeting and arrives 10 minutes late. In such a case, people attending the meeting get the message that agenda items are not as important.

It takes excellent initiative and a solid will to perceive and deal with all the questions during change. Change champions need to have the power to lead and be driven by their conviction.

The sports events are full of many examples of value-driven leadership. For example, Jesse Owens was the most outstanding Black star of field and track events in the 1936 Berlin Summer Olympics. Hitler was furious when he came to know that Jesse Owens had a gold medal-winning performance.

He said, "Americans ought to be ashamed of themselves for letting Afro-Americans win their medals. I would never shake hands with one of them."

It was a long jump event, and in two attempts, he stepped over the limit line, and a third foul meant he would be out of the finals.

Luz Long, a German athlete, was his closest and most bitter rival. The atmosphere in the stadium was charged and Hitler would have been annoyed if the German did not win. He took a towel, laid it a foot before the foul line, and advised Owens to use the towel to secure qualifying. Owens did that and won. This was evidence of the highest form of going beyond the call of duty and he demonstrated the highest standards of ethics and values. Playing fair is both by choice and attitude. Hitler handed out punishment to Luz Long by sending him to the Russian front, and he died there.

Years later when Long's daughter got married years, Jesse Owens walked her down the aisle to pay respect.

It was 1964 Innsbruck Winter Olympics. An Olympic gold medal is the dream of every individual and team and invariably the dream of every team in a bobsled event. The British squad driven by Tony Nash was sure to win the gold. But, to their horror, they found out they had a broken sled with a broken bolt on the rear axle. This would have been heart-breaking for any team which had worked hard and drained every nerve to the limit to reach the final.

They were left with no other choice but to quit the competition. Eugenio Monti was leading the Italian team, and Monti's team had made their last run. When he understood the British team's issue, he took the bolt out of his rear axle and sent it up to Nash without even blinking.

One could not imagine that the British team would win the gold medal and Monti's team the bronze. Nevertheless, Monti said from his heart. "Tony Nash did not win because I gave him a bolt; Tony Nash won because he was the best driver and deserved to win."

Think, also, of the final few minutes of the Euro 2012 final, when the Spanish captain, Casillas, pleaded with the referee to end the game early out of respect for the Italian team.

Of course, winning the Euro 2012 was important, but Casillas was a true athlete and respected Italy so much that he could not insult them through another goal and hand over massive defeat.

There was the third cricket test match between Australia and South Africa in Perth, Australia, on 3 December 2012. Ricky Ponting, nicknamed Punter, had captained the team from 2004 to 2011.

As he walked out for the last time in his test cricket career as the highest run-scorer in cricket test history, the rival South African team, led by captain Graeme Smith, gave him a guard of honour and applauded him. Pointing scored 13,378 runs in 168 test matches, surpassing only one man — India's Sachin Tendulkar.

The South African captain and team displayed the rarest show of values and principles.

Another story of "values in action", an example of value-driven leadership, will illustrate the point further. It was the last week to decide champions in Australia in two of the high-profile sports viz., Australian Rules football and Rugby League. The teams were lined up for their previous games to determine who would be crowned champion. The matches had the same intensity as the Super Bowl in America or the Champions League football final in Europe.

A week before that, Melbourne Storm had played their arch-rival, the Manly Sea Eagles. They had won by a narrow margin 26-22, but the game had been very bloody and bruising, and it had taken its toll on the players. When the bus got back to their hotel, it was close to 1 am, and every player was bruised and battered.

While all the players started alighting from the bus, Australian half-back Cooper Cronk and New Zealand back-rower Sika Manu dutifully collected the garbage from the bus's rear end to the front seats. They collected all the empty bottles or the trash left behind by their teammates.

Both players had received the same hammering in the game and suffered cuts and bruises.

Once they finished collecting the garbage, they handed over the rubbish to the bus driver and apologised for inadvertently leaving a few things. That was a fine display of personal principle and value-driven culture that they all had worked hard to create at the Melbourne Storm.

For change leaders leading a transformation, no single approach or prescriptive guidance or model can ensure success. Instead, expected results can come by targeting leadership actions of making the change meaningful, reshaping mindsets and behaviour, building a solid and committed team, and relentlessly pursuing the end goal with speed.

These elements powerfully generate the energy needed to engineer the escape.

A leader must be a well-informed and enlightened dictator in trying to change. At the very young age of 36, Jan Carlzon became the youngest CEO of Scandinavian Airlines with a mandate to turn around the business, which he did. His values and principles guided his actions. Action is the proof of the pudding, and the result is eating it. Therefore, unless people act, there won't be any movement towards expected change.

Everyone must guard against people indulging in the motion of aligning with change and not exhibit an action. Activities and rituals do not produce any results Leaders have the responsibility to create conviction by role modelling.

That is a miracle that Gandhi performed. Mandela, Martin Luther King, too, died with an imponderable weapon called non-violence.

CHAPTER 15

UNDERSTANDING THE PEOPLE BEHAVIOUR PATTERN

During change, employees in the organisation will have different concerns, and they express their concerns differently based on their personality type. Therefore, when developing strategies for managing change, it is helpful for managers to understand the personality types. Many studies and tools for assessing personality types are available. For example, Myers Briggs Type Indicator or MBTI, 16 PF are the widely used tool. It classifies personality types as:

1. Extroverts

This type seek to meet in groups and love to discuss and offer feedback. They are known to seek information in writing well before interactions in groups, and they expect giving feedback in smaller groups.

2. Sensing Types

These people need to be told the reason of how the change will improve the status, and details of the change plan. They always like to deal with facts.

Sensing type get influenced immediate impressions and use the "raw data". They derive meaning out of concrete information and rely on experiences to guide their future actions. People with this preference are pragmatic. They like to live the moment.

3. Intuitive Types

Such people would be happy if they were told about the big picture and why change is needed. These types can comfortably align their personal goals with the broader vision for change.

4. Thinking Types

They will look at the criteria that prompted a particular choice of the change strategy. These types focus on aligning with the organisation's core values and plan to address adverse impacts.

5. Judging Types

They will evaluate the implementation schedule and what the contingency plans are for failure. this type is all clear about the course of action.

They prefer to have backup plans than facing events as they unfold. They are prefer sticking to the plan rather than moving with the flow. It's as if they have a mental checklist for the actions and are open to rethinking. Appear as rigid and stubborn with rigid need for structure always.

Surprises can frustrate and stress them easily. Whether a long term or emergency they can place actionable plan. They have strong work ethic and place priority is the duties and responsibilities.

Rules, regulations, and guidelines are main appealing factors. They are driven by goal of fairness and results.

6. Perceiving Types

Although we may leave a few decisions open for discussion or debate, perceiving types want to know them.

A change process customised in a few respects to suit the needs of the individual is likely to render more fruitful results.

Personality type theory offers insights on addressing all the key players' concerns to establish that the change initiatives speed up and gain momentum.

The medical theory of the four senses of humour form the base which held that four bodily senses of humour (blood, yellow bile, black bile, and phlegm) are causing the illness. The terminologies sanguine, choleric, melancholic and phlegmatic to describe the effect of humour on personality originated when the Greek physician Delius Galenus referred to it first.

World experts are aware of the four temperaments for many years and the concepts stayed popular in the writings of several well-known spiritual leaders. Change leaders must be aware of people patterns, and it is to understand who will be worth conscripting in change.

The Choleric

Choleric people are easily angered and short-tempered; they are the proud, extroverted, dominating, capable leaders who can give directions. They seek to be in control. It doesn't mean they are greedy to be in leadership roles, but they would love to be one-up. They use commanding language, which may sound more like commands than requests, radiate confidence and sustain an aura of certainty, and their vocabulary reflects such an attitude. Nevertheless, these people are stable in their approach to problems.

They accept being tough and try to take on the challenge to prove that something is wrong. Choleric people will confront someone if the latter opposes them and defend themselves, constantly prevailing on others, and louder than those around them. Choleric can bully others and will stand by those who bully others. High-level confidence and demanding nature make others view them as natural leaders, though they may not enjoy leadership positions. They are highly sociable, open and straightforward.

They will rise to the challenges to prove themselves. They look for opportunities and be tough and strong.

Famous people of the choleric type are:

Julius Caesar, Napoleon Bonaparte, Adolf Hitler, Bill Gates, Donald Trump and Michael Jordan.

The Sanguine

Sanguine people are sociable and love the hard days. They love to be popular. They build a network of friends, love to help each other, and are always curious. They are comfortable in the company of many people, and they're not picky about friends. They talk more than listening. They enjoy social events and agree that everyone else around will too. Their vocabulary is always meant to convince people to come along. They make statements like, "You don't know what you're missing", they aren't careful with secrets, and they will easily spill others' secrets.

The Theatrical

This type exaggerates to make things appear more dangerous than they are. They appear to care for their looks. If they do not get noticed, they will rush into a conversation or speak something to attract attention.

They are very uncomfortable when they are left out.

The Melancholic

Several studies found the role of serotonin in causing imbalance and impulsive aggressiveness. If serotonin is deficient or functions below standard of the neurotransmitter a person becomes impulsively aggressive. Scientists indicate that serotonergic dysfunction makes the dopamine system malfunction. Melancholic is linked to serotonin, suppresses aggressive tendencies. Melancholic types remain calm and self-confident; they are family and community-centric. They are trustworthy, methodical and don't like unreliability. They are definite in planning and keeping schedules. They are thoughtful, analytical, profound, and they love details. Melancholic people are exposed perfectionist introverts. Their defining feature is perfectionism. Being idealists who expect a particular way, and they get distraught when the anticipations don't go as per their wish; they may hold high standards and that leads to distress when these standards are not met. This leads to being reticent and critical of others. Being good learners, they wish to know the details of even small thing; they are over-analytical, neurotic worriors, leaning towards being stubborn.

They react adversely to praises, often negating by maintaining they're not great to deserve that praise.

Usually, such people will blame themselves for mistakes, as they are aware of their inadequacy. They prefer tidiness, and are organised. They are hypersensitive. (Ref: Psychologia)

The Phlegmatic

The phlegmatic type is a peaceful person and remains stable, patient, and has compassion. They always keep calm when others around are in confusion. Those are humble, silent, controlled, listen well and always remain happy with their life. They are always the mediator and are easy to get along with.

Personal Mastery

Organizations learn when individuals are learning, though individual learning does not ensure organisational learning. Without continuous learning as corporate ethos, an organisation can rarely learn. Personal mastery is the sine qua non for achieving the dream of both the organisation and the people. In the words of Peter Senge, "Self-mastery is accepting the fact that we have a resistance to positive change. Therefore, to remain on course to attaining self-mastery one needs to negotiate with resistance to change."

It's easier to do self-correction when dealing with own mistakes. Personal mastery is the way of obtaining clarity and a more profound commitment to a unique vision. Other forms focus on energies, emerging patience, and seeing future reality objectively and stabilising internal stability. Self-mastery is above competence and skills, although they are essential ingredients. It involves the transcendental rise and not supremacy.

Personal mastery cannot be another profound idea worth pursuing if it needs to succeed. People seeking mastery do so with self-discipline and consistently through the process of continuous learning and reinventing. Personal mastery is not innate and is not another skill or competency. It is a process-driven self-learning capability. It is a discipline, and people pursuing personal mastery are conscious of their deficiencies, incompetence, and development needs.

They are confident, principle-centered, value-driven, and vision-aligned. It may be paradoxical, but this quality of seeking self-mastery drives people to intense learning.

A few of the learning approaches for organisations and individuals are worth knowing.

2,000 years ago, the dialectical form evolved as a learning philosophy. In an alternative world, this form of enquiry is still relevant. The two units are individual and the organisation, or the organisation and its environment form the thesis and antithesis engaged in debate.

Autopoiesis means self-creating, and it refers to self-producing, self-preserving, self-repairing, and self-relational features of living systems. The principle is that living organisms represent self-producing mechanisms. They support a particular form through self-regulation, even in the middle of material inflow and outflow.

It combines equipoise and systems thinking, proposed by Chilean scientists Humberto Maturana (1928-) and Francisco Varela (1946-2001) in the late sixties or seventies.

The autopoietic organisation is defined as "a unit and a network of components which participate following a repeatable process."

CHAPTER 16

CHANGE MANAGEMENT COMMUNICATION STRATEGIES

Telling more, that too, excessively through every available channel is the key to organisational change progress. The internet and social media play a crucial and relevant role in information dissemination to ensure multi-geographical, multi-cultural spread. Therefore, enterprises need to focus on continuous and constant communication during change programmes.

Several psychological factors and behavioural issues affect the way information is received and understood. It is the cognitive biases which affect people's way of processing data.

We examine these thoughts, affecting communication.

1. Confirmation Bias

Across the globe, the judicial and legal system depends even today on eyewitness accounts, which were the only basis for prosecution in most criminal cases before forensic science became handy. But confirmation bias has influenced many eyewitnesses to make assumptions leading to faulty delivery of justice. Confirmation bias does have bad effect. It does not permit one to change views even based on fresh evidence.

People who perceive that dogs are inherently dangerous animals when they see a dog sniffing a child would perceive that as an attack that affirms their own belief; on the contrary, those who love dogs see this as usual. Reliability on both eyewitness' accounts is not reliable because of confirmation bias. Confirmation bias can influence people to make assumptions that are based on nonfactual information.

While dealing with confirmation bias in change communication one could ask about the trustworthiness of the source; how one's view is challenged or reinforced; how many other people are differing.

On social media, even a small news gets noticed and shared by those with their biases. Friends and relatives who agree with you always post messages that align with your bias, and you are tempted to like or share them.

Confirmation bias is difficult to overcome, and communicators must be extra careful when dealing with change resistance.

2. Streisand Effect

Barbara Streisand, the famous Hollywood actress, was responsible for attracting over a million people when she threw a tantrum over a trivial issue of hiding California coastal records. The posting was initially viewed by only three people in 2003 in social media. When people feel that information is kept away, the psychological reactance makes them to get somehow. There is more curiosity and publicity when legal restraint is sought from publishing any information.

The Barbara Streisand effect is thought to occur when attempts to suppress, remove or censor a juicy piece of online information backfires and ends up making things worse.

3. The Backfire Effect.

The Backfire Effect concept is a highly relevant for OCM communication strategies. Backfire effect is defined as the effect in which "corrections increase misperceptions among the group in question." So often, one faces this situation when we present facts and data to prove a point, even with friends, which only ends with people hardening their stances further, despite hard facts.

When we see or read a news story that presents two sides of an issue, we choose the side which we agree with, and that choice reinforces our beliefs and viewpoint. Unfortunately, few individuals don't resist oppositions to their views but adhere to their original opinion even more effectively.

A way to get people on our side is not to treat the exercise as a battle to win but as a collaboration and co-creation accomplishment, especially while engaging in communication.

The normal human inclination is that if the beliefs are challenged even with facts and data, one must not alter the stand and adapt to change the thought process. However, when contradictory views challenge the most profound convictions, the original beliefs get stronger.

Therefore, any correction can push one away from the facts and data based on the issue's intensity, especially when the use is dearer to heart.

For example, those newspaper blurbs hidden on every page in newspapers are the most powerful forces shaping the thought process and what one thinks and decides. This is a behaviour hindering acceptance of the truth. The evidence is in the following experiment.

The University of Michigan and Georgia State University in America set up an experiment by creating simulated newspaper articles on popular political issues. The reports were written in such a way that they would affirm widespread misconceptions regarding problems in American politics.

The participants were given the second genuine article as soon as a person read a fake article which corrected the first viewpoint.

The manipulated article reported the news of US intelligence finding weapons of mass destruction in Iraq. However, the genuine article suggested that such weapons had never been found. People who were opposed to the war disagreed with the first article and agreed with the second. Those who were in agreement with war believed the first article and strongly disagreed with the second.

These are not surprising outcomes of the experiment, but what was surprising was how those who supported the war were even surer than before, believing that WMDs and their original beliefs were correct. Similar experiments were setup with other popular issues, viz., stem cell research and tax reform and, the results showed that corrections increased the participants' misconceptions, especially if corrections contradicted their ideologies.

The corrections, therefore, backfired. Once something is added to the collective beliefs, the impulse is to protect it from damage.

Attitude-inconsistent information makes people reacting like this. Confirmation bias safeguards us when we actively seek information, while the backfire effect secures us when the information seeks us and renders us blind.

The bias is to align with the original beliefs but not challenge them.

When someone tries to correct us to change the misconceptions, it backfires and may consolidate original faith.

Slowly, the backfire effect helps in making a person less sceptical. It allows one to continue to perceive the beliefs and attitudes as accurate depending on the conviction developed, people take steps to participate in change attempts.

Change leaders and influencers have to be sensitive to the backfire effect.

Mere repetition of a message stating how significant change is might not even work to enlist people to support. Is it a new training, enduring modification?

One may start the process through cultural change with the group of people in each category; such action steps might ensure acceleration of the process.

The outcome is that the change process would be getting accelerated and absorbed by everyone.

One significant mental shift helpful in being fair-minded and focused in arguments, is to think of the opinion not as a platform to settle scores but reframing it in one's mind t as a partnership, a collaborative effort. The group together is trying to work out the right solution.

It is easier to evaluate which arguments are good and which are wrong because the motive is getting the right solution together rather than debating. The leaders must know the effect of the backfire effect in communication to start and accelerate changes.

4. Ambiguity Effect

The ambiguity effect bias comes from the tendency to associate missing information with negative information.

When we feel that someone is hiding the information from us the impulsive action is to expect something harmful. The ambiguity effect is rational bias; however, it can prevent us from trying additional steps. Change-related communication suffers from ambiguity effects. The sure way to tackle ambiguity bias is to clarify amply what one would get from the change. By communicating in simple way, people gain higher confidence.

5. Anchoring

Relying too much on the first and one piece of information is the anchoring bias is the effect. The tendency to 'anchor' all of subsequent decisions in that first piece and give it high influence, even when the data is out of context. That anchor comes from the first piece of information we received. Once the anchor is set, our bias is set in interpreting information around that anchor, even if the first information was false or age old and is recent information. A rational decision can be made after an unbiased analysis. It becomes difficult after the first anchor.

One method to deal with this, is to encourage people to have of the first impression as inapt when the change idea was proposed and encourage them to get rid of preconceived perceptions.

6. Availability Cascade

Humans are inclined to agree with that information if the message is repeated. Therefore, people always conveniently follow age-old proverbial statements which have been repeated numerously. The availability cascade effect is self-reinforcing process. A collective belief gains more and more acceptability when we mention it many times.

7. Framing Effect

The way the information is presented influences our decision and that is the framing effect. A typical example is the "2 for 2-dollar" slogan in the shop window.

People get lured into purchase action thinking it is a deal while the actual unit price might be one dollar. Therefore, your communication plan needs to communicate with consistency and repeatedly convey the same message.

8. Illusory Truth Effect

The illusory truth effect is the human tendency to accept and believe something if it is easy to comprehend or process, compared to difficult items which need deeper analysis. Illusory truth effect gives way to the positive state of mind when we meet with information that we know is true. This is similar to the feeling that occurs when we hear news we have listened to before and feel positive. In an experimental study by Lynn Hasher, David Goldstein brought out this effect.

9. Bandwagon Effect

If people see many adopting the new change ideas, they also fall in line. The change adoption rate of ideas increases as more people subscribe to it and jump on the bandwagon.

If people see many adopting the change ideas, they also fall in line. Therefore, it is worthwhile to focus on early adopters and allow others to follow along, while initiating change communication. Prescriptive social influence is phenomenon to conform with others due to a desire to fall in line with the crowd and gain peer approval.

10. Illusory Correlation

Illusory correlation happens when we perceive a relationship between people and events, though no such relationship exists.

In an experiment three experts were asked to identify people diagnosed as mentally disturbed among a group of normal people: The experts could not identify even when the experts could deploy activities designed to reveal the participant's characteristics.

It was in front of the TV audience. We can easily conclude that the psychological diagnosis is as accurate as weather forecasting. Unfortunately, the professionals, overconfident of their capabilities claim that they have the expertise and behave as experts or show off to be experts. They are most probably suffering from illusions.

11. Base Rate Fallacy

A base rate fallacy occurs when we judge a result without considering apriori knowledge. There is a probability that the fallacy can occur while focusing on other irrelevant information. The strategy of presenting too many statistics can create the base rate fallacy.

12. Pareidolia

When we look at the sky with white clouds, we see and recognise some patterns as elephants or horses in otherwise random or unrelated cloud patterns. We call this pareidolia. It's a version of apophenia for describing the human tendency to seek ways in random information. The word's origin is in the Greek word 'para', which means beside or beyond form or image. Thus, animals or plants can 'appear' to be the form in clouds or even on sand or dust. Pareidolia includes the crazy spotting of Jesus or Mary in everything from a piece of bread toast to tortoiseshell.

Summary

Change is inevitable in any dynamic organisation however, big or small. Organisations always face resistance during implementation of change.

Handling objections especially is the most sensitive issue, and one needs to be cautious about the backfire effect. People defend their beliefs, and any aggressive handling can ruin the progress.

While strategizing, communication evolves certain best practices more specific to the organisation's culture.

Slow but multiple channels work better rather than less frequent extended information.

Theory U

Harvesting the united capacities of people and nations often appears complicated propositions, and we are only returning with failures that create social chaos. We may call these as collective transformational failures. What holds good for nations is valid for organisations during transformation.

Be it global warming or climate change, the attempts to normalise sentiments fall apart because of lack of political leaders' and individuals' will. But unfortunately, many minds are stuck in the destructive thought patterns of leaders and have no genuine intention to clear the blind spots.

We live in an era of massive institutional and system failure, in which we collectively create results that nobody wants.

Whether climate change, eradication of poverty, terrorism, destruction of forests or nature, the collective betrayal is apparent. Unless collective leadership and the capacity to meet these with proper strategies exist, creating a better future for humanity is a distant dream; isolated attempts to tackle the obstructions often fail or meet with chaos leading to failure.

As part of social responsibility, even the organisations involved can hardly manage changes occurring across the globe. Every government is stuck in their action and biased institutional ways concerning global issues.

What is true of governments and institutions is true of individuals? First, individuals will be receptive to newer ways if it does not obstruct them.

With his Theory U (or U Theory), Otto Scharmer tries to give reference points so that we may dissociate ourselves from established preconceived ideas. He outlines how an individual could contribute to solutions that are aligned with society's actual needs. Theory U describes personal leadership and an alternative way of thinking. Through "presencing", one needs to shift the focus to the emerging future.

An individual has to be open in mind to receive new ideas without thoughts and emotions impeding ideas. Until and unless these obstructions are lifted, one will not embrace change wholeheartedly. This is a prerequisite for establishing good "presencing" or listening.

Scharmer has identified four levels of listening:

1. **Downloading:** People only listen to reconfirm what they know when transferring familiar information.

2. **Factual listening:** We focus when the information differs from what we know.
3. **Empathic listening:** Understanding is possible by empathising and listening
4. **Generative thinking:** This is listening without personality interference.

Leaders who initiate change can use this tool to enhance leadership effectiveness to let go of the prevailing ideas.

CHAPTER 17

PREPARING FOR ESCAPE VELOCITY

Escape velocity is the minimum speed an object is required to reach the getaway gravitational field of another thing. Escape velocity is independent of the mass of the escaping object. However, the heavier object will require more energy to escape. The large global enterprises need massive change need substantial energy.

V_escape: 40,000 km/hr or 11 km/sec from the surface of the earth.

What is the relevance of escape velocity to organisational change management? First, when architecting the change, the escape velocity principle must be applied. A minimum level of push speed is required to escape from the pull of the past organisations' past culture and comforts of status quo conviction. Second, leadership must guide the organisation on what to do when one reaches that fork in the road and answer questions about why the right or left path is chosen. When the organisation comes to a crossroads, procrastinating on which road to choose for the journey ahead can be disastrous. This dilemma to change or not to change occurs either because of an internal crisis or ineffective management, resulting in shrinking margins and lower growth.

Once the trigger is pulled, there should be an essential minimum time spent in architecting the change plan and identifying the minimum time spent at each of those steps stated in the model.

The focus is on the barest minimum time to obtain the escape from the pull of the past. This is particularly true of migration projects from the traditional standalone system to ERP.

Crucial questions need to be asked by change leaders.

Change needs holding a crucial conversation by leaders with significant people.

To stay away from tough talk because of fear of disagreement makes the change initiative go slowly as tough questions remain unanswered. While a whirlpool has a relatively consistent form, it does not exist separately from the movement of the river.

The following are the tough questions that appear confrontational but must be faced and clarified:

Why is there still too much preoccupation with the present?

Are you all putting in any or enough endeavours to shape the future collectively?

How much leadership commitment does there need to be to shape the future?

Is there enough talent around all of us to manage the future job demands?

Resource shortage cannot be tackled overnight, and lack of resources cannot be the reason for not changing. Is there enough steam in the team?

When the market share is shrinking in a high growth market, the only reason for sluggishness can be a loss of steam.

Is there the right talent mix, when the complete business model is being changed as the skills required to face new offerings and customers are different? This question is to be addressed even before the programme launches.

The flapping of wings by the butterfly doesn't cause the hurricane, but the tiny change it causes in its environment leads to another change and thus, a chain of events is created which snowballs into a storm.

While embarking on large-scale transformation programmes, there will be resistance from individuals. Is there a way to help people change patterns of behaviour that are not helpful to the change and the organisation's resolve?

One can draw a few clues from the DPT, or Dialectical Behaviour Therapy.

People can increase their emotional and cognitive regulation by applying appropriate coping skills in the sequence of events, thoughts, feelings can help avoid adverse reactions. Behaviour modification starts with the assumption that people lack the skills or are influenced by positive or negative reinforcement that interferes with functioning appropriately.

How can managers and leaders cope with changes in the face of chaos and complexity?

Key Ideas: Learning the art of managing and changing contexts, learning how to use minor changes to create significant effects is the butterfly effect. One must be open to noncorporations that can facilitate processes of reorganisation.

Visionary Leader's Mindset

The unique thing about the minds of visionary leaders is flexibility, and they do not take a stand unless convinced. The innovative leader has the skill to make the mindset shift, which supports adaptive behaviour. Their adaptive mindset is deeply ingrained in their belief system, and that impacts their behaviour that is perceptible to others.

Their blind-spot area is tiny. Many leaders can articulate an adaptive mindset. The 360-degree appraisal process can be used in understanding the perception of people. The term 'adaptation' refers to alteration in the physical or behavioural characteristics to establish survival. If an ability to adjust to recent information and experiences is enabled, adaptation is feasible. The essence of learning is essentially altering oneself to a changing environment.

Through transformation, one can exhibit new behaviour that allows one to cope with change.

Leaders are able to balance inquiry (questioning) and advocacy (stating a standpoint or position). They express their assumptions and describe the data that led them; they also explain those assumptions and make their reasoning more explicit.

Visionary leaders take pains to explain the context of their point of view. They refrain from defensiveness when ideas are questioned or challenged. When advocating, they listen, stay open and encourage others to give different opinions. They improve inquiry by walking others through their mental ways or process and finding out which data point they are operating. They stay unaggressive and ask questions in a way that does not provoke defensiveness.

The reasons for inquiring are explained as one's own need for clarifying concerns.

They listen for new viewpoints that may emerge when people are complaining about the outcome of change.

Change leadership requires a conviction that healthy conflicts are necessary and belief that mistakes are learning opportunities. To win people over, change leaders must embrace and encourage critique. Visionary leaders must display their skills to articulate vividly an inspiring view of the future state integrating with sharp business acumen tempered by deep industry and market knowledge through technology understanding, skill in planning and strategic actions.

During the progress of change, the ability to motivate and inspire requires taking charge.

There are necessary steps that leaders need to take charge of the organisation's destiny confidently:

(i) Identify core talents, abilities, competencies, and skills.

(ii) Encourage everyone to do an activity more than anything and care more about one thing. The linkages must be identified to marry vision and values to an individual's professional contribution.

(iii) Identify fears. Fear is a paralyser. "Behold the turtle-that only makes progress when he sticks his neck out!"

(iv) Push forward by continuously asking:
What is keeping me from actively pursuing?
What's the payoff? What's the damage?
Is it a "mistake"? What is blocking?

(v) Name role models, identify the role models' with their supporters' behaviour and identify the network.
Everyone impacted by change must be asking themselves, "Who are the people we trust and admire?
What are their qualities which make them adorable people?
How can we embrace these admired qualities into one's way of being while preserving a sense of self-integrity?
Who are the people look-up to when we need specific measures and the results?"
"If you argue for the limitations, you get to keep them!" said Jonathan Livingston Seagull.
"Indecision is a decision," said James Bryant.

Impactors during change are the cheerleaders, skill builders, and recommenders. Each one must be identified as an influencer. Change champions are challengers, and they must question people who spent over six or seven years in the company. Do not induct new entrants; however senior, the person is in the hierarchy.

(vi) Question what the view of success is, with everyone affected by the change. Many will be confused about success.

Identify what constitutes success. If encouraged properly, people raise questions:

What does success mean?

What does success mean to me?

What does success mean to others around me?

What does success in my job in my profession mean?

What is the definition of success for me by my organisation?

How do I define success in my personal life?

Do I suspect that my definition of success will change as I grow older in the same organisation?

How can I broaden my definition of success?

These introspections trigger the thought process for awareness of the need for change initiatives at personal and organisational levels.

(vii) Identify a coach. Many wonder why one needs a coach. Coaching is essential since the coach is a person who has been there and done it (BTDT). Every participant in change must trust the person who will help them to see the blind spots. Anyone who holds your hand and walks you through dark hours of the career path, aka, a coach, can lead through change.

(viii) Triumph criteria and success must be identified. The success criteria are highly personal, though driven by organisational intentions.

(ix) Spell out action steps. Unless the steps to take are defined, it will be challenging to decide which should be the first item to be tackled on the list out of all those that matter. Not everyone gets support or the well-wishers. It is useful to know whom to rely on. Few people unconditionally support changes in organisational matters. Thus, managers must identify,

Who will be spot lighters?

Who will be esteem builders?

Who will be the link for connecting the dots?

Who will be handling political issues?

(x) Walk the talk. The proper brain exercise of mind-mapping or building a collage on the destination of the profession helps. Map out with words like, "doable, possible today" steps to move forward, call for action.

Give yourself a KITA and take action; any action is better than inaction; most times, it's better to take action and find out if it's a mistake than not taking any step.

(xi) Expand the circle of Influence for change acceleration.

Steven Covey, in his work, differentiates effectiveness from efficiency. While efficiency is merely obsessed with output, effectiveness is about balancing production capability with production.

The concept of expanding the circle of influence by proactive people is useful in change management. The circle of influence works from the inside out, empowering the influence to expand to change those who cannot see the bigger picture due to change.

As Mahatma Gandhi said, "If you want to change something, be part of that change and not be a mere observer." Being principle centred and value-driven enabled Gandhi to influence millions of Indians. However, the change to be successful must be through effective leadership.

An issue that tested his principle and personal philosophy towards life once confronted Gandhi.

A woman follower of Gandhi would attend his ashram (a small, humble hut-like personal residence) with her five-year-old son every day and sit in the front row during the morning prayer. It is common knowledge that in India's state of Gujarat, people eat plenty of sweets. Therefore, almost every special dish is infused with sweetness. One day, Gandhi enquired with the woman that he understood her attendance in the prayer session every day but did not comprehend why she brought her son along.

The woman complained that her son had a medical issue, and requested Gandhi to tell the boy not to eat sweets, so that the diabetic condition of the child could be kept under check.

She complained that her son would listen to Gandhi because he was a prominent leader and not to her own advice.

Gandhi smiled and said nothing at that time. Weeks went by, and after two months, Gandhi called the boy and nicely told him that eating sweets was not suitable for his health, and that he should give it up.

The boy, too, nodded his head in agreement. The boy's mother got curious and asked Gandhi because he took two months to express those simple words of advice. Gandhi replied that for him, it had not been such a simple matter. From the day she had requested for help, Gandhi had stopped eating sweets and tried giving up altogether. Then he realised how difficult it was for a grown-up man like him to give up an old habit. He wanted to experiment with his own willpower to develop conviction before he gave the advice. Once he gave up the habit, he could talk to the child with conviction.

A fine example of principle-centred leadership requires leaders who are eager to change things to be like Gandhi. They should not speak words without conviction. Instead, they must encourage the participants in change processes to ask themselves, "What is that one small but positive act I can put into action today?

Everyone must be in a state of mind to ask, "What two other actions can I do within a defined and reasonable time, e.g., the next 30 days, to move me towards a changed condition?"

It must motivate everyone to, "What are at least two strategies for networking with others (who have something in common with me) that I am comfortable implementing immediately?" How many ways can I continue to expand my Circle of Influence (CI)?"

Transformation Through a Shared Vision

The words "I have a dream!" echoed throughout America and brought change. Whether Martin Luther or Gandhi, their efforts with determination and dedication to the cause changed the nation's mindset. They did not begin with exaggerated promises of material things, like the modern jargon-crazy managers of the corporate. Instead, the leaders converted their dream to a powerful positive future vision and shared that vision with people.

What is a shared vision? Extensive sharing, and not mere statement of the vision, is essential. The vision must be comprehensible to draw a mental picture of that better future state and support it.

The significant purpose of the vision is to generate additional inspiration and energy levels to change the current condition and create a new future.

Managing the Political Process

Whenever human involvement is involved, one cannot escape politics because of power and status mongering. Therefore, depending on the extensiveness of change, one needs to realign the power equation in the organisation.

If the change is more radical or transformational, it must involve the reconfiguration of power centres.

The momentum for change will need powerful lobbying within the organisation, commonly from the chief executive, board members, union and other influential outsiders. In an organisation, a combination of the interest and power of individuals or groups decide to change acceleration; understanding the political context in and around the organisation is essential for successfully achieving change.

A power group and the hidden opposition are the new normal in any organisation.AS we bring along our emotions and insecurities to work, all organisations have the workplace politics.

Members of the organisation are perceived to be on either side. However, the nature of resistance varies according to the industry, sector and size of the organisation.

A similar influence is from the power elite. People are appointed in key positions based on personal loyalty and trust so that control is not lost. Change may be perceived as a threat for existing elites or perpetuation of their rule. They manipulate people, regulations and resources. Successful change implementation requires deeper management of the organisation's politics.

Personal Vision and Shared Vision

Personal vision begins with self-inquiry.

A shared vision emerges when people align their vision with that of the organisation.

Strength and commitment come from an individual's own deepest drives. Shared visions come from a common attitude of caring towards a unique esoteric future. But should visions be based on situation analysis? No.

The right rational way should be aiming for what one truly wants to change in the current climate. The personal vision combines one's abilities, interests, personality, values, goals, skills, experience, family background and stage of mental development.

Self-limiting mental models can weaken creativity and intelligent processes that enable change.

Organisational learning efforts that prepare people's minds to appreciate alternative ways to define problems and seek solutions enables mindset change. In change management, learning to understand the power of shared vision and its importance is essential.

Enabling change is learning to look at something from many angles and ask, "Is there only one way or many alternate ways? How can we collectively develop multiple perspectives? How can we make any difference if we think we can't do it?"

Usually, any existing system in organisations is designed perfectly to produce a current level of results. If the expectation is for different results, keeping the same method with no change is not influencing or enhancing the chances of any other outcome. For example, most governments want poverty to go away. Still, it never goes away because the bureaucracy creates and works on the same systems and processes to address the outcome level.

If we require new results, the existing systems need to change with an elevated level of thinking and mental models, free from fixed mindsets and biases.

"The most pathetic person in the world is someone who has sight, but has no vision," said Helen Keller.

While employees will be concerned with the present, the leadership must focus on the future and build a compelling future image.

"Vision without action is a dream. Action without vision passes the time. Vision with action can change the world," said Joel A Barker. The leaders must examine what self-limiting mental models are blocking the progress and how those hardened mindsets influence the thought processes.

The mental models that limit or choke ambitious aims are those assumptions or beliefs that define what is easier to do or possible, brand it as realistic or achievable, and block what people aspire to.

Many innovations that have become part of every day life are met with stiff resistance from industry leaders that thrive on innovation. The mental models were no different. The motion picture with sound was received this way: "Who the hell wants to hear actors talk?" Harry Warner, Warner Brothers, had declared in 1927 on the launch of motion picture with sound.

A few other predictive mindsets are enumerated here:

"No likelihood exists that man can ever tap the power. If someone did not think differently, the world would have been darker,"

"I think there is a world market for about five computers," said Thomas Watson Jr, founder and chairperson of IBM, 1943.

"Everything that can be invented has been invented," Charles H Duel, Commissioner, US Office of Patents, had urged President William McKinley to abolish the patents office in 1903.

Ford was advised by the then president, Michigan Bank, not to invest in Ford Motor. "Horses are here to stay. The automobile is only a novelty, a fad," he was told.

The advice was not accepted, and he invested USD 5,000, which later became USD 12.5 million. "There is no reason for any individual to have a computer in his home" Ken Olsen, president, Digital Equipment. A successful computer company from 1960 to 1990 declined and soon got acquired by Compaq. Compaq did not understand the new business and ultimately Hewlett-Packard took over Compaq.

Moral is that every change can be trauma unless handled by the leadership effectively.

CASE STUDIES-BUSINESS TRANSFORMATION

Case 1: IT Start-up

This bay area IT services company who was only a speciality skill provider witnessed a steady decline in profits and revenue after a decade of success. It was a worrying sign for the organisation's decline in market share, in the growth market. Any marketing pundit would spell trouble when market share declines in growing market. The company was pushed to do an analysis about the newer market opportunities for repositioning and rebranding.

The outcome was a three-year "strategic change management plan" that, when implemented, would enable them to become category killer in data analytic-BI- segment, reduce operating costs, and realise the long-term business objectives.

The company had on-site and offshore operations in the USA and India.

The employee headcount consisted of 600 full-time staff and another 200 contracted staff. They served more than 1,400 active and semi-active clients across the globe. So, the initiative became imperative for survival and growth. The aspect of the plan was the successful rebranding with existing customers -the replacement of the organisation's 10-year-old heritage. The project began in 2010. The requirements for the initiative were identified as a credible set of reasons for this change. So, they retooled the existing people to fit into change.

Eliminating Resistance Removing Fears: Stakeholder's Communication

The initiatives were implemented across global operations.

A formal process to identify a strong programme manager and set up a PMO was initiated. A conscious decision was taken to look internally. After a thorough internal search, the company selected one who was in a similar role of project management and programme management; the candidate had a sound track record of success, having implemented the many BI projects on time and within budget for multiple clients. In May 2010, the organisation launched the project with widespread excitement and support.

Engineering the Escape: Challenges Emerge

The project kicked off with solid momentum. Project participants were excited about the prospect of a new initiative that would improve the company's ability to serve existing customers and respond to new business with changed offerings.

Though the initial project had gone well, challenges surfaced as employees found difficulty adjusting to their new roles. Nevertheless, everyone feels assured of the project's success.

It wasn't long before the team felt the positive effects of organisation wide change. Almost everyone showed signs of fear and apprehension. A sense of doubt and frustration replaced eagerness and excitement. Employees began questioning "Will this new strategy yield the benefits as envisaged? Is it worth the extra effort?"

Strain bore heavily on staff members: especially on those doing double duty of working on the project while attending to their day-to-day client site responsibilities. In addition, those who absorbed the extra workload of co-workers were preoccupied with the project.

Whether because of miscommunication or a lack of it, the rumour mill churned, and messages were circulated to the indicating, "What if I can't rise in my competency level? Will I retain my job?"

The senior management team had a concern about the general morale. Resources and monetary constraints had forced a decision about not increasing the staff for the PMO.

The CEO doubted about keeping up with daily operations, and a growing sense of job loss threatened the holding of capable staff members.

The programme manager who had created the entire process could only work part-time as his current manager was under pressure to complete the billable assignment. The project timelines appeared shaky and it was clear to the leaders that some step had to be taken.

Seeking Help to Manage Change

After six months, with roughly 20 per cent of the project complete against a target of 40 per cent, the leadership took action to mitigate any further delay risks - time and cost overrun- related to the "human component" of the project.

The first part of this OCM strategy challenge involved finding a replacement for the current billable project assignment because the selected programme management candidate had a dual job role. The HR global director was made a full-time change management consultant.

They initially worked with practice area leads - senior-level managers- to develop an integrated strategy to reach milestones on time and budget. The major task was mapping transition-related risks and having a detailed plan that balanced the need for strong leadership, project management, and change management at all business unit levels.

Re-examine Reasons: Why Change?

Internal perception vs external perception found a wide gap and identified it as the first thing to fix. The message strategy was focused on "Salespeople cannot get better rates unless the customer sees value addition."

Everyone understood that change management exists to help transition from a current business to a new industrial state —IT staffing service provider to BI consulting services, and further up the value chain. As an effective transition exercise in people competency, the consulting and customer engagement skills were identified as skills to manage the people aspect to reposition the category killer.

The second step was to get people on board to participate in reskilling and retooling to focus on the OCM project, allowing creative time to improve, champion the new cause, and develop leadership skills.

When changing the existing organisation structure or processes, people naturally experience anxiety. If not managed well, that anxiety can grow and sabotage the transition.

It was identified as a crucial step for unit-level managers to safeguard. Top leaders were fully aware and appreciated that they are entering into along drawn process.

They armed themselves with a set of new tools and techniques and understood that they couldn't afford to lose patience or steam on the way.

HR was to work on every individual's response to change and determine how group dynamics support or subvert operations. Key manager's and individuals' leadership patterns were identified through data from 360-degree assessment for the previous three years. Knowing specific skills, the manager had displayed, HR could leverage it to determine the style range and adaptablity of sponsors and the influencers.

The first step was to identify the areas of the organisation that are ready for early adoption and those under-prepared or unprepared. With assessing one's strengths and that of the organisational unit and its leadership, HCM recommended simple and powerful skill map to tackle the burden of guesswork to find people who could solve problems. One solution was to take off the responsibility from the shoulders of the executive leadership team. A key message to managers was, "When one is deep-rooted an organisation's culture, it is difficult to see the interconnectedness of issues."

The change management process started with need assessment by using SurveyMonkey for interviewing executive leaders, and holding focus group sessions with staff members both in and outside the project.

The assessment focussed on possible challenges faced by the programme management team.

The need assessment covered several aspects of the company's experience with change that is envisioned. These included past changes.

The point raised was about the past decision of branding transition struggles and the lessons learnt. This implied an absence of continued and consistent internal and external marketing push. If one is not aware of the state of one's systems, how can one expect the change to begin?

If the attempt is to make progress, it cannot be piecemeal, and done through ad hoc approaches. Alignment of the organisation to change programme, vision, and goals is inevitable. The data gathered aided one to begin an organisational redesign - this was achieved through a project to define the current state of the organisation's layers, and was followed by a discussion to create new structures. Execution steps were also clarified to establish and prescribe a new organisation chain of command.

As is common in organisations that make small incremental changes, organisational structure rarely is re-assessed and revamped. It was a key challenge for HCM. Strengths and weaknesses (SWOT) analysis needs to be done by the executive and unit-level team managers. This information is vital to identify the strengths required for successful project implementation. It draws up a realistic baseline for all interventions and established powers. The individuals feel recognised and can see how they can champion the new environment. Understanding the root cause that lead to weaknesses revels the perspective of on the current ways of operating.

Findings from the Needs Assessment

The assessment identified numerous issues that contributed to staff's low morale and the difficulty of the transition. Those issues included:

1. **Lack of Resources:** Decisions not to staff-up for the project because of budget created obstructions, which had negative consequences as the project progressed.

They were not adequately distributing decision-making authority among managers. Managers were pre-occupied with operational work with no time for managing change.

2. **Lack of (or Errors in) Communication:** A few essential resources were aware of the entire scope of the OCM project; but no sharing of timelines happened.

    The grape wine was active while people assumed things and spread rumours about the whole motive.

    There were no proper standards to support continuous and ongoing two-way communication between project leadership - PMO and the organisation.

    Not enough communication went through regarding change project development and daily department issues.

3. **Inconsistency:** The inconsistent decisions by local managers who did not know where to go was the next reason.

    Leadership had difficulty in working as a united front, whether a single leader or collective leadership. Employees move from one manager to another until they get an answer, and they end up wasting time.

4. **Delayed Decision-making:** It took too long to make decisions because many practice area leads understood the "why" behind some processes but knew "how" they got to work for change.

    Time was in short supply always to explain every decision. Managers tried to procrastinate and held on to their existing power within the current structure. Delays cost more money, and time was spent in non-crucial activities.

5. **Negative Attitudes:** Documentation proved to be too technical, intimidating targets and deadlines. The frustration of being left out of important meetings added to the neglect. The belief was only "key people" got to know.

6. **Perception Over Reality:** The employees were uncertain of their future, not being rewarded for taking on more work, not made aware of the training support and the cost. Who could bear such a thing?

7. **Lack of Buy-in:** Leaders always feared that they were sabotaging the project.

8. **Loss of SMEs / Lack of Knowledge Transfer:** Most PALs didn't fully understand the "why" of change. Without proper guidance for the personal transition, many Practice Area Leads felt threatened about their position in the organisation and their jobs. In addition, champions of the project were tired of battling the resistors.

Strategies

After identifying the challenges and risks, the project leaders went along to design and implement the strategic change management plan. Based upon the needs assessment survey they initiated a three-pronged strategy for eliminating the challenges and moving forward.

Those key areas are summarised below.

Prepare local Leadership for early adoption

The key initial step is to groom the leadership team to lead the organisation through the transition and overcome the new challenge.

Preparation

Leadership training for managing transition throughout the life cycle of the project was initiated. A tool called LPI, or Leadership Practices Inventory was used. Leadership skill and team development plans, for utilising the project for organisation-wide improvement, communication skills and a comprehensive communication plan were developed.

One worked with the local project sponsors to take a more active role.

Immediate Outcome

The leadership team were propelled by the vision while actively exploring individual members' strengths and using the strengths to advance unified team effort.

Leadership development sessions and coaching continued for the project's duration, unfolding extra levels of leadership staff as they created a new organisation structure and implemented many changes.

In addition, they provided change management training to principals / engagement managers.

Armoured employee programme-evaluation dates and tools were kept ready. Initial briefing sessions for all at all locations were completed.

Organisational Redesign

The second step was to carry out a restructuring process. The change management strategy included restructuring the organisation to create a new structure that allowed to match the organisation's agility to the latest market offerings - solutions than services-focused solutions- for three verticals. A subject matter expert or SME to fill the competency gap was also hired.

Managers were also urged to reorganise to build subject knowledge, create career paths and execute succession planning.

The strategy also included clearly defining the chain of command and adding several layers above principals. The structure distributed the decision-making among leaders to be more responsive and agile in the changing skill landscape.

It precisely defined employee roles and responsibilities, performance measures, career paths, opportunities, and ongoing training requirements. The organisation also decided that future salary hikes would have incentive plans for growth across five levels of competency.

Outcome

Realisation dawned that without a change in building an entirely new BI (Business Intelligence) solution, there was no point in tinkering around with the existing offerings.

The new model was timely to reassess the organisation structure.

It had placed a reorganised structure that allowed the domain's expertise to be more alert in managing market positioning and to develop specialists.

Over Communicate.

Another facet of the change strategy is in building robust channels for two-way communication between employees and leaders. For example, regular, monthly, all-hands staff meetings with mid-month "stand-up" staff meetings were implemented.

A change network group that monitored the change management activities had acted as a communication conduit.

An in-house newsletter was created for sharing project information, that kept staff abreast of project developments, change management activities and other important information.

Result

As steps were implemented, there were more ways to involve staff members in planning, developing, and implementing the change plan which increased morale. Staff members felt a part of the mission with a clear stake in the project's mission success. They knew "why and not the how" which made all the difference by reducing misinformation and wild rumours. Many employees were seeking opportunities to participate in competency development. The staff members were aligned in their career goals. The company is now on the verge of a bright future as an agile, aligned organisation, equipped with BI solutions in three verticals that meet the strategic business objectives for years to come. They are closer than ever before reaching their CEO's vision of each staff member seeing themselves as "a genuine BI consultant". The company emerged as a category killer in the data analytic segment.

Gartner's magic quadrant identified the business as the fastest-growing BI boutique in 2012.

As for the gains to many employees, the experience of adding competency to manage programmes for change became a significant achievement given the success of the programme. With formal OCM programmes, every manager who championed the cause can now offer clients a comprehensive BI service. People speak of their new capabilities through genuine HCM efforts. Everyone believes change management is vital for every organisation and that static organisations never stay alive for long. However, responsible people know that responsible leadership will not willingly let that happen.

Model for Employee Empowerment: Integrated HCM and OCM-armoured Employee

In the Hollywood movie *Rambo*, starring Sylvester Stallone, the character played by Stallone becomes a one-person army skilled with many forms of combat survival skills. The character was trained in handling AK47s, grenades, bows and arrows, practising hand combat and guerrilla warfare. This character inspired the creation of the model for transformation. It changed competency by developing high-level consulting skills in BI and armouring them with different connected skills. The model of armoured employee was created as a support mechanism for the transformation management programme.

Any change initiative cannot succeed without a concurrent formal structured competency building strategy to meet new skill needs when the business transforms.

The transformation model answered two crucial questions that would come out during the introduction stage of the change initiative:

1. What is in it for me?
2. How do I cope with changes if I do not have the skills?

This armoured employee model provided answers to the issues leading to resistance to change initiatives by addressing the change initiatives, skill and competency gaps.

Instead of telling the people about lack of consulting skills, we initiated steps to assess everyone, including the managers in pre-defined skills. For every level, there was pre-defined weightage for skills.

We defined the organisational maturity as lifting the individuals in the organisation to progress gradually from Level 1 to Level 5

We defined the learning and competency development model through five levels of competency maturity and growth path:

Level 1: Squirrel

These included the following kinds of people:

Those with competency domination in one dimension.

People with mainly technical skills in software coding, tool maintenance, and database administration.

Employees with three to four years of experience in software development database or software tools maintenance and support. They needed to install, configure tools and have some basic knowledge of project management as well as conceptual understanding of BI tools and data management. They may have low ability to capture customers' requirements holistically and without consulting skills.

Assessment scores should be below 35 per cent in six of the seven dimensions

Level 2: Steward

They should have competency in technical project management and have technical problem-solving skills. They should have a moderate level of customer-facing skills and no consulting skills.

Anyone who scored in the assessment below 45 per cent in five of the seven dimensions was labelled this way.

Level 3: Crusader

They should have competency in technical project management, account management, average consulting skills, below-average sales skills.

Around 55 per cent in four areas may be at knight level in one of the seven dimensions — an assessment score at 85 per cent.

Level 4: Knight

They should have competency in client management, account management and can generate new business through superior diagnostic skills for the customer, as well as above-average consulting skills. They should have high-level problem-solving skills.

Assessment score should be 65 per cent in five areas. Should have an overall score of above 80 per cent.

Level 5: Fellow

Should have high competency in consulting skills, programme management and can make consulting sales. Can convert existing business to large scale, and have an overall score of 95 percent or above in six of seven dimensions.

Each consultant is to be assessed after they complete the requisite number of courses every year.

These courses would be:
Support systems: Prescriptive career guidance plan or PCGP, which describes the path to progress oneself from Level 1 to Level five.
Web-based training aids: 250 pre-recorded video / audio courses across seven dimensions-learning target 40 hours per quarter - used external programmes selectively.

Assessment canter-annual assessment-online:
180 questions in 100 minutes. No negative marking. No pass-fail.
The cut-off score for each level is different.
Difficulty increases with every section of questions.

Project Planning.

This would include the following steps:
Analysis of gaps that exist between the current state and the anticipated state.
The process steps to review the progress of changes.
Impact analysis of a change.
Knowhow of change management processes used in the past.
The list of key stakeholders.
Change management tools.
Project monitoring / scheduling the change programme.
Information requirements to change requests.
Estimated schedule changes.

The information included in a project plan.

Techniques to prioritise changes.

Define change failure indicators.

Lessons learnt when a change attempt fails.

Crucial change management leadership issues.

Leadership style adaptability for changes.

Leader behaviour during a change when the requirements aren't known; dealing with ambiguity.

Leader behaviour during change when the impact of the change is unclear.

Leadership in dealing with resistance to change.

The oratory reflecting in communication skills.

The articulation of strategies to counter resistance to change.

The competency to convince people about benefits.

The commitment to ascertain that all stakeholders are informed at each step of the process.

Leadership in ensuring trust through transparency across the organisation.

Risk management.

Risk assessment plan.

Skill to differentiate between constraint and a risk.

Sample list of risks (in change management).

List of high risks areas.

Prioritised risk management order..

Metrics to be used to measure risk.

The quality of output in change management tasks.

Review methods of time and cost overruns.

Quality strategy for improvement.

Metrics to be used to measure quality level and cost of quality.

Benchmarks, best practices or methodologies for change management.

Improvements to the change management process.

List of soft skills and benefits.

Influencing actions that will convince team members, which can accelerate change.

Envision: The ability to look at the grand picture and create organisation affinity.

Empower: Coaching and hand holding-created sense of caring.

Enlist: The ability to mobilise support. Can enable team spirit.

Encourage: Recognising, applauding. Can motivate and accelerate change.

Motivate: Skill to influence with appreciation and reward. Can accelerate change.

Constant feedback to every member to create a change of heart.

Give presentations to large audiences and create confidence.

Manage political obstacles to change and thereby eliminate resistance.

Quick, timely and complex decision-making to eliminate setbacks.

Manage a stakeholder expectation to create fulfilment.

Case 2: The British Airways

The never-ending problem of change and transformation at British Airways is one everlasting lesson that positive change results once achieved cannot replicated. It is because the shift cannot be a one-time exercise or one dimensional.

Transformation of BA was a massive project of change that lasted 12 years and involved complex steps, far more than mere structural change. Marshall rode a rough ride in BA when he was staring at an enormous loss of GBP 140 million per year, and BA even earned the nickname of "Bloody Awful" airline. Passenger associations rated BA as the first airline to avoid.

That image has lasted till today; British Airways has slowly developed a negative image as the least preferred, most under-performing and unprofitable international carrier. Redeeming an organisation from this rotten state to a profitable and admired airline was more difficult than climbing Mount Everest and a risky task for any CEO. BA needed someone similar to Lee Iacocca, who led Chrysler out of trouble. The transformation involved mainly work culture transformation and change in every operational area within the airline, besides courageous leadership to drive these changes.

Margaret Thatcher was the prime minister; she took a bold step and assigned the task to John King, the chairman, to find the most suitable candidate. King picked Marshall to head BA. John King took up immediately the cost-cutting, and Marshall started rebuilding the airline's image and reshaping its customer service. They strongly agreed that BA to turn around with these steps. King initiated harsh measures such as resizing, modernising the fleet, eliminating unprofitable routes and making marketing agreements with other foreign airlines. Marshall went after wooing back the lost customers and restoring employee morale.

The supervisors in BA earned a scandalous reputation as "balcony management", which needed a different tone. Marshall, an influential leader and a better fit for driving the culture shift in the organisation, was troubled by bureaucratic muddles.

Virgin Atlantic, the rival airline, was rapidly gaining ground at the time, and it posed major threat as an emerging competitor. The questions raised at the behest of Lord King. were, "Will British pride allow that?".

BA resorted to a few tricks to kill competition, which were mere "dirty tricks", aka, campaigns to malign Virgin Atlantic. However, they merely earned substantial legal penalties. The way to kill competition is through three positive methods:

1. There should be quality focus. Earlier, we talked about the six-sigma standard ISO and TQM, embracing one model is crucial to ensure zero defect.
2. Secondly, hunger to provide exceptional customer service at every level, and it is a cultural development issue.
3. The third is having the best user-friendly website and effective social media management. Many companies only parade their senior team and their biodata on their website. No customer ever got interested in that. Make it sleek and simple.

BA's worldwide operations needed massive modernisation. The plan consisted of multi-dimensional decisions on cost-cutting, downsizing, aircraft fleet replacement, improved infrastructure, e.g., computerised reservations systems, hub and spoke operations.

Priority was given to decentralisation, resetting of pricing, revamping terminal facilities and creating an exclusive Terminal 4 at Heathrow. The re-branding of the airline's classes of service was a significant decision. Delegation of decision-making power to line managers was one of the change initiatives.

The performance management system got reworked to focus on management bonuses to measure customer service.

In addition, strategic alliances, mergers and acquisitions, were initiated, strengthening the position of the airlines at Heathrow Airport.

The attitude of the airline's employees was not helpful, as they were all casual and indifferent. Moreover, the philosophy of senior managers was one of arrogance, and even managers considered customers as a nuisance. Everyone knows that excepting the government employees, private companies cannot afford this attitude.

The biggest challenge for Marshall was to redefine and reinforce British Airways' business priorities to refocus on customer service as the turnaround strategy. Marshall diagnosed that the lazy, conservative belief and the attitude of employees needed change. They were to look differently at their role in British Airways, their jobs, and their day-to-day conduct with customers.

The national airlines of every country reward their employees for ensuring on-time performance. United Airlines staff made the right call to delay a connecting flight for a passenger who wanted to see his dying mother before she passed away.

Quality customer service was what BA needed, and Marshall established the norm that staff must stick to quality as service attitude.

The major steps towards the transformation were changing the organisation's culture.

A bold step was taken to downsize the headcount by 40 per cent. The culture change comprised several retooling initiatives towards customer handling and cost-consciousness, and Marshall's "led from the front" style sped up the moves.

He totally detested armchair leadership and demonstrated his unique style of being hands-on. He flew hundreds of miles to be with the ground staff initiative, flight crew and cabin crew and travelled in coach-class or off-load himself from the flight based on seat demand.

He attended nearly all training session on "Managing People First" session. Marshals would never miss the event scheduled every Friday afternoon, with a no holds barred question answer session with the participants. If he did not make it, he would call for the meeting in the boardroom without fail.

Sharing the lunch table with the employees, the leader established trust, which drove them to love their leader.

The culture change initiatives and programmes lasted from 1983 to 1995. They included continuous solid and consistent training interventions across the organisation, with each programme focusing on a customer-first approach. Change is all about the leadership challenge.

Not every CEO or chairperson can be like Marshall but they can learn to become one.

Colin Marshall later became the chairperson of the board, replacing Lord King.

Robert Ayling was promoted to the CEO's job. Thus, even when BA was termed a sick airline, the culture change initiatives continued until the trend was reversed.

The airline's finances had to become healthy, and it earned the reputation as the most favoured carrier for international travel by business travellers. Customers voted BA as the dream airline that most college graduates would work for. BA became the second most admired airline in Europe by 2000.

These results were not the outcome of culture change that Marshall led but came from a systems approach that saw many changes implemented over 13 years. A robust change management strategy worked, and BA became profitable as per the plan.

A hard-hitting communication strategy laid out the reasons for the restructuring and privatisation to enable escape to the future. Strong leadership steered BA through a hard time that could have otherwise turned into a disaster. However, the changes were not permanent as BA lost the effect of change initiatives and soon faced the crisis.

Single attempt to change however massive is not a permanent solution.

REFERENCES

A

Ackoff, *A Concept of Corporate Planning*. Wiley Interscience, 1969.

Adler Mortimer Jerome, *Dialectic*, p 4. Routledge, 2000.

Alan Dix, Janet Finlay et al., *Human-computer Interaction*, 3rd edition. Hertfordshire UK, Prentice-Hall, Europe.

Anand Adhikari, YES Bank, said 'Yes' to all bad boys of Indian banking'. *Business Today*, 6 March 2020.

Alan Cooper, *About Face: The Essences of User Interface Design*. IDG Books, Foster City CA, 1995.

Ann Menninger, Suzanne Hidi, Andreas Krap, *The Role of Interest in Learning and Development*, 1st edition. Psychology Press, 2015.

B

Barton Laurence, *Crisis in Organisations: Managing and Communicating in the Heat of Chaos*. South-Western Publishing, 1993.

Bryan, 'The Coming Revolution in Issues Management: Elevate and Facilitate', Communication System, 15 July 1997.

Bruno G Bara, *Cognitive Science - A Developmental Approach to the Simulation of the Mind*. Hove UK: Lawrence Erlbaum Associates, 1995.

Barings Case Study. *Risk.com*, February 2004; *ERisk*, May 2004.

Bendaley Nicole, Three Things the Most Effective Leaders Will Do In 2021, Forbes, January 3, 2021

Branch Melville; The Corporate Planning Process; American Management Association, 1962.

Bryan Smith, *The Dance of Change: The Challenges to Sustaining Momentum in Learning Organisations*. Doubleday, New York, 1999.

Bunce Dr Peter, "Transforming Financial Planning in Small and Medium-sized Companies." **Beyond** Budgeting Round Table, 2007. Drucker, Peter. Hope and Fraser, 2003

Bunge Mario Augusto, 'A critique of dialectics. *Scientific Materialism*, Episteme 9, pp 41-63, Kluwer Academic Publishers, Dordrecht, Boston, 1981.

Bunge Mario Augusto, 'Evaluating Philosophies'. *Boston Studies in the Philosophy of Science*, pp 295, New York, 2012.

C

Charles Duhigg and Keith Bradsher Jan, *How the US Lost Out on iPhone Work*. New York,2012.

Craik KJW, *The Nature of Justification*. Cambridge University Press, Cambridge, UK, 1943.

Champy and Nitin Nohria, *Fast Forward: The Best Ideas on Managing Change*. McGraw-Hill, New York, 1996.

'Challenging Resistance to Change'. *Journal of Chuck Williams, Management, Innovation and Change*, Chapter 7.

D

'Dialectic', AMCIS 2001 Proceedings. 383, http://aisel.aisnet.org/amcis 2001/383, 2001.

Drucker, 'Planning for Uncertainty'. *Wall Street Journal*, 22 July 1992.

Dronke, *A History of Twelfth-Century Western Philosophy*, Phil Papers 1988 p198.

E

Elwell Frank W, 'C. Wright Mills on the Power Elite', 1966 Wikipedia.

F

Faulkner Christine, *The Essence of Human-computer Interaction*. Prentice-Hall, Hempstead, UK, 1998.

Craig Fearon, 'The Budgeting Nightmare'. *CMA Management*, May 2000.

Ference Marton, Shirley A Booth, *Learning and Awareness*. L Erlbaum Associates, 1997.

G

G Gigerenzer, in *International Encyclopaedia of the Social & Behavioural Sciences*, 2001.

Gordon, Kim Under Fire: Will a Crisis Take Your Company Down? Here's How Deft Handling Can Turn Public Opinion Around'. *Entrepreneur*, April 2001.

Gorski, 'A Blueprint for Crisis Management: Understanding What It Takes to Weather the Inevitable Storm'. *Association Management*, January 1998.

Gentner and Albert L Stevens, ed, *Mental Models*. Lawrence Erlbaum Associates, Hillsdale, NJ, 1983.

Gribbons William M, *Knowledge-Infused Design (The "Ultimate Solution" to Product Usability*. Help 99 Proceedings, November 1999.

H

How Leeson Broke the Bank'. *BBC Online*, 22 June 1999

Hampton John J, *AMA Management Handbook*, 3rd ed, New York, 1994.

Hajdamach Charles R, Jane Shadel Spillman, Thomas P Dimitroff, Frederick Carder and Steuben Glass, *American Classics Book*. Corning Museum 1998.

Haynes, *John, Philosophical Foundations of a Dialectical Analysis as a Research Methodology: Transformation of the Self in Hegel's Dialectic*. AMICIS 2001, Proceedings 383.

Hix, HR Hartson, *Developing User Interfaces: Ensuring Usability Through Product & Process*. John Wiley & Sons, Inc., New York, 1993.

Hope, Jeremy, Robin Fraser, Peter Bunce, and Franz Roosi, "Beyond Budgeting". Round Table, 2009.

I

Irvine, Robert B. 'What's a Crisis, anyway?' *Communication World*, 15 July 1997.

IBM Corporation, *"Object-Oriented Interface Design: IBM Common User Access Guidelines"*. 1992.

J

Jack B ReVelle, *Quality Essentials: A Reference Guide from A to Z*, pp 8–9. ASQ Quality Press, 2004. James W. *The Principles of Psychology*. Holt, New York, 1990.

Jones, Sue. 'Choosing Action Research'. *Organisational Analysis and Development: A Social Construction of Organisational Behaviour*, Ian Mangham, ed, pp 23-45. John Wiley & Sons, Ltd., 1986.

Joydeep Ghosh, Sebi lifts ban on seven brokers, *Business Standard*, September 2013.

Johnson-Laird, *Mental Models - Towards a Cognitive Science of Language, Inference and Consciousness*. Harvard University Press, Cambridge, MA, 1983.

K

Keating, Lauren. "'Proactive Approach Minimises Damage to Image'. *Atlanta Business Chronicle*, 10 November 2000.

Karen E Klein, 'Better Business Through Budgeting'. *Business Week*, 19 January 2006.

Knowledge @wharton. Scandal at Satyam: Truth, Lies and Corporate Governance. Wharton, 9 January 2009.

Kolb, DA RE Boyatzis and C Mainemelis, 'Experiential learning theory: Previous research and new directions. *In Perspectives on Cognitive, Learning, and Thinking Styles,* Sternberg and Zhang, eds. Lawrence Erlbaum, NJ, 2000.

Kolb, *D. A. Experiential Learning: Experience as the Source of Learning and Development*. Prentice-Hall, New Jersey, 1984.

L

Lise Alves, http:// riotimesonline.com/Brazil-news/Rio-business/Brazil-"petrobras-registers-highest-net-loss-in-history; 22 March 2016.

M

Managing Change and Transition. Harvard Business School Press, Boston, 2003.

Marginson, David and Stuart Ogden, 'Budgeting and Innovation: Do Budgets Stifle Creativity?' *Financial Management*, April 2005.

Markham, *Arthur B, Knowledge Representation*. Lawrence Erlbaum Associates, Mahwah, NJ, *1999*

McKeon, Richard (October 1954) 'Dialectic and Political Thought and Action', Ethics 65 (1): 1–33. October 1954.

Medin and Ross, *Douglas). Cognitive Psychology*, 2nd edition. 1996, Amazon.

Mayhew, *Deborah J. (1999); The Usability Architecting Life Cycle: Morgan Kaufmann.*Sanfrancisco 1999.

Morgan, *Images of Organisation*, Chapter 8. Sage Publications, Thousand Oaks, CA, 1997.

Mueller, *The Hegel Legend of Thesis-Antithesis-Synthesis*, Philosophy Journal of history of ideas, p 166. June 1958.

N

Nielsen j, *Usability Architecting*. The Diego California Academic Press, 1993.

Norman, *Donald (1988). The Design of Everyday Things*. Doubleday/ Currency, New York, 1988.

O

Obert, *S.L "The Development of Organisational Task Groups*. Case Western Reserve University, PhD dissertation, 1979.

P

Patterson, 'Crises Impact on Reputation Management'. *Public Relations Journal*, November 1993.

Peirce Hector, 'AIG's Collapse: The Part Nobody Likes to Talk About'. *American Banker*, 16 June 2014.

Postan Michael M 'Function and Dialectic in Economic History'. *The Economic History Review*, 14 (3): 397–407, April 1962.

Preece Jenny, *Human-computer Interaction*. Addison-Wesley, Reading MA, 1994.

PJ Paul Whalen et al., *A Functional MRI Study of Human Amygdala Responses to Facial Expressions of Fear Versus Anger, Emotion,* National Library of medicine abstract, Vol 1: No 1 70-1983. March 2001.

Purser Ronald E., and Steven Cabana, 'Mobilising Large-Scale Strategic Change: An Application of the Search Conference Method at Xerox' 19/10 1996.

R

Rebecca J Compton, *Behavioural and Cognitive Neuroscience Review,* Advances in Cognitive Science Sage Vol 2 No 2, pp 115-129.June 2003.

Reale, Giovanni. (1990), *History of Ancient Philosophy,* five vols, John R. Catan, Vol 2, p 150. Albany State University of New York, 1990.

Robert J Ristino, *The Agile Manager's Guide to Managing Change.* Velocity Business Publishing, Bristol, VT.2000

James Reason, *Human Error.* Cambridge University Press, Cambridge, UK, 1990.

Reason, 'Tim; Building Better Budgets'. *CFO,* December 2000.

Rescher, *Nicholas (2007). Dialectics: A Classical Approach to Inquiry.* Ontos Verlag, New Brunswick; Frankfurt, 2007.

Rabbi Nachman's Stories, Rabbi Arya Kaplan, tr. Breslov Research Institute, Jerusalem, 1985.

Rogers, Yvonne, Andrew Rutherford, and Peter Bibby, ed, *Models in the Mind - Theory, Perspective, and Application.* Academic Press, London, 1992.

S

Scharmer, Theory U: Learning from the Future as it Emerges. Berrett-Koehler Publishers, 2009.

Shabdita Pareekh, "Arjuna's Bird's Eye Test Teaches Us How We Should Set Our Priorities Right & Chase Our Goals", Life. November 18, 2015.

Scharmer and K Kaufer, *Leading from the Emerging Future: From Ego-System to Eco-System Economies.* Berrett-Koehler Publishers, 2013.

Sears Andrew, *An Introduction to Human-computer Interaction.* DePaul University, Chicago, 1997.

'Seven Ways to Greet a Neighbour'. *Ask Asia*, 2009; Archived from the original on 11 May 2009. Retrieved
3 May 2009.

Sims Ronald, *Changing the Way We Manage Change*. Prager, Westport, CT, 2002.Senge, Peter M Senge, Art Kleiner, Charlotte Roberts, George Roth, Rick Ross and

Simms j, 'Controlling a Crisis'. *Marketing*, 9 November 2000.

Stephanie Smith and Kim Hunter, 'Virgil Scudder Tackles Crisis Tactics'. *Communication World*, February 1997.

'Small Business Budgets and Budgeting'. *National Federation of Independent Business*, 2009.

Shneiderman, *Ben (1998). Designing the User Interface: Strategies for Effective Human-computer Interaction*, 4th edition. Addison-Wesley, Reading, MA, 1998.

Schneider William, *The Re-engineering Alternative: A Plan for Making Your Culture Work*. McGraw Hill, 1999.

Starkman Dean, 'AIG's Other Reputation'. *Washington Post*, 21 August 2005.

Springs Marta, *The Art of Dialectic between Dialogue and Rhetoric: The Aristotelian Tradition*. Controversies. 9, 2011.

(This book reconstructs the tradition of dialectic from Aristotle's Topics, its founding text, up to its 'renaissance' in 16th century Italy, and focuses on the role of dialectic in the production of knowledge.)

Steven H Appelbaum, Sally Habashy, Jean-Luc Malo, Shafiq Hisham, 'Back to the Future: Revisiting Kotter's 1996 Change Model'. *Journal of Management Development*, Vol 31 Iss: 8, pp 764-82, 2012.

Susman, *Gerald I; "An Action Research: A Sociotechnical Systems Perspective*, G Morgan, ed, pp 95-113. Sage Publications, London, 1983.

Stacy Conradt, 'How Barbra Streisand Inspired the Streisand Effect'. *Mental Floss*, 18 August 2015.

T

Therese Borchard, '5 Tips for Managing Anxiety During Transition'. Every day Health October 2016.

Tilson James and Robert E Prasch, 'It Was Not a Free Lunch: The True Cost of the AIG Bailout'. *Neweconomicperspectives.org*, 24 January 2013.

Trist Eric, 'A Concept of Organisational Ecology'. *Australian Journal of Management Vol2*, 1977.

U

Uri Gneezy, Stephan Meier, and Pedro Rey-Biel. When and why incentives don't work to modify behaviour, *Journal of Economic Perspectives*, Vol 25, No 4, pp 191–210, Fall 2011.

V

Varela, HR Maturana and R Uribe, *Autopoiesis and Cognition: Realisation of the Living,* Springer Science and Business Media, Boston Studies in the philosophy of science 1928.

Van De Ven Poole Marshall Scott, 'Alternative Approaches for Studying Organisational Change' September 2005.

W

Wharton, University of Pennsylvania website 'Europe's Financial reforms: What are the Next Big Changes?', knowledge @Wharton, February 2016.

Williams Chuck, *Management*, 7th edition. Butler University.

Wilson Stephanie Mathilde Bekker, Peter Johnson and Hilary Johnson, *Helping and Hindering.* 27 March **1997**; Computer Sciences; Proceedings of the ACM SIGCHI Conference on Human factors in computing systems

GLOSSARY OF OCM TERMS

Brief explanations are given to facilitate an easy understanding of the jargons which are used in this book. These terminologies have contextual meaning different from the generic dictionary meaning.

Many of these terms have broader or slightly different meanings beyond OCM theory. Clarifications of these generic meanings can be found in the business dictionary and in Nudge Theory.

Accessibility: This is about the reach and the efficiency of the change communication message. It refers to the intensity to which the target group understands the message's intent and how the audience experiences the news.

The principle is simple and similar to the concept of reach in marketing. Regardless of the cleverness of the communication and the intervention itself, if only 10 percent of the audience experiences the emotions of the message, the communication will not work well. Likewise, it may not be effective if the intervention has 100 per cent reach with even multiple attempts.

Anchoring Bias: The normal human tendency is to rely on the most recent information, however non-relevant it may be. The tendency is to anchor decisions around first information.

Analytic: Method developed to analyse raw data. However, it has become a science examining unorganised data to conclude what the raw data conveys.

Data analytics focuses on inferring and deriving a conclusion.

Anchoring and Adjustment: A standard method of approximation or estimation of an unknown character or description of strange something by using similar perceived and prior reference as a basis for the guesswork.

Audience: In any communication effort, those receiving a message or getting informed are the target of an intervention.

Automatic Systems: It is a natural way human beings sense, though often irrational, instinctive, and unhelpful instead of thoughtful or 'System Two' thinking.

(System 1 operates automatically and quickly, with little or no effort and no sense of voluntary control. System 2 allocates attention to the effortful mental activities that demand it, including complex computations.)

Autopoiesis: A process by which a system, organism, or organisation produces and replaces its components and distinguishes from the environment.

Availability: Availability refers to the perceived scarcity or abundance. People assess the unknown in terms of credibility and social acceptance as a thumb rule. A broad alternative meaning is "visibility" or "commonness".

Bench Mark: A 19th century term used when land surveyors cut into the stone to secure measuring equipment. The modern meaning measures against a standard, usually the best in class or best practices to improve.

Bias: A firm adherence to a particular thought, taking a position and exhibiting the behaviour. We can call it prejudice. Our inclination and preference are based on our biases. Bias gets established by our own "subjective social reality" from our perceptions; our view of the world shows the behaviour. Much of what is registered in our brain comes through inputs from the culture. Besides the culture, race, gender, religion and sexual orientation creates biases.

Big Data: The Internet has generated extensive data sets structured and unstructured and too large and complex to manipulate with standard methods or tools. Yet, organisations use data to make informed, reliable, robust decisions. Volume, variety, and velocity are defining dimensions of big data, while veracity is a recent addition.

Business process Re-engineering: It is the act of recreating a core business process with the goal of improving product output, quality, or reducing costs. Typically, it involves the analysis of company workflows, finding processes that are sub-par or inefficient, and figuring out ways to get rid of them or change them. **Jul 18 2019**

The Butterfly Effect: This is a fascinating concept. The chaos theory describes this phenomenon as follows. Even a tiny event or change to a completely unrelated thing or condition can impact large, complex systems in simple language. The term might have originated from a novel thought about how a butterfly's flapping of wings in distant South America could create a storm in Texas, implying that even the tiniest influence on one part of a system can affect another part.

In a broader sense, the effect is a way of explaining how unaccounted elements can cause instability for large systems and remain impossible to predict with accuracy because too many unknown variables come into play.

Choice: Alternates or multiple options or events which One faces at decision points, preference of which may lead to a pleasant or unpleasant outcome.

Choice Architect /Architecture: Individuals and Organisations deploy nudge theory to design choices and influence people for change management. Choice architecture refers to the role of a leader, someone with authority who uses the entire range of heuristics (Process or methodology) in designing choices for people to adapt. This term has double interpretations: it also refers to stimulus-response compatibility, or in a broad sense, a system of options designed for people when initiating change.

The Choice Design: A core idea to the principle of Developing and initiating any interventions, it offers choices and free selection from the option. This includes the option of not deciding. Choice design is the responsibility of choice architect.

This concept is exploited by marketing and advertising professions and legal contracts (small print) designed to fool consumers.

Compliance: This implies strictly falling in line with legal provisions or industry-wide best practices and established rules, standards, laws and business practices.

Compliance Audit: Verification and validation by qualified professionals on the conformance to prescribed or adopted standards. Relevant to an activity or practice defined by a government regulatory authority, such as ISO, or accounting disclosures, etc.

Corporate Governance.

The good methods either prescribed by law or anyone who has expertise in running the business. It aims to assure the interest of all stake holders.

Clean Language: Somewhat related to Nudge. It is a methodology about the way communications are worded. Clean language can dramatically affect how meanings and moods are generated. Conforming refers to herd mentality, and in change management, relates to the tendency for people to adhere to familiar norms rather than sticking their necks out. Normal human tendency is driven by survival instinct, forcing one to align oneself to a bigger group, avoiding confrontation and risk.

It causes affirmation and a sense of safety through strength in larger numbers. It's an enormously significant feature of social and group behaviour without which there could be no social events, no religion, no political rally, religious gathering, etc.

Dashboard: An aeroplane pilot has various instruments on the panel that give visible data to decide, a dashboard is a visual executive information system that offers a set of customisable windows and data portals. The dashboard provides relevant and precise details that are helpful to decision-makers. The display is available on a dashboard, about various types of company-specific operational information.

Delayed Gratification: A way of resistance to temptation. People may postpone satisfaction for more significant rewards later. The lack of ability to resist temptation or delay gratification is a human weakness. People who invest in shares for the long term exhibit this behaviour. We usually are habituated to delay better gratification of health through laziness.

Default: Option of no action or decision in any computer setup. Default is the box unchecked. People effortlessly get into 'default' to inaction or indecision to change. If no decision is offered, the change progress can be slow. 'Opt in' and 'Opt-out' options are indispensable to change readiness surveys. Need assessment surveys therefore, cannot leave any action choices.

Design of Choice: choice design and design of choice have the same meaning; refers explicitly to architecting communications, creating different types of cues and interventions. The 'choice architect' or the plan offers helpful options to be easy to comprehend and follow.

Econs: We refer to imaginary people. The new paradigm of economics was developed to counter traditional theories based on rational human behaviour. For example, leaders and politicians represent a society and leaders and governments imagine being economists, but society consists of normal 'humans' with natural weaknesses. Econs think logically and rationally.

Empathy: Empathy is the ability to understand the receiver's mind. Active listening does not involve quick judgement while in communications. Leadership to practise empathetic listening when the audience's mood, personality, and needs influence what is understood from what is spoken. Overcoming resistance is easy when empathy is shown.

Escape Velocity: In change management, implementation plans to generate a minimum threshold level of speed to get out of the past, as a rocket needs the speed to escape gravity while propelling to a higher orbit.

Facilitation: It's a technique that is a profound concept by which we can help people think and decide, based on personal needs at suitable stages of change progress and during a process of engagement.

Fear: It is generated by loss aversion. It can substantially influence opinion and choices, and cynics often exploit this and the politicians and organisations seeking to manipulate others. However, it is helpful in many events, such as guiding people's belief and decisions concerning drunken driving, junk food, gun violence, smoking, drug addiction, and even AIDS. So, people use fear in shifting group mood, as with tobacco smoke and obesity, which can have fatal and painful consequences to health. Thus, fear can be beneficial in changing things unless misused.

Feedback: Soliciting the responses or reactions from the target or the participant, or the audience during and after decisions.

It is empowering adjustment and valuable to change behaviour.

Framing: The style or orientation of communication fitting to the audience's need and involves features such as positive or negative aspects, presenting advantages or disadvantages. Generally, it includes recommendation or dissuasion, endorsement, and aspiration. For example, those who train as salespeople develop a 'silky tongue' and are good at 'framing', which gives an option to increase the attractiveness of the proposition to the prospect.

Governance: The systems, processes, rules and regulations defined for an organisation by leadership to conduct its business operations ethically. Fairness and transparency are necessary to governance.

Herd Mentality: When individuals stay on with group norms, it is 'following the herd'. The need to be assertive is enhanced by strength in numbers or the courage of being part of the mob.

Heuristics: We use internal references and responses to form views and accept or defy change. Thaler and Sunstein would describe 'heuristic' to a 'nudge'. The word heuristics is derived from Greek heuriskein, 'find'. The term emanates from inner nature. Heuristic thinking is emotional and instinctive. Heuristic refers to the learning technique. The plural word heuristics refers to more than one thinking tendency. We, as humans, process numerous information and make our own choices. Heuristics help us decide most efficiently and drive decision-making easy by reducing cognitive load.

Mental shortcuts save enormous time for us and cognitive energy. Daniel Kahneman and Arnos Tversky identified heuristic types as:
Familiarity heuristic.
Attribution Error.
Representativeness.
Satisficing.

Normally, the human temptation is to rely on the most recent information, however unconnected. In the same way, availability heuristics demonstrates mental shortcuts.

Representativeness helps in categorising other people.

Satisficing is a method of deciding on the first choice which fulfils specific standards despite alternate decisions or strategies that guide decisions and judgements. Past learnings and readily available information fuel these instant judgments.

For example, if a car is speeding in your direction, the instinct is to jump away while crossing the road. It is a logical thought. The mind extracts experiences or knowledge to make a snap judgement.

Humans: Living people who represent the society and understand irrationally, emotionally, often wrongly. For example, a common tendency amongst business leaders to be ignorant or oblivious to reality and it is because of their belief that societies are populated by logical, rational 'Econs'.

Inertia: Inertia is a tendency to remain unchanged. It is a significant aspect of human nature in decision-making. Inertia is linked to the maintenance of defaults and the status quo. Inertia refers to the human tendency to do nothing when faced with making hard choices resulting in difficulty.

Input: A substitute for any change intervention idea. A helpful word in describing any intervention. Attempted alteration of the state by a choice architect.

Key Performance Indicator: It is measure of the results against objectives

Likeability: It is the reliability of leaders who are associated with change intervention. A simple conclusion about audience behaviour is, they are less likely to engage and respond to change intervention if they do not have faith in the source of the change intervention. When the audience is unaware of the integrity credibility of the source, the likeability suffers. Likeability is subjective, as audiences like and seek a different type of leadership and a leader's reputation is a relative concept. Therefore, a CEO's assertive statements on change outcome increases influence, if his past statements were credible and trustworthy.

It is similar to any amateur investor accepting Warren Buffett's statement of investment recommendation as credible than one from President Obama.

Limiting: Human impulse is to seek more when restricted. The tendency is to crave for anything perceived as scarce, as the availability is controlled by time limit or expiry. A recent example is the oxygen shortage in Indian hospitals.

Loss Aversion: Loss aversion is the human inclination to value something possessed more than when not possessed. This predilection produces a resistance to change, inertia or status quo bias. When any change idea is proposed, it is perceived to threaten or deprive the person of possession like status authority. The push comes from the sensitivity of the force in this habit of risk avoidance. Loss aversion works in opposite ways to optimism or overconfidence.

Motivation: Beginning with Abraham Maslow, many experts have laid the foundations for the behavioural push; Maslow's famous hierarchy of needs model is the most basic way and explained the ultimate driving forces behind the push. To quote Maslow, "Corporate and managerial power were damaging feature of society in suppressing people's free choice and natural potential."

Mindlessness: 'Mindlessness' is more like negligence, trying to avoid, not concentrating, etc. Some illusionary trick on the brain causes mindlessness. When designed, poor change communication interventions and mindlessness can cause significant group-wide effects of flawed thinking, leading to poor decision-making.

Mood and Mood-changers: Mood affects our feelings, and this influences how we respond to change interventions. 'Mood-changers' are interventions which affect consciousness and inspire, amuse and enthuse. Mood increases engagement and receptiveness. People's attention to change is enhanced by getting rid of fear, stress, pressure, isolation, low self-esteem, etc.

Neurolinguistic Programming (NLP): Neuro Linguistic programming is a subset of linguistics, computer sciences, and artificial intelligence. It is a concept of communication like Transactional Analysis (TA). NLP offers ways to interpret and manage the effects of communication signals between people.

Nudge: Thaler and Sunstein's 'brand' name for mental shortcuts influences individuals or groups' cognition and decision-making. Heuristics is about a passive and a constant tendency, while nudge refers to an intentional intervention.

Optimism-Overconfidence: People's tendency to overestimate the ease with which they can handle issues. Optimism increases complacency and has positive influences on decisions to change. However, optimism can lead to overconfidence. This has an opposite effect to loss aversion, which restricts reasoning and decision-making.

Opt-in or Opt-out: Opt-in means being part of the contract and allowing third-party intervention. Opt-out is the option to exit a contract.

Positioning: The term is used in marketing and refers to product's location or relocation in a specific customer segment that influences targeted people's understanding or behaviour; for example, Steuben was positioned as an upscale market premium product

Political Will: It refers to the courage in conveying passing any new rule which involves substantial political risk. The new rules may upset some people and please few others. 'Political will' refers to the collective gains and costs that would result from making drastic changes by any political party.

Priming: The process by which people are prepared before taking action. The methods adopted are visualisation, role modelling, building belief, educating and giving information before exercising options, and not directions. It is a sophisticated method of facilitation.

Psychological Contract: It is the leadership's fairness level that drives the bonding. More than a legal contract between the employee and the employer, determining what the employee does matters. The concept application is increasingly complex and significant in the workplace and people management at a different level. Especially in change management, in large organisations, emotional bonding works favourably.

Reach: This is a technique used in marketing to ensure the depth of understanding by the target audience of any advertisement, communication, or intervention. Reach is vital in all change communications designed to impact a group. With the poor spread, not enough of the audience get the intended message. Aiming at 100 per cent reach is not practical.

Reach determines the success of group interventions. For example, the change intervention could be significant step, but the impact will be poor with poor reach.

Recipient: In a group or team briefing situation, it refers to team members who are the subject to a targeted communication or intervention. The recipient is the same as a respondent in change communication.

Relevance: Refers to the needs of the recipient and how well the message matches the need. This requires that the option given for the audience is meant for change.

Representativeness: It refers to similarity and stereotyping. People use or refer to known stereotypes while assessing or characterising an unknown thing or option.

Mass media and social media communications spread or create and spread stereotype references, and people form faulty opinions and decisions.

Respondent: Commonly, in research surveys, a respondent is one who receives a message and replies. However, in change management, the respondent is anyone receiving change communication or intervention.

Rule of thumb is a general substitute term for instinctive comparison, calculation, or assumption based on preconceptions.

Self-control Strategies: People develop self-control routines and habits to overcome self-perceived weaknesses. For example, these could be general habits people develop to save money to avoid liability of spending. Many people keep alarm clocks out of reach to overcome the temptation to switch them off. What started as a countermeasure, these routines become part of the lives and influence reasoning and response to change communications and interventions.

Self-image: Self-image is significant and relevant for change management communications and interventions. Change architects design interventions and communications suitable to the personalities and moods people have. People's personalities and philosophies are quite different, despite huge cultural influences. Misaligned interventions and communications are inappropriate and stay away from the intervention. People do not recognise the change intervention to be relevant or meaningful depending upon their self-image.

Semiotics or Semiology: A subject of study of signs and symbols. Signs are extensively used in traffic signs or hospitals to warn people. Semiotics includes any activity, conduct, or process involving signs. Characters communicate meaning that is not seen or understood as a symbol itself to the sign's interpreter. Semiotics is a significant aspect of nudge theory. The heuristic (problem-solving method) is called stimulus-response compatibility. Semiotics is related to linguistics, particularly to language, architecture and meaning. Semiotics is about the language and signage, the figure of speech and symbolism. The processing part of semiotics is termed semiosis. The core is of logical elements and anthropological elements.

It bases the effects on unchanging logic (e.g., big is more impactful than small) and partly on human elements such as genetics, evolution, culture, and conditioning (Wikipedia).

Sensory: Other than language, symbols, signs, etc., sensory inputs affect people's understanding and decision-making. Films with better music influence people's moods and so also the decision-making in everyday life. When we enter Starbucks, the smell of freshly brewed coffee has an immense effect on us and vividly registers in our minds. Heat and cold affect human moods. Hundreds of other stimulants act as sensory nudges.

Signage: It refers to visual signals which convey specific meaning to an audience. These could be colours, symbols, graphic design, headings, visual media, layouts, signposts, notices, etc., all of which are full of potential to convey meaning through signals easily.

Signal: Communication or any other non-verbal cue that conveys meaning to the receiver. Signal assumes a broader sense of forms of messages, which influences humans who are receptive to cues. For example, a change of colour, size or even style of text is a signal. So also, is the direct eye contact or repositioning of an object. Movement equates with effective thought intervention.

Spotlight Effect: When people are isolated, they are prone to develop anxiety. This creates mental pressure and enhances the fear of making errors, typically inertia or conforming (herd mentality). People maintain a sense of self-significance while passing judgements, as they believe they can exaggerate the visibility of their actions and decisions.

Status Quo Bias: The tendency to conserve a state of affairs and indulge in inertia. The behaviour model is "take no action". This does not mean powerlessness but exploitation by corporations.

It is maintaining an existing state of affairs or the present condition. The Latin word 'status quo' is 'situation in which' always. Protecting the current situation is the status quo. It identifies with inertia and is mostly the default mode in organisations.

Stimulus-Response Compatibility: It is the design and use of symbols or emblems and language appropriate to the message intended to convey. For example, universally adopted warnings use signs and, irrespective of language, Red represents a 'no' or 'stop' message, and a green tick conveys a meaning of yes or positive. Compatibility is a concept of message alignment.

Sympathy: It refers to the ease with which the audience aligns with any intervention. A communicator can be more efficient when they pay attention to the mood and personality of the audience. The communicator must check if the communication is in aligned and vibrates with the audience. Self-image and empathy contribute to effectiveness in dialogue.

Syntactics-Syntax: The structure of words in a language contributes to the actual meaning of communication. Especially within sentences, the order of words seeks to clarify clear meaning.

Temptation: It refers to tendencies seeking a maximum reward for minimum effort - just as people try to win millions by betting one dollar. Greed, ego, insecurity, desperation, etc., drive temptation. Vulnerability in the modern era or when it can be a trap is temptation. Delayed gratification is closely linked to getting tempted. A large-scale crisis has been created because of an attraction to amass wealth or power.

Transactional Analysis: TA is beneficial in interpersonal communications. Being a powerful model for personal and organisational development, interpersonal change, Transactional Analysis tries to explain why we react to communications and interventions on an emotional level. Originally, the idea was developed by Dr Eric Berne in his book *Games People Play* and subsequently popularised by Thomas Harris in the book, *I am Ok You're Ok*.

A Few Famous Must-read Works for Leaders

Erikson's Psychosocial Theory of Human Development.
John Adair's an Action-Centred Leadership.
Herzberg's Motivational Theory.
McGregor's X-Y Theory.
Thomas Harris, *I am Ok; You Are Ok*.
Malcolm Gladwell, *Tipping Point. Outliers,Blink*
Adam's Equity Theory.
McClelland's Motivational Theory.
Victor Frankl, *Man's Search for Meaning: Logo Therapy*. Victor Frankl, *The Unconscious God*.

ABOUT THE AUTHOR

Dr. E. J. Sarma is a strategic management consultant specialising in organisational change management and human resource management. He has been training, mentoring employees and executives for leadership skills in a global environment. He has written over 500 articles in leading journals. In addition, he has conducted over 1,000 seminars. He is the author of the book *Different Strokes: How to Reward and Recognise Employees*.

Dr. Sarma has 35 years of experience in working with global organisations. He is PhD and MBA in Business Administration from Mumbai University.

He is trained in leadership Practices inventory, and Certified Quality Auditor.